What people are sa[illegible]

When History Had Other Plans

The central theme of this remarkable book is that while real engineering is an experimental science that works because it is based on a mass of real-world experiments, social engineering is only based on hope and abstract theory, which is why it regularly fails. A whole wish list of fashionable causes, past and present, are dissected, from making the world safe for democracy, communism, and feminism, to the minimum wage, foreign aid, renewable energy, the cancel culture and immigration, and their fatal weaknesses displayed in brutal and eloquent detail, backed with a massive apparatus of notes. A few hours of easy reading will tell you things you never imagined.
C.R. Hallpike, Emeritus Professor of Anthropology, McMaster University, Ontario and author of *Savagery and Civilisation*

A fast-paced, engaging, and well-documented look at how our intertwined world is difficult — if not impossible — to design and control. Their book provides a plethora of twentieth- (and now twenty-first-) century examples of the old saying: "The road to hell is paved with good intentions."
Elizabeth Weiss, PhD, Professor of Anthropology at San Jose State University and author of *Repatriation and Erasing the Past*

An arresting comparison of slavery in the United States with slavery in the Soviet Union. These similarities and contrasts should be better known.
Stephen Hicks, PhD, Professor of Philosophy at Rockford University, Illinois and author of the *Pocket Guide to Postmodernism*

The book is well composed and well written, persuasive and supported with a long list of appropriate citations.... It invokes the critical thinking and understanding of our past and contemporary world.

Boyka Anachkova, PhD, professor, D.Sc., Bulgarian Academy of Sciences, Sofia

When History Had Other Plans

When History Had Other Plans

Vladislav Bogorov

and

Allison McKenzie

London, UK
Washington, DC, USA

First published by Chronos Books, 2025
Chronos Books is an imprint of Collective Ink Ltd.,
Unit 11, Shepperton House, 89 Shepperton Road, London, N1 3DF
office@collectiveinkbooks.com
www.collectiveinkbooks.com
www.chronosbooks.com

For distributor details and how to order please visit the 'Ordering' section on our website.

ISBN: 978 1 80341 609 0
978 1 80341 639 7 (ebook)
Library of Congress Control Number: 2023943739

A CIP catalogue record for this book is available from the British Library.

Design: Lapiz Digital Services

UK: Printed and bound by CPI Group (UK) Ltd, Croydon, CR0 4YY
Printed in North America by CPI GPS partners

The authors thank the doctors who saved Vladislav's life: Associate Professor Yulee Vanev, Valentin Zlatev, and the late Georgy Bogdanov.

We wanted the best, but it turned out like always.

Viktor Chernomyrdin
Prime Minister of Russia

Contents

Acknowledgements

The editing of this book was assisted by Professor Boyka Anachkova, Marieta Ganeva, and Maureen Allison. The authors also thank Candace Mckenzie, Mississippi Department of Archives and History, for providing them with a much needed reference.

Chapter 1

Making the World Unsafe for Democracy

In 1914, the British were told that they were at war "to make the world safe for democracy".[1] But their involvement in WWI made the world less democratic. To see how this came about, we need to remember how the war progressed.

The Stalemate

The Schlieffen Plan was Germany's idea to fight a two-front war by not fighting a two-front war. Under this plan, France had to be knocked out of the war first, while Russia mobilised, and then Russia had to be dealt with. There were flaws both with the plan and in its execution. However, the plan almost succeeded in the first weeks of the war. That is why the French called saving Paris in 1914 a "miracle" (the Miracle of Marne), when they managed to stop the Germans. One of the reasons the plan failed was that Germany had to unexpectedly fight Britain on top of Russia and France. Scottish historian Niall Ferguson claims that:

> If the British Expeditionary Force had never been sent, there is no question that the Germans would have won the war. Even if they had been checked at the Marne, they would almost certainly have succeeded in overwhelming the French army in the absence of substantial British reinforcements. And even if the BEF had arrived, but a week later or in a different location as a result of a political crisis in London, Moltke might still have repeated the triumph of his forebear.[2]

The failure of the Schlieffen Plan led to a bloody stalemate. If the plan had succeeded, the war would have been shorter and therefore less destructive.

Moreover, protracting the war (and therefore making it so destructive) set the atmosphere for punishing Germany with the Treaty of Versailles. British politician Sir Eric Campbell-Geddes expressing the public mood that led to the treaty, saying "we shall squeeze Germany until the pips squeak".[3]

Without the Versailles Treaty, there would have been no German-speaking territories incorporated into Poland and Czechoslovakia, no reparations leading to hyperinflation, no national humiliation for Germany, no "stab in the back" theory, no confiscation of German properties and colonies.

The British participation also made the war truly global.[4] In particular, the USA fought because Britain did. Britain cut the German transatlantic telegraph cables making sure that the German and the Austro-Hungarian version of the events could not reach the American press. Britain spread lies of raped nuns and the Belgian babies tossed onto German bayonets.[5] Britain transported munitions on RMS Lusitania and hid this fact when it was sunk by the Germans, thus manipulating US public opinion in favour of entering the war.[6] Britain intercepted and decoded the "Zimmerman Telegram", which finally pushed the USA into the war.[7] It is little wonder that the Americans went to war adopting the British "safe for democracy" phrase, coined by H. G. Wells back in 1914.[8]

German civilians were starved by the Royal Navy blockade thanks to British participation. It was not lifted even after the Armistice.

> With her merchant ships and even Baltic fishing boats sequestered, and the blockade still in force, Germany could not feed her people. When Berlin asked permission to buy 2.5 million tons of food, the request was denied.[9]

Thousands of men, women, and children died as a result. The architect of this policy, Churchill, said that his aim was to "starve the whole population – men, women, and children, old and young, wounded and sound – into submission".[10]

A British general stationed in Germany said that his troops could no longer stand the sight of "hordes of skinny and bloated children pawing over the offal from British cantonments".

It is not surprising that "Freedom and Bread" later became a Nazi slogan.[11]

Hitler tapped into the resentment these policies caused in Germany and this is how he came to power in 1933.[12] Kaiser Wilhelm II's Germany, a state that used to hold free elections, eventually ended up as one of the worst totalitarian regimes in history.

Technology

There is an argument that there would have been a stalemate on the Western Front with or without Britain for purely technological reasons – namely that a manoeuvrable war was not possible with machine guns and barbed wire. But as deadly as this combination proved to be, many more casualties were inflicted by artillery.[13] This detail matters because the efficiency of the artillery depended on spending enormous quantities of expensive shells, which, in turn, depended on economic resources. In short, the technological development was not enough. Each warring nation needed to match the resources of its opponent in terms of steel production, precision tools, chemical industry, etc. Although the French had modern guns, France was no match for Germany industrially, could not manufacture so many shells, and therefore no stalemate was possible if it faced Germany alone, without Britain.

Moreover, both sides found ways to overcome the barbed wire and the machine guns: the Germans with stormtroopers, the Allies with tanks, and both sides with "undermining" – literally mining under the enemy's position in order to place explosives and blow their trenches up. The Russians, under the command of General Brusilov, found a way to overcome the stalemate as early as 1916 and they were not even using any new technical means.

That none of these tactics led to a strategic breakthrough was, again, a result of resources, not of technology. Behind each line of defence there was another, and another. The attacking party was slowed down and this gave the defenders time to move troops from elsewhere and counter-attack. The stalemate was a matter of quantity and not of quality because the many lines of defence, and the reserves available to plug a bridge in these lines, was a matter of having enough economic and human resources. Germany could initially match the combined industrial power of France, Russia, and Britain because they were not well organised.[14] But they were improving and, by 1917, the powers were unequal.

To make things worse, the USA joined the war. With it, the Allies had far more men, tanks, aeroplanes, shells, food and, sure enough, the German line was decisively broken in 1918. Furthermore, the German defensive fortifications that were broken in 1918 were superior to the ones that were successfully held at the Somme back in 1916. This indicates that resources mattered more than the quality of fortification used: the poor fortifications held while the good fortifications failed.

Russia

The conditions that brought about the February Revolution in Petrograd in 1917 would not have occurred if Germany had not had to fight Britain on top of Russia and France. It was the dragging on of WWI and not the historical development of Russia that led to socialism being established there.

Despite the efforts of generations of Soviet propagandists claiming technological failings and impoverishment, Russia was in fact an industrial giant. It was the fourth most industrially developed country in the world and was rising through the ranks with an astonishing 19 per cent increase in production per year. The wage of the Russian worker was second only to the US worker. If the difference in food prices between the two countries is taken into account, the wage difference was a mere 15 per cent.[15] It is hard to imagine this now, but Westerners used to immigrate to Russia in order to be paid more. The Russian industrial output continued to grow even during the war, while it was falling in Germany and Britain.[16]

Lenin and Trotsky could not have come to power in October 1917 if the soldiers had not brought down the government in February 1917. The two played no role in the February Revolution (they were not even in the country) when the Petrograd garrison soldiers invaded the hall where parliament members were gathered. It was these soldiers who pressured the frightened Members of Parliament into issuing the infamous Order number 1. (There were also students and workers, but it was the soldiers that were armed and in those days that was what counted.) It stated that from that moment onwards, the soldiers would elect their officers. In theory, the Order was intended for the Petrograd garrison only, but it reached the front as well. It disintegrated the army. It was these soldiers who then sent representatives to the front in order to agitate the other soldiers to give up the fight, to disobey and attack their officers, and then to return to the rear to plunder the estates of the rich. It was they who toppled the Russian state and prepared the ground for the Bolshevik's coup that followed in October.

However, the Petrograd soldiers did all this just because they didn't want to be sent to the front to fight and they would not have had to go to fight if there was peace in 1917. They were indifferent to socialism and hadn't heard of Lenin, although he would not have come to power without them. All of these events point to one summary: USSR would not have been created if the war did not carry over into 1917.

No USSR would have meant no WWII. It was the Soviet leadership that instigated the war between Nazi Germany on the one hand and Britain and France on the other. (This is covered in "Attempts to Prevent WWII Made It Happen".) Then, after WWII, USSR almost caused WWIII. Stalin planned to take over Western Europe in the late 1940s or early 1950s.[17] Fortunately, he was dead by 1953, likely murdered by some of the Politburo members who were against a new war.[18] The "doves" had killed the "hawk". Still, this did not prevent the Cold War which resulted in hot Proxy Wars that caused a number of casualties comparable to these of WWI, to the risk of nuclear annihilation of humanity, and to tens of trillions of dollars wasted.

Of course, the British politicians could not have predicted this long chain of events back in 1914. Nobody could. But that is the point. The consequences of our actions are far more numerous and extensive than we know.

Still, forecasting some calamities was possible. Russia was another country that blundered into WWI. Peter Durnovo, a civil servant, advised the Russian Tsar not to go to war.[19] He exhibited a remarkable foresight by predicting that socialist slogans would be raised as a result of the war; that properties would be snatched; that the Russian state would be toppled, a "most extreme social revolution will become inevitable", he said, and foretold of the anarchy and the radical elements that would come to power and devastate the country. That turned out to be an accurate summary of what followed under Lenin, Trotsky, and Stalin. The USSR exterminated about 62 million people.[20] To put this figure into chilling perspective, Nazi Germany exterminated about 21 million.[21]

The Dominating Power

It can be objected that making the world safe for democracy was just a propaganda slogan, like saving "poor little Belgium".

(The Schlieffen Plan called for seven-eighths of the German army in the West to "smash" into Belgium in order to attack France. Belgium was in the way and Germany violated its neutrality. This, along with the news of the German atrocities, most of them fabricated, was used as a pretext for Britain to go to war.[22]) It can be further argued, as many historians do, that Britain really entered the war because it did not want a single power to dominate the continent, a policy it has pursued since the Napoleonic Wars.[23]

If this was the case, then the results were the opposite of what was intended. First Nazi Germany became the dominant power on the continent (in the late 1930s) and then the Soviet Union did (in the late 1940s). In effect, the National Socialists and the Communists came to power as a result of the British involvement in WWI. Worse still, Britain itself was weakened and therefore less able to oppose them:

> By fighting Germany in 1914, Asquith, Grey and their colleagues helped ensure that, when Germany did finally achieve predominance on the continent, Britain was no longer strong enough to provide a check to it.[24]

The same argument can be made about Britain and USSR. In a sense, the only dominance Britain destroyed by going to war was its own.

As was already shown, the war would have been short without British involvement. The surviving documents suggest that Germany would have annexed neither Belgium nor French territory. There would have been a union where the member states would not pay any custom duties. The Russian power in Eastern Europe would have been reduced. Poland, for example, would have been independent.[25] Here's how Niall Ferguson sums it all up:

Had Britain stood aside – even for a matter of weeks – continental Europe could therefore have been transformed into something not wholly unlike the European Union we know today – but without the massive contraction in British overseas power entailed by the fighting of two world wars.... With the Kaiser triumphant, Adolf Hitler could have eked out his life as a mediocre postcard painter and a fulfilled old soldier in a German-dominated Central Europe about which he could have found little to complain. And Lenin could have carried on his splenetic scribbling in Zurich, forever waiting for capitalism to collapse – and forever disappointed.[26]

Endnotes

1 Patrick J. Buchanan, *Churchill, Hitler, and "The Unnecessary War": How Britain Lost Its Empire and the West Lost the World*, (New York, Crown Publishers, 2008), pages xx, 50, 51.

2 Niall Ferguson, *The Pity of War*, (London, The Penguin Press, 1998), page 458.

3 "Squeeze Germany Until the Pips squeak", Richard M Langworth website, published on September 14, 2014, consulted on May 11, 2020, https://richardlangworth.com/squeeze-germany.

4 "How The World Went to War In 1914", Imperial War Museum website, published on February 5, 2018, consulted on May 10, 2020, https://www.iwm.org.uk/history/how-the-world-went-to-war-in-1914.

5 Patrick J. Buchanan, *Churchill, Hitler, and "The Unnecessary War": How Britain Lost Its Empire and the West Lost the World*, (New York, Crown Publishers, 2008), pages 68, 106.

6 Centenary News, First World War 1914–1918, published on May 2, 2014, consulted on September 26, 2019, https://centenarynews.com/article?id=1616.

7 "Zimmermann Telegram: United States-European history (1917)", Britannica website, consulted on September 26, 2019, https://www.britannica.com/event/Zimmermann-Telegram.
8 Patrick J. Buchanan, *Churchill, Hitler, and "The Unnecessary War": How Britain Lost Its Empire and the West Lost the World,* (New York, Crown Publishers, 2008), page 51.
9 Patrick J. Buchanan, *Churchill, Hitler, and "The Unnecessary War": How Britain Lost Its Empire and the West Lost the World,* (New York, Crown Publishers, 2008), page 77.
10 Patrick J. Buchanan, *Churchill, Hitler, and "The Unnecessary War": How Britain Lost Its Empire and the West Lost the World,* (New York, Crown Publishers, 2008), pages 79.
11 Patrick J. Buchanan, *Churchill, Hitler, and "The Unnecessary War": How Britain Lost Its Empire and the West Lost the World,* (New York, Crown Publishers, 2008), page 80.
12 Laurence Moyer, *Victory Must be Ours: Germany in the Great War 1914–1918,* (London, Leo Cooper, 1995), page 6.
13 "Shrapnel from mortars, grenades and, above all, artillery projectile bombs, or shells, would account for an estimated 60 percent of the 9.7 million military fatalities of World War I." Caroline Alexander, "The Shock of War", World War I: 100 Years Later, Smithsonian Magazine website, published on September 2010, consulted on September 16, 2019, https://www.smithsonianmag.com/history/the-shock-of-war-55376701/.
14 Niall Ferguson, *The Pity of War,* (London, The Penguin Press, 1998), pages 259, 260.
15 Marina Svanidze, *Estoricheskiye Hroniki si Nikolaim Svanidze, (Historical Chronicles with Nikolai Svanidze*), Volume one, (Amphora Publishers, Saint Petersburg, 2007), pages 24, 25.
16 Niall Ferguson, *The Pity of War,* (London, The Penguin Press, 1998), page 250.

17 Kaystoot Zakoretskiy, *Tret'ia Miravaya Voina Stalina (Stalin's World War III),* (Moscow, Yauza-Press, 2009); Edvard Radzinsky, *Stalin,* (Great Britain, Hodder & Stoughton, 1997), pages 543–547.

18 Abdurakhman Avtorhanov, *Zagatka Smyearttee Stalina (The Mystery of Stalin's Death),* (Moscow, Ex Libris Slovo Soviet-British co-operative venture, 1992).

19 Paul Robinson, "How Russia Might Have Stopped World War I", The American Conservative website, published on February 4, 2014, consulted on April 28, 2022, https://www.theamericanconservative.com/articles/how-russia-might-have-stopped-world-war-i/.

20 R. J. Rummel, *Death by Government,* (New Jersey, Transaction Publishers, 1995), pages V, VI.

21 R. J. Rummel, *Death by Government,* (New Jersey, Transaction Publishers, 1995), pages V, VI.

22 Patrick J. Buchanan, *Churchill, Hitler, and "The Unnecessary War": How Britain Lost Its Empire and the West Lost the World,* (New York, Crown Publishers, 2008), pages 35–52, 106.

23 Niall Ferguson, *The Pity of War,* (London, The Penguin Press, 1998), page 443.

24 Niall Ferguson, *The Pity of War,* (London, The Penguin Press, 1998), page 461.

25 Niall Ferguson, *The Pity of War,* (London, The Penguin Press, 1998), pages 170–172; Patrick J. Buchanan, *Churchill, Hitler, and "The Unnecessary War": How Britain Lost Its Empire and the West Lost the World,* (New York, Crown Publishers, 2008), pages 60–62.

26 Niall Ferguson, *The Pity of War,* (London, The Penguin Press, 1998), page 460.

Chapter 2

Freeing the Workers Enslaved Them

The stated goal of Karl Marx was to free the exploited. "Workers of the World, Unite. You have nothing to lose but your chains!" was one of his famous quotes.[1] In accordance with this, we – those living in the Soviet empire – were taught from an early age that we have been liberated from the exploiters. Socialism equalled freedom.

But what if the "liberation" that began in 1917 actually ended in slavery in the early 1930s? This startling fact has been acknowledged by many authors since 1948 when Dallin and Nicolaevsky published their extensive study of slavery in the USSR, which covers all aspects: how slaves were made to work, how the methods used affected mortality rates, what living conditions were, etc.[2] A lot of data can also be found in the memoirs of those who survived the Soviet concentration camps, from Solzhenitsyn[3] and Shalamov,[4] to hundreds of others. It is not surprising that those witnessing the transportation of prisoners to the concentration camps by barges compared it to that of slaves shipped across the Atlantic.[5]

In the West, slavery is associated with Hollywood props such as chains and images of black people lashed under the hot Caribbean sun, not white people worked to death in concentration camps in Siberia. But the very word "slave" comes from the word for Slav because the Slavic people, all of them white, were enslaved by both Arabs and Western Europeans for centuries. As Professor Thomas Sowell observed, slavery has nothing to do with race or racism because people of all skin colours have been enslaved or have enslaved others throughout history.[6]

However, there was a difference between the slavery under socialism and slavery in the Caribbean. The number of slaves under socialism massively outnumbered any other example throughout human history. The same goes for the number of deaths resulting from slavery in the USSR, as Professor Rummel has observed:

> In some 70 years it likely chewed up almost 40 million lives, well over twice as many as probably died in some 400 years of the African slave trade, from capture to sale in an Arab, Oriental, or New World market.[7]

Incidentally, that is not counting the slaves in the National Socialist concentration camps, who were also white.

The acquisition of slaves in the USSR was organised like any other economic activity in a socialist state: there was a quota for it.

The government planned in advance the number of prisoners that would be needed for the next year, and would place an advance order for the arrests with the People's Commissariat of Internal Affairs (NKVD).[8]

In most countries, the law determines the number of the people behind bars: if more activities are criminalised, more people will be jailed. It was just the opposite under socialism where the number of those locked up determined the law. The law was changed so that a pre-planned number would be reached. New articles were enacted if the number of slaves in the concentration camps was not sufficient so that more people could be sentenced to forced labour.[9]

The word "sentenced" used here does not mean what it does in the West today. It was not the decision of a court of law (let alone of an *independent* court of law). The sentence could not be appealed and was not reached following a transparent procedure.

Moreover, the camp administration could refuse to release prisoners who had served their term if it found that necessary for economic reasons.[10] Finally, the administration could, at its own discretion and without a new charge, re-arrest a freed prisoner just because he had already been sentenced once before.[11] In short, the state was not constrained by law regarding who could be forced to work and for how long.

The fact that the slaves under socialism were public property had another consequence: their mortality rate was higher than in countries where the slaves were private property like, for example, the privately owned slaves in the USA during the nineteenth century. Statistically speaking, life expectancy was better even for inmates in Nazi concentration camps.[12] A private slave owner ensured that his property was maintained and used for as long as possible. The officials who managed the slaves under socialism had no such incentive.[13] They hadn't paid for them and would not lose their investment if the slaves died. They could afford to be callous. In the words of Naftaly Frenkel, one of the early ideologists of the Soviet concentration camps: "We have to squeeze everything from a prisoner in the first three months. We will not need him later."[14]

It made sense that the concentration camp prisoners were forced to work without proper shoes, clothes or food in sub-zero temperatures: they had to survive with the clothes and the shoes they were arrested in. For the women, that often meant pushing wheelbarrows through deep snow in high heels.[15] It is no wonder that few survived beyond the first few months.

One additional reason for the disregard of the well-being of the slaves was their availability. It was much easier to arrest people locally than to carry them across the Atlantic Ocean. They had less than 4 million slaves in the southern United States.[16] As was pointed out, the Soviets had way more.[17]

The popular assumption is that those sent to concentration camps were enemies of Stalin's regime, in other words that they must have been rich in the past or must have told a political joke.

This was not necessarily so. For example, there was a campaign to catch those without passports in the big Soviet cities in the early 1930s. (It was the peasants who had no passports, and they were fleeing from their villages in a desperate attempt to save their lives as at this time the famine artificially created by the Soviets was underway.) Apart from catching peasants, those who took part in these "hunting parties"[18] sometimes caught people with passports in order to fulfil the quota.[19] Enemies or not, the camps needed workers.

Some of the secret police reports from the 1930s frankly stated that the need for qualified personnel would be satisfied by arresting "suitable" (in terms of qualification) persons.[20] In other words, the usefulness of one's qualifications was grounds for imprisonment. Lavrentiy Beria, the head of the secret police, suggested that specialists working in the secret police research bureaux should be sentenced to lengthy terms of imprisonment in order to make them work harder by promising them a reduction of their prison terms.[21] So, their freedom had to be taken away in order to be offered back to them in exchange for work.

That it was clear to the rulers that imprisonment was about economic results and not punishment was evident in what Stalin said, too: "In August 1938, as the penal terms of a generation of convicts drew to a close, he playfully asked the USSR Supreme Soviet whether such convicts should be released on time. He declared that 'from the viewpoint of the state economy it would be a bad idea' to set them free since the camps would lose their best workers."[22]

This reasoning makes sense given that people under socialism are an economic resource in the same way oil is. In the words of a Russian historian, Stalin read the monthly reports about those sentenced for "spying, diversion, and terrorist activity" along with the "ones on the harvesting of grain, the mining of coal, and the smelting of steel".[23] When abortions were banned in the

USSR in 1936, Stalin said: *We need people. This is not a personal affair for the women.*[24]

It makes sense that North Korea, the last surviving Stalinist state, ensures the prisoners will not commit suicide by punishing their surviving relatives.[25] After all, those who kill themselves destroy public property and sabotage the economy. Neither is a private matter and therefore they cannot be left to decide when to end their lives.

The same economic reasoning was applied on lower levels. To illustrate, a Soviet concentration camp commander reported in the 1930s that 15.3 per cent of the prisoners have been lost during the last year, quickly adding: "Given the task of colonizing the enormous territory of Nareem, which was achieved as quickly as possible, the population loss figure should not be considered significant."

The author of the report gives further numbers to substantiate that he hasn't overspent too many people.[26]

Viktor Kravchenko, a prominent Soviet defector who worked in a war production office in Moscow, observed the mindset of the regime and "the complacency with which these people used human life ... like so much inert raw material for their plans, experiments and blunders".[27]

Slavery in the USSR was distinct from private slavery in another way too. In accordance with the propaganda, it was never called "slavery".

Slavery Outside Soviet Concentration Camps

The concentration camps were only the most extreme form of slavery. Those who were not imprisoned were slaves too. Leaving the government farms was forbidden in the USSR in 1930. Essentially, serfdom was restored. It was ordered to use women as beasts of burden for ploughing. Even pregnant, they were put in teams of four to the yoke. In 1933 this was regulated formally as well by the Prohibition of Leaving Act.[28]

The same went for the cities. One had no choice whether to work or not for the state according to the regulations in the Soviet Union. Both men and women were slaves in all but name since they had no choice where to work, for how long or for how much money. Their bosses had full power over them, which had life and death consequences for the "employee".

Eventually, the rules became even stricter.[29] A Decree "On the Transfer to the Eight-Hour Working Day, the Seven-Day Work Week, and on the Prohibition of Unauthorized Departure by Laborers and Office Workers from Factories and Offices" was passed on 26 June, 1940.[30] The severity escalated with the Decree "On the Mandatory Procedure for the Transfer of Engineers, Technicians, Masters, Skilled Laborers and Office Workers Between Certain Factories and Institutions" from 19 October, 1940. People were not only forbidden to quit work but were dictated where they must work.

And this was just the official part of the process. People were coerced to work with or without regulations. An engineer, for example, was forbidden from leaving his workplace for months on end until he developed a certain tool.[31]

Children absent without leave from their factory were sent to concentration camps.[32] The same went for adults who did not fulfil their quotas.[33] People all over the country were tied to their jobs or sent to concentration camps if they were late for work.[34] Women were frequently forced into sexual slavery in the USSR during WWII.[35]

The word slavery, when applied to countries like the USSR or North Korea, is not to be taken metaphorically. The people were deemed property of the state in everything but name because they were used by it like a resource. They were not bought and sold, however, because they were public property rather than private. There was no one to sell them to and no one to buy them from – the owner of all means of production in the land was just one: the state. They were forced to work and were deprived of the right to leave (not just the country but often their town or village, without a travel permit, a system that still exists in North Korea today).[36] They could not negotiate their conditions. In theory, they received wages (if they were not in a concentration camp) but the size of the wage was determined unilaterally by their "employer" (By the way, being paid does not necessarily exclude slavery as some slaves in USA were also paid.[37]) That wage was often just a token gesture.[38] Moreover, the people had no choice whether to work for it or not.

Even if the people under socialism were free to change their jobs (as they eventually were under Brezhnev), they could not choose a better pay because they were still working for the same employer – whether you were working as a miner or a minister, a poet or a plumber, a teacher or a turner, you were all employed by the government.

Why the "Liberation" of the Workers Backfired

Many people say that slavery had nothing to do with "true" socialism, that slavery happened because of who was in charge in the USSR. (Interestingly, the same argument is not made about the National Socialism. Nobody claims it was good but that it was corrupted by Hitler.) They blame Lenin and Stalin for socialism being bad; if only Lenin and Stalin were nice guys who excelled at pressing wildflowers, the system would have been different.

However, who the leaders were was a consequence and not a cause as F. A. Hayek demonstrated in *The Road to Serfdom*. (The relevant chapter is aptly called "Why the Worst Get on Top".) Lenin and Stalin happened to be the most suitable to implement Marxism, but that does not mean that others would not have come forward if those two men did not exist: just think of Trotsky, for example, who was no less bloodthirsty. He dreamt of what the Khmer Rouge realised decades later in Cambodia. Trotsky said in his speech at the IX Party Congress that everyone was to be "a soldier of labour" who would not have the freedom to choose what job to have and for how much, because if he did not obey orders, he would be court martialled as a "deserter". Trotsky was not just talking the talk but walking the walk and he was brutal enough to enforce Marxism upon the population. The Red Army committed horrible atrocities under his command. When the White Army advanced in 1919, they uncovered mass graves full of people who had dirt in their lungs. They had been buried alive. Others had been skinned alive. Some women's breasts were cut off while they were alive, and others had been tortured by having their hands skinned so that gloves could be manufactured from their skin.[39]

Leninism and Stalinism are often presented as not true Marxism. However, just like we may find the hints of everything Stalin did in Lenin's policies, so we can find the hints of what Lenin did in what Marx preached. To illustrate, people associate starving the Ukrainians with Stalin, but Lenin did it first.[40] The same goes for the secret police infiltration and the concentration camps, both invented under Lenin. Likewise, Lenin is supposed to have strayed from Marxism because the latter predicted a revolution in a highly industrialised country while Lenin forged a coup in a country where most of the population were peasants. But Marx wrote as early as 1882 that this was not a problem as long as there was a revolution in Russia.[41] The message was that everything was acceptable so long as it yielded results. Lenin displayed this lack of principle as well. Julius Martov, a prominent politician at the time, observed in October 1917: "Lenin is neither interested in peace nor in war. He is interested in revolution only and the only good revolution for him is the one that will allow the Bolsheviks to come to power."[42]

In hindsight, it should not be surprising that a plan to free the labour ended in enslaving the labourers. As Napoleon observed, there are only two forces that unite humans: fear and interest.[43] If you remove the interest (which is what you do when you dispense of the private property as Marx prescribed), you are left with only fear to make them work. Fear, therefore, becomes the currency of your new economy. Instead of voluntary transactions, you must rely on coercion. There's a phrase for that: forced labour. In effect, this amounts to reversing history given that it progresses "from status to contract", as Henry Maine put it.[44]

Let us see in detail how losing all freedoms was inevitable whatever the leaders wished for. Lenin's rule was marked by hundreds of peasant revolts.[45] The White Armies, there were several of them, were on top of it, not to mention the Kronstadt Rebellion. To overcome this resistance, the Communists needed ever more effective means of population-control. This is how they came up with the one-party rule (in 1917 they ruled with the Essers and there were other parties in the country[46]). They closed the borders (initially they allowed immigration), opened the concentration camps (initially they just shot people), introduced the press monopoly (there were still some opposition newspapers in 1918[47]). The Communists developed the secret police infiltration (at the beginning they were arguing whether they needed secret police), and eventually adopted the personality cult of one supreme leader (there were many leaders at first).

The Communists started by expelling their enemies. These were the times of the infamous "Philosophers' Ship" when some of the leading intellectuals were driven away from the country. (Actually, there were two ships and neither of them were officially called "Philosophers".) In 1922, Lenin even envisaged a death penalty for those who might try to return (Article 7 of the Penal Code).[48] This sounds strange today because throughout the twentieth century, millions strived to escape socialism and almost no one wanted to go back. It seems that Lenin could not have imagined the Berlin Wall at this point. After all, the Berlin Wall was erected to keep the people living under socialism in.

The Communists quickly realised their mistake. They not only lost human resources by expelling people but also allowed the truth of what was going on in the USSR to be spread throughout the West and an anti-Soviet lobby to be established. That is why the regime stopped banishing its enemies abroad.

Moreover, their enemies had less chance to travel abroad than the general population (which they had very little chance to do themselves). This feature of socialism was kept to the last throughout the Soviet empire. Everyone who wanted to go on an excursion to a "capitalist" country (that is how we named non-socialist countries, the ones that could give political asylum to somebody coming from a socialist country), had to be given permission to travel by the local secret police and party branch.[49] Such permission was not given unless one had a clean record. Not having a clean record did not necessarily mean that you had committed a crime. It could have been that, at any time in your past, you had been reported for telling a political joke, or that your uncle had been sent to a concentration camp (because having such an uncle suggested that you had reason to hate the government and if you hated the government, you may decide not to return from a trip abroad and therefore you must not be allowed to leave the country). Having close relatives left behind to pay the price for your flight was another way to guarantee that you would return. So, contrary to what Lenin was doing initially, people were not allowed to go abroad precisely because they may not return.

Travelling abroad was just one area where reality corrected the Communists and showed that their whims did not matter. A totalitarian state is inconceivable with free press and yet many Bolsheviks argued that they should keep this freedom at first.[50]

It sounds unimaginable now, but the Communists also discussed whether to close down the secret police after the Civil War. Its officers and collaborators were so badly paid that some of the females had to work as prostitutes.[51] Even some of the leaders thought they should get rid of the secret police as police and public prosecutors could suffice.[52] They were corrected by the reality yet again finding out that without it their authority would not be viable.

If the borders were not closed, the population would flee and that would be the end of that state. This was what was about to happen with East Germany before the Berlin Wall was built. Alternatively, the totalitarian state would have to make concessions as the Khmer Rouge were forced to do at the beginning of their rule for fear of losing their population. They could not consolidate their power if the borders were not shut.[53] You cannot make an open-borders socialist state work any more than you can inflate a punctured tyre.

And if the socialist state is not isolated from the world, the propaganda will not work as the population will have access to alternative information. That is what partially happened with the population of East Berlin who were able to watch Western TV, and this is what eventually happened throughout Eastern Europe when part of the population started to listen to Radio Free Europe; the foreign radio stations subsequently had to be jammed and those caught listening had to be punished. The state borders had to be impenetrable to radio waves as well, not just to people. (The internet did not exist at the time, but North Korea lived to see its invention and therefore had one more problem to take care of.) The system would crumble if there was either freedom of movement or freedom of information. The borders, as the Soviet Communists used to put it, had to be "padlocked". (They even made movies illustrating this idea.)[54]

The same would happen if there was freedom to exchange information within the borders. To stop people talking, they had to fear it. Terror was needed and, to know where to direct this terror, snitches were needed. Exercising terror required "eyes and muscles" – data on those who opposed socialism (eyes) and the force to arrest, torture, and shoot them (muscles).

It required that every sphere of life was infiltrated by secret police informants.

To ensure there was no armed resistance, the army had to secure a given territory and confiscate the weapons of the population. (This is how it was in Russia after 1917 and this is how it was in Eastern Europe after 1944 when the Red Army occupied it and thus gave free rein to the local Communists to establish totalitarian governments.) As Mikhail Tukhachevsky, one of the top Soviet military commanders, summarised, the end of the war is not the end of the violence but its beginning because not having armed resistance means the Communists may exercise terror freely.[55]

To defeat the enemy's armed forces, the Communists needed to compel their own forces to fight since their soldiers were not volunteers. Blocking troops were needed to make sure that their own soldiers would follow orders because they, being drafted, were part of the same population that needed to be subdued. The blocking troops were there to shoot their own fellow soldiers if they tried to escape. But that was only one half of the solution because if they were to simply shoot all opponents right away, the state may be depopulated as Cambodia was under the Khmer regime (who succeeded in wiping out 31 per cent of the population in three short years).[56] That is why concentration camps were needed – where the opponents were defused and yet still economically utilised.

Using such logical considerations, we can deduce most of the vital elements of a totalitarian state. In hindsight, we can work it out as a theorem. Every step was a necessary continuation of the previous one and made it necessary to follow in the same direction towards making the state ever more powerful and individuals ever more powerless.

The Communists had no choice once they started to shoot the protesters in 1918[57] but to go on shooting or give up power and answer for their crimes. The choice was simple: to be powerful and alive or to be powerless and dead. The terror caused resistance and this, in turn, necessitated more terror. This process was self-perpetuating, it left "mounds" of human corpses as contemporary reported.[58] There was no one left to resist eventually and the totalitarian state was complete under Stalin.

The Communists had to control every sphere of life to keep their power. If just one sphere was left uncontrolled, it would have been used as a rallying point to resist the Soviet system. A single freedom may quickly be exploited by the opponents of the regime and become a widening breach of security. The Catholic Church in Poland, for example, was left independent and it contributed to the creation of Solidarnost which, in turn, was quickly transformed from a trades union to a political party.[59] This party eventually toppled the state. Any totalitarian state is a pressurised system because of the stresses that accumulate and cannot be safely released. One small hole is all it takes for a catastrophic decompression.

The National Socialists had the benefit of an example of an established totalitarian state, the USSR, when they began constructing their own in Germany in 1933. Yet they too went through trial and error. To illustrate, Hitler had an agreement with the Vatican which allowed the church to educate some of Germany's youth, initially. Hitler soon sensed that this arrangement spread an ideology hostile to National Socialism. Since Christianity and Nazism contradict each other, Catholic schools had to be closed.[60]

Marx and Engels must have anticipated the need for extreme violence in order to establish socialism, although they didn't describe the workings of a concentration camp in detail. Engels expected that the prisons would not be large enough for the enemies of the new regime, and therefore recommended that special guarded places were to be established.[61] Marx wrote about something resembling what we saw in the USSR, a state of universal asceticism and uniformity.[62] He also advocated the use of terror and forced labour, state monopolism, indoctrinating the population from an early age, the abolition of private property and, finally, social engineering.

The bottom line is that socialism doesn't work if people are given a choice of where to go, what to do, what to own, what to say, and what to read. In other words, socialism and freedom are incompatible. Gorbachev introduced freedom in a socialist country and the result was the collapse of the system. So, we may dream of a non-violent socialism, a socialism with a human face, as they used to call it during the Prague Spring in 1968, but the hard experimental data doesn't agree with these ideas.

Normal state machinery, like the one in Western Europe, works well enough if you want to raise the taxes. If you want to go further than that, say to confiscate the houses of the people or force them to work, a more coercive state is needed. If you want to take it all, an all-powerful state is necessary and we call such a state totalitarian. The more it gives (like free healthcare, free education) the more it has to take (taxes, property, freedoms). As has been observed, "A government big enough to give you everything you want is big enough to take everything you have."[63] Which just echoes what Plato said thousands of years before, namely that "extreme freedom can't be expected to lead to anything but... extreme slavery".[64] Pierre Boiste echoed it in the nineteenth century: "If everybody is equal, nobody is free."

Endnotes

1 Karl Marx and Frederick Engels, "Manifesto of the Communist Party", Marxists Internet Archive website, page 67, consulted on June 15, 2022, https://www.marxists.org/archive/marx/works/download/pdf/Manifesto.pdf.

2 David J Dallin and Boris I Nicolaevsky, *Forced Labor in Soviet Russia,* (London, Hollis and Carter, 1948).

3 Aleksandr Solzhenitsyn, *The Gulag Archipelago, 1918–1956: An Experiment in Literary Investigation*, (The Harvill Press, London, 1986).
4 Shalamov, Varlam, *Kalimskiyeh Raskazee (Kolyma Stories), Completed Works in Four Volumes*, (Moscow, Vagrius, 1998).
5 Anatolii Fedoseyev, *Zapadnya: Chelovek i sotsializm (Trap: Man and Socialism)*, (Frankfurt/Main, Germany, Possev-Verlag, 1976), page 82.
6 Thomas Sowell, *Applied Economics: Thinking Beyond Stage One*, Basic Books – a member of the Perseus Books Group, The United States of America, 2009), pages 20, 21, 41.
7 R. J. Rummel, *Death by Government*, (New Jersey, Transaction Publishers, 1995), page 9.
8 Viktor Suvorov, *The Chief Culprit: Stalin's Grand Design to Start World War II*, (Annapolis, Maryland, Naval Institute Press, 2013), page 24.
9 Kaystoot Zakoretskiy, *Tret'ia Miravaya Voina Stalina (Stalin's World War III)*, (Moscow, Yauza-Press, 2009), pages 361–363.
10 Kaystoot Zakoretskiy, *Tret'ia Miravaya Voina Stalina (Stalin's World War III)*, (Moscow, Yauza-Press, 2009), page 363.
11 Kaystoot Zakoretskiy, *Tret'ia Miravaya Voina Stalina (Stalin's World War III)*, (Moscow, Yauza-Press, 2009), pages 364, 365.
12 Peter Kenez, *A History of the Soviet Union from the Beginning to the End*, (Cambridge, Cambridge University Press, 2006), page 136.
13 R. J. Rummel, *Death by Government*, (New Brunswick, New Jersey, Transaction Publishers, 1995), page 182.
14 Marina Svanidze, *Estoricheskiye Hroniki si Nikolaim Svanidze, (Historical Chronicles with Nikolai Svanidze*), Volume one, (Amphora Publishers, Saint Petersburg, 2007), page 340.
15 Marina Svanidze, *Estoricheskiye Hroniki si Nikolaim Svanidze, (Historical Chronicles with Nikolai Svanidze*), Volume one, (Amphora Publishers, Saint Petersburg, 2007), page 426.

16 "Slavery in the United States", Economic History Association website, consulted on May 5, 2021, https://eh.net/encyclopedia/slavery-in-the-united-states/.
17 R. J. Rummel, *Death by Government*, (New Jersey, Transaction Publishers, 1995), page 9.
18 The phrase "hunting parties" was unofficially used in People's Republic of Bulgaria in the 1980s. There were "hunting parties" for all kind of campaigns, for example, when the Turkish and Arab names of the local Turks and Bulgarian Muslims were forcibly changed into Bulgarian; people used to warn each other not to leave their passports at home as this may have grave consequences.
19 Mark Solonin, *22 Yunya: Anatomya Catastrophyee, (June 22: Anatomy of the Catastrophe)*, (Moscow, Yauza-Press, Eksmo, 2009), page 404.
20 State Archive of Russian Federation, Fund 9414, Inventory 1, Case 1805, Sheet 66, quoted after www.memo.ru/history/NKVD/GULAG/artcles/Chapter3prim.htm.
21 Alter Litvin and John Keep, *Stalinism: Russian and Western Views at the Turn of the Millennium*, (United Kingdom, USA, Canada, Routledge an imprint of Taylor & Francis, 2005), page 13.
22 Robert Service, *A History of Modern Russia: From Nicholas II to Putin*, (The Penguin Group, 2003), page 251.
23 Roy Medvedev, *Let History Judge: The Origins and Consequences of Stalinism*, Revised and expanded edition, (Columbia University Press, 1989), page 11.
24 Marina Svanidze, *Estoricheskiye Hroniki si Nikolaim Svanidze, (Historical Chronicles with Nikolai Svanidze)*, Volume two, (Amphora Publishers, Saint Petersburg, 2007), page 58.
25 Blaine Harden, *Escape from Camp 14: One Man's Remarkable Odyssey from North Korea to Freedom in the West*, (London, Pan Books an imprint of Pan Macmillan, 2015), page 86.

26 "SibLAG of OGPU Report on the Economic Development of Nareem by the Special Settlers from May 1931 to June 1932, towards 7 August 1932", published on the Estoricheskiye Materialy (Historical Materials) website, http://istmat.info/node/58244 , consulted on September 1, 2021.

27 Paul Hollander, *Political Will and Personal Belief: The Decline and Fall of Soviet Communism*, (Yale University Press, page 53), quote from Google books UK website https://books.google.co.uk/books?id=vJwC34GQnhEC&pg=PA53&lpg=PA53&dq=%22like+so+much+inert+raw+material+for+their+plans%22&source=bl&ots=IjRPVHmG_B&sig=ACfU3U0Li-Y8tJa_rSsfceZjT-XFIa-GXA&hl=en&sa=X&ved=2ahUKEwidk-nE-ZL0AhXoQ_EDHRe1AWUQ6AF6BAgEEAM#v=onepage&q=inert&f=false, consulted on 12 November 2021.

28 Marina Svanidze, *Estoricheskiye Hroniki si Nikolaim Svanidze, (Historical Chronicles with Nikolai Svanidze)*, Volume one, (Amphora Publishers, Saint Petersburg, 2007) page 374.

29 Vadim J. Birstein, *SMERSH – Stalin's Secret Weapon*, (London, Biteback Publishing, 2011), pages 81, 82.

30 Hugo S. Cunningham, "On the Transfer to the Eight-Hour Working Day, The Seven-Day Work Week, and On the Prohibition of Unauthorized Departure by Laborers, and Office Workers from Factories and Offices", published December 28, 2000, consulted on August 2, 2020, http://www.cyberussr.com/rus/uk-trud-e.html.

31 Viktor Suvorov, *Dien M: Kakda nachalas vtayara meeroviya voyna? (M-Day: When Did World War II Begin?)*, (Moscow, AST Publishing, 2000), page 235.

32 Viktor Suvorov, *Dien M: Kakda nachalas vtayara meeroviya voyna? (M-Day: When Did World War II Begin?)*, (Moscow, AST Publishing, 2000), page 226.

33 Viktor Suvorov, *Dien M: Kakda nachalas vtayara meeroviya voyna? (M-Day: When Did World War II Begin?)*, (Moscow, AST Publishing, 2000), page 232.

34 Mark Solonin, *22 Yunya: Anatomya Catastrophyee, (June 22: Anatomy of the Catastrophe),* (Moscow, Yauza-Press, Eksmo, 2009), page 408.

35 Nikoulin N. N., *Vospomenania O Vineyneh (Memoirs About the War),* (St. Petersburg, The State Hermitage, 2008), page 25.

36 Barbara Demick, *Nothing to Envy: Real Lives in North Korea,* (Granta Publications, 2010), page 53.

37 Thomas Sowell, "Thomas Sowell: Even with slavery, power is limited", Washington Examiner website, published on April 21, 2010, consulted on June 15, 2022, https://www.washingtonexaminer.com/thomas-sowell-even-with-slavery-power-is-limited.

38 The wage of a Soviet worker during WWII was typically enough to buy food for two days on the black market and nothing else. People survived on the rations the state distributed. Soldiers in my time received a monthly wage which was enough to buy two boxes of shoe-polish. Something like this goes on in North Korea today. The essentials are administratively distributed by the state, there is virtually no shopping and no money. (Barbara Demick, *Nothing to Envy: Real Lives in North Korea,* (Granta Publications, 2010), page 62.)

39 Marina Svanidze, *Estoricheskiye Hroniki si Nikolaim Svanidze, (Historical Chronicles with Nikolai Svanidze*), Volume one, (Amphora Publishers, Saint Petersburg, 2007), page 163.

40 R. J. Rummel, *Never Again: Ending War, Democide, & Famine Through Democratic Freedom,* (nonfiction supplement), (The United States of America, Llumina Press, 2005), pages 93, 94; Marina Svanidze, *Estoricheskiye Hroniki si Nikolaim Svanidze, (Historical Chronicles with Nikolai Svanidze*), Volume one, (Amphora Publishers, Saint Petersburg, 2007), page 137.

41 Karl Marx and Frederick Engels, "Preface to the 1882 Russian Edition" of the Communist Manifesto, Marxists

Internet Archive website, 2010, page 5, consulted on September 23, 2019, https://www.marxists.org/archive/marx/works/download/pdf/Manifesto.pdf.

42 Marina Svanidze, *Estoricheskiye Hroniki si Nikolaim Svanidze, (Historical Chronicles with Nikolai Svanidze*), Volume one, (Amphora Publishers, Saint Petersburg, 2007), page 113.

43 "How to Unite your Team: Advice from Napoleon", published on December 31, 2012, on The Grassy Road, consulted on February 16, 2021, https://pennyherscher.com/2012/12/31/how-to-unite-your-team-advice-fro/.

44 Katharina Isabel Schmidt, Henry Maine's "Modern Law": From Status to Contract and Back Again?, published on June 13, 2017, consulted on March 9, 2021, https://academic.oup.com/ajcl/article-abstract/65/1/145/3867144?redirectedFrom=fulltext.

45 S L Feerosov, *Eestoria Rasee: Oochebnik diliya Srednyeevah Prasfessionalnava Abrazavania, (History of Russia: Textbook for Intermediate Professional Education),* (Moscow, Yourite Publishing, 2019), page 226; There were 245 big peasant uprisings in 1918 alone, Igor Bunich, *Zlatoto na Partiata (The Party's Gold),* (Sofia, Prozoretz publishing house, 1993), page 24).

46 Some were abolished as late as 1923: See, for example, Thomas de Waal, *The Caucasus: An Introduction,* (Oxford University Press, New York, 2010), page 79.

47 Roy Medvedev, *Let History Judge: The Origins and Consequences of Stalinism,* Revised and expanded edition, (Columbia University Press, 1989), page 53.

48 Marina Svanidze, *Estoricheskiye Hroniki si Nikolaim Svanidze, (Historical Chronicles with Nikolai Svanidze*), Volume one, (Amphora Publishers, Saint Petersburg, 2007), page 221.

49 Vadim J. Birstein, *SMERSH – Stalin's Secret Weapon,* (London, Biteback Publishing, 2011), page 175.

50 Peter Kenez, *A History of the Soviet Union from the Beginning to the End,* (Cambridge, Cambridge University Press, 2006), page 33.

51 Leonid Mlechin, *Lenin: Soblaznenie Rossii (Lenin: The Seduction of Russia),* (Peter Publishing, Moscow, 2012), page 291.

52 Leonid Mlechin, *Lenin: Soblaznenie Rossii (Lenin: The Seduction of Russia),* (Peter Publishing, Moscow, 2012), pages 294–297.

53 R. J. Rummel, *Death by Government,* (New Jersey, Transaction Publishers, 1995), page 175.

54 Granitza Na Zamkye (The Border is Padlocked), 1937 film, produced by Syoozdyetfilm, directed by Vasily Jhuravlov, all soviet movies on RVISION YouTube channel, published on May 27, 2013, consulted on June 15, 2022, https://www.youtube.com/watch?v=VFnmKhkHn8A.

55 Viktor Suvorov, *Icebreaker,* (London, Hamish Hamilton Ltd, 1990), Internet Archive website, consulted on June 15, 2022, https://archive.org/stream/IcebreakerWhoStartedTheSecondWorldWar/SuvorovViktor-Icebreaker.WhoStartedTheSecondWorldWar_djvu.txt

56 R. J. Rummel, *Death by Government,* (New Jersey, Transaction Publishers, 1995), Chapter 1.

57 Marina Svanidze, *Estoricheskiye Hroniki si Nikolaim Svanidze, (Historical Chronicles with Nikolai Svanidze*), Volume one, (Amphora Publishers, Saint Petersburg, 2007), page 128.

58 This word was used by one of those who used machine-guns against the peasants armed with pitch-forks: Igor Bunich, *Zlatoto na Partiata (The Party's Gold),* (Sofia, Prozoretz publishing house, 1993), page 25.

59 Vladlen Sirotkin, *Stalin: Kak Zastavit Liudeay Rabotat, (Stalin: How to Make People Work?),* (Moscow, Algorithm Publishing, 2004), pages 346, 347.

60 Zhelyu Zhelev, *Fascismut (The Fascism)*, (BZNS Publishing, Sofia, 1990), page 244.

61 Viktor Suvorov, *Poslednata Republika: Zashto Savetskiyat Sayooz Zagoobi Vtorata Svetovna Voina? (The Last Republic: Why the Soviet Union Lost World War II?)*, (Fakel Express publishing, Sofia, 1996), page 35.

62 Vladlen Sirotkin, *Stalin: Kak Zastavit Liudeay Rabotat, (Stalin: How to Make People Work?)*, (Moscow, Algorithm Publishing, 2004), page 166.

63 Fred Shapiro, "Quotes Uncovered: Big Government and Peculiarities", Freakonomics website, published on October 1, 2009, consulted on April 19, 2020. https://freakonomics.com//2009/10/01/quotes-uncovered-big-government-and-peculiarities/?utm_source=feedburner&utm_medium=feed&utm_campaign=Feed%3A+FreakonomicsBlog+%28Freakonomics+Blog%29.

64 Siobhan McLoughlin, "Freedom of the Good: A Study of Plato's Ethical Conception of Freedom", UNM Digital Repository website, published in 2012, consulted on August 20, 2020, https://digitalrepository.unm.edu/cgi/viewcontent.cgi?article=1014&context=phil_etds.

Chapter 3

Attempts to Prevent WWII Made It Happen

Germany's invasion of Poland in 1939 is considered the beginning of WWII. This would not have happened had Britain not given a war guarantee to Poland. Ironically, Britain did it in order to prevent a new world war.

The British Guarantee

Not many people remember now that all Germany wanted from Poland in 1938 was the "reunion" of Danzig and consent to the building of "an extra-territorial motor road and railway line" across the "Corridor". Berlin offered to leave Warsaw in control of the economic and railway facilities in Danzig and guaranteed Poland's frontiers.[1]

Let's explain what these words mean. It was called a "reunion" because Danzig used to be part of Germany – it was 95 per cent German and its population wanted to be reunited with Germany. Besides, Poland should have returned it under the Treaty of Versailles since it already had another port on the Baltic. The "Corridor" itself was also former German territory. Hitler did not want it back, he just wanted a passageway through it so that the Germans may reach Danzig. The demand was "remarkably moderate", as the British historian Basil Liddell Hart observed.[2]

To put this into context, Hitler was trying to reverse the results of WWI. The Munich Agreement gave him the Sudetenland. That was another territory inhabited by Germans who were not consulted as to whether they wanted to be citizens of Germany when the Treaty of Versailles placed them inside Czechoslovakia.

However, Hitler got greedy after this. He violated the Munich Agreement when he invaded the remainder of Czechoslovakia in 1939. This showed not only that he could not be trusted but that he wanted more than simply uniting the Germans. The message Britain got was that there was no point in making any more allowances to keep the peace. Prior to this, the West was prepared to give Germany some concessions in order to prevent a new and devastating war. Now it became clear that concessions did not work.

It was against this background that on 31 March, 1939, Britain declared an unconditional guarantee of the Polish independence, hoping to deter Hitler from aggression against Poland.

Observers were appalled by this move. British soldier turned military historian Liddell Hart said:

> The Polish Guarantee was the surest way to produce an early explosion, and a world war. It combined the maximum temptation with manifest provocation. It incited Hitler to demonstrate the futility of such a guarantee to a country out of reach from the West, while making the stiff-necked Poles even less inclined to consider any concession to him, and at the same time making it impossible for him to draw back without "losing face".

In the words of the former First Lord of the Admiralty, Lord Duff Cooper, "the decision whether or not Britain goes to war" was left in the hands of Poland.[3] The French shared the view that the British guarantee was madness but had to follow its ally's lead. The result, now that Poland had her war guarantees from the two great Western democracies, was that it was not willing to make any concessions to Germany.[4] A peaceful solution was no longer possible.

Still, this development was not enough to ignite a world war by itself. Invading Poland was dangerous to Germany for a number of reasons, not least of which was the potential position of the USSR. The latter, just like Poland, was a predominantly Slav country. Also, it bordered on Poland and therefore could send a lot more military equipment and "volunteers" than it did to Spain during the Civil War there.

The Chief Culprit[5]

The war guarantee story converged on another that is less known today. A series of new studies reveal that the Soviet Union was looking for a way to instigate a big war in Europe and, after the "capitalist" countries exhausted each other fighting amongst themselves, to conquer it. As Birstein points out, the literature on this is growing.[6] Some of the drafts of the Soviet war plans to attack Germany in June/July 1941 were found,[7] and these neatly correspond with what the Red Army actually did on the ground.[8] There were also Russian-German phrasebooks containing strange questions that could have been asked only on German soil, and the fact that the Red Army had excellent topographic maps of Germany but not of its own territory.[9] Then there was the numerous non-documentary evidence that has been compiled so far, such as the type of weaponry developed. For example, the Soviet navy hardware was suited for an offensive and not a defensive war,[10] the main type of war plane developed was suited for a situation where the Soviet Airforce attacked first,[11] the Baltic Fleet was useless in a defensive war, but crucial in an offensive one,[12] the location of the Soviet air bases was suitable for an offence but not defence,[13] the fact that USSR had not only 7 times more tanks than Germany, but that these tanks were of superior quality,[14] that the munitions factories were located near the border and the way munitions were stored on the ground,[15] the massive airborne forces,[16] and so on. The evidence is too numerous to squeeze into a paragraph. In fact, it is too large to squeeze into a single book, given that the literature on it already runs into thousands, if not tens of thousands, of pages and dozens of books.

Britain and France did not know that the USSR was trying to instigate a war at the time, but they should have. Soviet propaganda was not hiding the intention that socialism must be spread all over the world as a result of a great war. Lenin was talking of a war that would spread socialism before WWI had even ended in his Military Programme for the Proletarian Revolution.[17] Zinoviev, another Soviet leader, said:

> If Russia makes peace, this peace will only be temporary. The Socialist Revolution in Russia will only win when it is surrounded by a ring of sister socialist republics. A peace made with imperialist Germany would only be an episodic phenomenon. It will provide a short break, after which war will boil once again.[18]

Britain and France did not need to have access to top secret Soviet documents as the very Soviet code of arms expressed this idea clearly. It featured the whole Earth with a hammer and a sickle on it, representing a borderless state spread over the globe. Fittingly, there wasn't anything national in the national anthem of the Soviet Union. The anthem was "L'Internationale", the French song that was used by the international socialist movement. It was translated into Russian with minor changes, and it still referred to freeing the workers all over the world and not particularly in Russia. An enormous number of overt publications openly expressed the same idea: from the speeches of government leaders published in *Pravda Daily* to the movies shown in the theatres. (The movies in the USSR were scripted, produced, and directed by the Soviet government just like the newspaper articles were.) For example, a war is the prelude to spreading socialism to the West in the most popular Soviet movie at the time: *If War Comes Tomorrow* (1938). *The Great*

Citizen (1937) went even further, with a scene explaining how the USSR would have 30–40 new republics after a "good war".[19] (The scene was cut after WWII, when the war turned out to be not so good for USSR.) One day after *The Great Citizen* was released, Stalin wrote in *Pravda Daily* that the one thing which guarantees capitalism cannot be restored is the international victory of socialism.[20]

Then there were the many Soviet policies that had one explanation only: the USSR was preparing for a large, aggressive war. Its industrialisation was aimed at production of weapons – offensive weapons at that. A Western nation like Britain should have been aware of this as most of the factories built in the Soviet Union were bought from the West. The USSR had developed one of the largest airborne forces in the world since the 1930s and these could be utilised only in an offensive war. The newsreels showing Red Army paratroopers were not kept secret; British intelligence missed clues that were accessible to the general public.

Incidentally, many scholars underestimated Soviet movies as historical sources. Of course, movies under socialism reflected not the reality but a virtual reality – they were propaganda – but this virtual reality could tell an experienced viewer a lot about the actual reality. In a sense they were government documents under socialism because they were produced only by the government. Everyone involved, from the director to the actor, was a government employee in the same way as the policemen or teachers. These movies accurately reflected the intentions of the political leadership and not the artistic preferences of their scriptwriters or directors. Stalin personally watched every movie before it was released[21] and gave instructions to its director. As historian Roy Medvedev aptly put it, Stalin "edited" the movies.[22]

We may argue whether the USSR really wanted a big European war or not, but one thing is certain: what Stalin did next made it happen. The Soviet Union was informed by British and French representatives in Moscow in August 1939 that their governments were serious about stopping Hitler and that they would declare war on Germany if it attacked Poland. But the USSR did not join Britain and France.[23] It did just the opposite and allied itself with Germany, backing it to confront Britain and France. Instead of cautioning Hitler to leave Poland alone, the USSR incentivised him to invade it by offering him more than Danzig (which was all Hitler demanded). Hitler himself admitted he would not have had the courage to invade Poland if it was not for the Soviet position.[24] It was the USSR that proposed the Molotov-Ribbentrop Pact, according to which Germany would get half of Poland. Furthermore, the USSR supplied Germany with oil and other resources to make it possible for the latter to wage war in Europe.

This policy was in accordance with what Stalin said privately:

> The war is between two groups of capitalist nations... but we are not against it, if they fight a bit and weaken each other. It would be good if Germany could destabilise the positions of the wealthiest capitalist nations (of England especially). Hitler, without knowing it, is weakening the foundations of the capitalist system.... We, in the meantime, are able to manoeuvre, to nudge one country on against the other, so that the fight will be more intense.[25]

It is not surprising, then, that Stalin was so happy after he signed the Molotov-Ribbentrop Pact, boasting that he had deceived Hitler.[26]

Indeed, he had. While Germany attacked on 1 September 1939, the Soviet Union did not. Germany repeatedly reminded the USSR that it is supposed to invade as well.[27] However, the Soviet Union waited until Britain and France declared war on the only aggressor, Germany, and until Germany had done most of the most of the dirty work crushing the Polish resistance. Only then USSR took its own share.

The History of the History

Stalin's trick worked so well that it still works. If you stop a passer-by on the street in any country in the West today, the chances are that they will know about Germany invading Poland but will not know that the USSR invaded the same Poland in the same month of the same year. Woody Allen summarized the public perceptions: "I just can't listen to any more Wagner, you know... I'm starting to get the urge to conquer Poland."[28]

If Wagner is replaced with Shostakovich, no one will get the joke. The laypeople will know even less about the fact that the USSR, not Germany, came up with the whole idea of partitioning Poland. Somehow it does not matter that the Molotov-Ribbentrop Pact was published as early as 1948 and it does not matter that even the USSR eventually admitted its existence (the Soviet government claimed it was a forgery at first) and condemned it in 1989.[29]

In 2019, the European Parliament declared that the USSR should be equally blamed alongside Germany for starting WWII.[30] Albeit the adopted resolution said nothing that would be new to historians, it is an indication that the facts finally began to match the conventional wisdom. It only took 71 years. Incidentally, it took the European Parliament even longer to recognise other historical facts. For example, it declared as recently as December 2022 that it now recognised the 1933 Soviet starvation of Ukrainians as genocide.[31]

The slowness of the European Parliament explains this delay to some extent. Stalin's deviousness also explains why it takes so long for certain facts to be recognised. He was exceedingly good at hiding behind the scenes whenever there was dirty work to be done. Stalin organised the collectivisation in the early 1930s which ended with seven million peasants being starved to death and with about as many more sent to concentration camps (these events are explained more in the "Stalin Lost Because He Prepared Too Well" chapter) and yet it was low-level officials who were blamed for it all.[32] He launched the Great Terror in the late part of the same decade which ended with several million more exterminated, but it was Yezhov, Stalin's NKVD chief, who was blamed for it. (This period became known as "Yezhovshtina" in the USSR, a name derivative from Yezhov.) Stalin gave the appearance of legality to everything he did: from show trials to the invasion of Finland and South Korea which, supposedly, both attacked their socialist neighbours and thus provoked the respective wars.[33]

The Molotov-Ribbentrop Pact was more of the same. Even its name reflected this: it was signed in Moscow and yet was not named after that city (like, say, the Munich Agreement of 1938), it was signed by Stalin and yet it did not bear his name. It was Hitler's turn now to be a pawn in Stalin's game and he was: he, alone, was blamed for starting WWII.

As can be expected, Putin doesn't share this opinion. He said that blaming Stalin for the German invasion is "the height of cynicism".[34] In this respect, the majority of Western authors are in full agreement with him.

The West Lost WWII

Because WWII had losers, people assume there were winners. However, wars are not boxing matches where the winner ends with a hefty sum of money, a win in his career, and a few bruises that will heal in a week. Usually everybody loses in a war, even the winner. Pierre Boiste observed a long time ago that, "War is a process that impoverishes those who win it."

Germany and Britain fell into Stalin's trap in 1939. They were at war, exhausting each other, while the USSR rested on the sidelines. The Communists had their big war at last.

Although it did not go as planned (something covered in the "Stalin Lost Because He Prepared Too Well" chapter), it was still to bring Stalin a substantial expansion of his empire by 1945 and it was to cause Britain to eventually lose its own empire.[35] Thus, a genocidal totalitarian empire became enlarged while a "civilising" liberal empire became diminished.

Moreover, the West as a whole was weakened. A murderous totalitarian system, that of National Socialism, was no more, but it was replaced by an even more powerful totalitarian system that exterminated three times more people: that of Soviet Socialism.[36] National Socialism was destroyed but so was Germany and therefore it was in no position to protect Europe against invasion from the East during the Cold War. The USA had to predominantly shoulder this burden. While Britain and the USA had enemies they could vanquish before WWII (like Germany and Japan), they had enemies they could not possibly defeat militarily afterwards (like USSR and China).

One of the consequences of WWII was that China and North Korea became socialist countries. This is a problem the world still has to deal with in the twenty-first century.

Knowing what we know now, we should be amazed at how ahead of his time Harry S. Truman, the future President of the United States, was when he said in 1941: "If we see that Germany is winning the war, we ought to help Russia; and if that Russia is winning, we ought to help Germany, and in that way let them kill as many as possible..."[37]

Soviet Socialism and National Socialism were both genocidal, aggressive, and dangerous. Instead of Britain (and later the USA) exhausting itself by fighting one of the two monsters, it could have left the two monsters to fight each other. That was easy to achieve because all Britain had to do was to do nothing: to stay out of it by either not giving a war guarantee to Poland or, if it did that, by accepting the German peace offer once France fell instead of continuing the war.

If Truman had his way, whichever of the two totalitarian states won would have been weakened and therefore been less able to take over Europe. However, the war between the two totalitarian states was shortened as the West got involved early on (just as Stalin wanted). Thanks to this, the war between National Socialism and Soviet Socialism did not drag on into 1946 and the Soviet Union did not emerge so exhausted as to be less dangerous. What Britain effectively did was to do some of the Soviets' job. It expended British blood and British treasure in order to save Soviet blood and Soviet treasure. This made sure the USSR is capable of waging a Cold War and threaten the West with a "hot" one. In a sense, the British government served Soviet interests better than its own.

As for Poland, the country where it all started, it lost far more than Danzig. All of its territory was lost to the Soviet empire, an empire that was no less brutal than Hitler's given that it murdered three times more people than the National Socialists did.[38]

WWII is tragic not only because tens of millions perished in it, but because its stupidity seems so obvious in hindsight.

Endnotes

1 Patrick J. Buchanan, *Churchill, Hitler, and "The Unnecessary War": How Britain Lost Its Empire and the West Lost the World*, (New York, Three Rivers Press, 2008), pages 241–242.

2 Patrick J. Buchanan, *Churchill, Hitler, and "The Unnecessary War": How Britain Lost Its Empire and the West Lost the World*, (New York, Three Rivers Press, 2008), page 245.

3 Patrick J. Buchanan, *Churchill, Hitler, and "The Unnecessary War": How Britain Lost Its Empire and the West Lost the World*, (New York, Three Rivers Press, 2008), page 256.

4 Patrick J. Buchanan, *Churchill, Hitler, and "The Unnecessary War": How Britain Lost Its Empire and the West Lost the World*, (New York, Three Rivers Press, 2008), pages 257, 258.

5 Viktor Suvorov made the case in his book *The Chief Culprit: Stalin's Grand Design to Start World War II*, (Annapolis, Maryland, Naval Institute Press, 2013.

6 Vadim J. Birstein, *SMERSH – Stalin's Secret Weapon*, (London, Biteback Publishing, 2011), page 46; Mark Solonin, *22 Yunya, ili Kogda nachalas' Velikaya Otechestvennaya Voyna? (June 22, or when the Great Patriotic War began?)*, (Moscow, Yauza-Press, 2005) (in Russian); Anatolii Tsyganok, 'K kakoi voyne gotovilas' Krasnaya armiya? Chast' pervaya,' Polit.ru, June 18, 2006 (in Russian), http://www.polit.ru/analytics/2006/06/16/whichwar.html, retrieved September 4, 2011."

7 Mark Solonin, *22 Yunya: Anatomya Catastrophyee, (June 22: Anatomy of the Catastrophe)*, (Moscow, Yauza-Press, Eksmo, 2009), pages 174–182.

8 Details see in Viktor Suvorov, *Vzemum Si Dumitay Nazad, (I Take it Back)*, (Sofia, Fakel Express publishing, 2004), pages 134–138.

9 Viktor Suvorov, *Poslednata Republika: Zashto Savetskiyat Sayooz Zagoobi Vtorata Svetovna Voyna? (The Last Republic: Why the Soviet Union Lost World War II?)*, (Fakel Express publishing, Sofia, 1996), pages 191–205 and 223–230.

10 Viktor Suvorov, *Dien M: Kakda nachalas vtayara meeroviya voyna? (M-Day: When Did World War II Begin?)*, (Moscow, AST Publishing, 2000), pages 88, 89.

11 Viktor Suvorov, *Dien M: Kakda nachalas vtayara meeroviya voyna? (M-Day: When Did World War II Begin?)*, (Moscow, AST Publishing, 2000), page 128–144.

12 Viktor Suvorov, *V Syankata Na Pobedata (Shadow of Victory)*, (Sofia, Fakel Express publishing, 2003), pages 41–46.

13 Viktor Suvorov, *V Syankata Na Pobedata (Shadow of Victory)*, (Sofia, Fakel Express publishing, 2003), pages 76–80.

14 Viktor Suvorov, *Poslednata Republika: Zashto Savetskiyat Sayooz Zagoobi Vtorata Svetovna Voyna? (The Last Republic:*

Why the Soviet Union Lost World War II?), (Fakel Express publishing, Sofia, 1996), pages 209–217.

15 Viktor Suvorov, *Dien M: Kakda nachalas vtayara meeroviya voyna? (M-Day: When Did World War II Begin?),* (Moscow, AST Publishing, 2000), page 123, 124.

16 Viktor Suvorov, *Poslednata Republika: Zashto Savetskiyat Sayooz Zagoobi Vtorata Svetovna Voyna? (The Last Republic: Why the Soviet Union Lost World War II?),* (Fakel Express publishing, Sofia, 1996), pages 273–291.

17 Viktor Suvorov, *Icebreaker,* (London, Hamish Hamilton Ltd, 1990), page 17.

18 Viktor Suvorov, *The Chief Culprit: Stalin's Grand Design to Start World War II,* (Annapolis, Maryland, Naval Institute Press, 2013), page 28.

19 "The Great Citizen (1937)", published on February 28, 2018 on the Mair Nur-Bek YouTube channel, consulted on October 11, 2019, https://www.youtube.com/watch?v=iXQo1o4RrpI; "Pakt o Nyenapadeynee Molotova na Ribbentropa. Zveyzdnyeh chas Stalina, chast 2", (The Molotov Ribbentrop Pact. Stalin's finest hour. Part 2), Mark Solonin YouTube channel, published on December 2021, consulted on June 7, 2021, https://www.youtube.com/watch?v=6hUwDIrLrms.

20 Viktor Suvorov, *Razgrom (Defeat),* (Moscow, AST publishing, 2010), page 85.

21 Roy Medvedev, *Bleejnee Krug Stalina: Saratnikee Vajdyah. (The Inner Circle of Stalin: Associates of the Chief),* (Yauza-Press, Eksmo), 2005), page 113.

22 Roy Medvedev, *Bleejnee Krug Stalina: Saratnikee Vajdyah. (The Inner Circle of Stalin: Associates of the Chief),* (Yauza-Press, Eksmo, 2005), page 124.

23 Viktor Suvorov, *The Chief Culprit: Stalin's Grand Design to Start World War II,* (Annapolis, Maryland, Naval Institute Press, 2013), page 108.

24 "The pact between Stalin and Hitler: a triumph or tragedy", (Pact Stalina suh Gitlerom: trioomph eleh tragedia), Radio Liberty YouTube channel, streamed live on August 26, 2019, consulted on November 5, 2021, https://www.youtube.com/watch?v=E-7CnMRS-Xw

25 Viktor Suvorov, *The Chief Culprit: Stalin's Grand Design to Start World War II*, (Annapolis, Maryland, Naval Institute Press, 2013), page 109.

26 "The Molotov-Ribbentrop Pact: Secretly and Suddenly", BBC website, published on July 31, 2009, consulted on February 16, 2021, https://www.bbc.com/russian/russia/2009/08/090731_ussr_germany_pact_history.

27 Viktor Suvorov, *The Chief Culprit: Stalin's Grand Design to Start World War II*, (Annapolis, Maryland, Naval Institute Press, 2013), page 112.

28 "100 Woody Allen Quotes That Highlight His Take on Life", The Famous People website, consulted on August 27, 2022, https://quotes.thefamouspeople.com/woody-allen-3439.php.

29 "Postanovleneyeah Sayezdah Narodneekh Deputatov SSSR o Paktyeh Molotova Ribbentropa ot 24.09.1989" (Decree of the People's Deputy Congress of USSR about the Molotov-Ribbentrop Pact from 24.09.1989), Documentee Dvadsatava Vyekah website (Documents from the 20th century website), consulted on June 1, 2020, http://doc20vek.ru/node/3261.

30 European Parliament resolution on the 80th anniversary of the start of the Second World War and the importance of European remembrance for the future of Europe, European Parliament website, consulted on September 30, 2019, http://www.europarl.europa.eu/doceo/document/B-9-2019-0098_EN.html.

31 "Holodomor: Parliament recognises Soviet starvation of Ukrainians as genocide", European Parliament website, published on December 15, 2022, consulted on December 15,

2022, https://www.europarl.europa.eu/news/en/press-room/20221209IPR64427/holodomor-parliament-recognises-soviet-starvation-of-ukrainians-as-genocide.

32 "J. Stalin, Glalavokruzhaynieh ot Oospyehav. K Vaprosam Kalhosnavah Dveejaniah" ("Dizzy with Success. Concerning Questions of the Collective-Farm Movement"), 100(0) key documents website, Department of History, Friedrich-Alexander University, consulted on June 15, 2022, https://www.1000dokumente.de/index.html/index.html?c=dokument_ru&dokument=0007_erf&object=translation&l=ru

33 On South Korea see Kaystoot Zakoretskiy, *Tret'ia Miravaya Voyna Stalina (Stalin's World War III)*, (Moscow, Yauza-Press, 2009), page 146; On Finland see Vadim J. Birstein, *SMERSH—Stalin's Secret Weapon*, (London, Biteback Publishing, 2011), page 76.

34 RIA Novosti, Putin Raskriteekaval Ziyavleneeya O Razvyazeevanee Stalineem Voinee (Putin Criticised The Statement About Stalin Instigating The War) published on October 3, 2019, consulted on December 9, 2022, https://ria.ru/20191003/1559415462.html?in=t.

35 Andrew Stewart, Empire Lost: Britain, the Dominions and the Second World War, (London, New York, Continuum, 2008).

36 R. J. Rummel, *Death by Government*, (New Jersey, Transaction Publishers, 1995), pages V, VI.

37 Kristine Phillips, "'He is honest – but smart as hell': When Truman met Stalin", Washington Post website, published on 17 July 2018, consulted on 3 November 2021, https://www.washingtonpost.com/news/retropolis/wp/2018/07/17/he-is-honest-but-smart-as-hell-when-truman-met-stalin/.

38 About 62 million as opposed to about 21 million: R. J. Rummel, *Death by Government*, (New Jersey, Transaction Publishers, 1995), page V.

Chapter 4

Stalin Lost Because He Prepared Too Well

The beginning of Operation Barbarossa in 1941 is usually presented as an unstoppable advance of the superior Nazi war machine against a technologically backward Soviet Union. (This looks plausible on the surface – after all, the Germans conquered most of Europe very quickly, while Russia had a long history of being technologically old-fashioned.) The initial success of the Germans was also explained in terms of what in historiography is often referred to as Stalin "decapitating" his army in 1937–39. The capable officers were supposedly executed during the purge, leaving the army without experienced commanders.

But what if the technological obsolescence and the "decapitation" were myths invented by the Soviet propaganda? There is evidence that the first – regarding Russia's tech inefficiency – was started by Stalin himself, and the second was created by his successor, Nikita Khrushchev. Both claims have been debunked since the Soviet Union collapsed. It turned out that it was the USSR who had technological superiority in 1941 and that there was no "decapitation".

So, if this is true, how were the Germans able to reach Moscow in 1941? The ironic answer is that this was because the USSR was technologically better prepared for war. It enjoyed modern, well-designed weaponry while the Germans had antiquated and inadequate models in 1941.

USSR Better Armed Than Germany

The only proof of Germany's technological superiority was that this was claimed by the USSR. The first reference to it is in Stalin's speech given in the Mayakovskaya Metro station on 6 November 1941. He explained the German success in terms of the Red Army not having enough tanks and aeroplanes.[1] What the Soviet leader said became the cannon of Soviet propaganda. No Western scholar ever checked the validity of these assertions on the ground, studying and counting actual tanks and aeroplanes, nor would they have been allowed to. Since historians in the West had no access to actual proof, they uncritically began to repeat the assertions of the Soviet government.

Soviet propaganda, as usual, was asserting the opposite of what was true.

Soviet tanks were superior to the German tanks in every respect: firepower, armour, cross-country passability and reliability. Moreover, the USSR had over seven times more of them. (These details are given in Appendix 1.)

The situation was similar with the artillery. While the German howitzers were WWI models (FH-13 and FH-18 – the digits show the year that these were adopted, namely 1913 and 1918), the Soviet ones were designed in the late 1930s and were so advanced that some models were still being used at the start of the twenty-first century. On top of that, the USSR had a lot more of them.

The USSR also had more aeroplanes: 24,488 to Germany's 6852.[2] Moreover, many Soviet models were superior to the German ones. For example, the MiG-3 was faster than its counterpart, the Messerschmitt 109.[3] Unlike Germany, the USSR had heavy bombers, which was how it was able to bomb Berlin in 1941. The TB-7 bomber was invulnerable to the German fighters and air defence because it could fly at 12,000 metres while Germany had no aircraft that could go that high.

The list could be continued with the automatic firearms, the towing vehicles, the parachutes. The USSR had more and better of everything. So, there was technological superiority, but it was the Soviets who enjoyed it. Whatever the reason for the German success in 1941, weaponry does not explain it.

No Decapitation

The Red Army was poorly led in 1941, the story goes, because it was "decapitated", between 1937–1939 when 40,000 officers were allegedly executed. The good Soviet officers were supposedly shot and the junior ones who filled the vacancies lacked experience in their new posts. Also, according to this story, the replacements lacked initiative because they were scared that they too may be purged.

The decapitation myth was invented under Khrushchev in order to discredit Stalin when he denounced him, and has been used by many others since, in order to explain how a small and relatively poorly-armed German Army succeeded in reaching Moscow[4] in 1941 despite fighting a better-armed opponent.[5] A document stating that 40,000 officers were discharged,[6] some of them honourably because of old age, was deliberately misquoted by the Soviet propaganda which claimed for decades that 40,000 were shot. Incompetent officers who were indeed executed, like Mikhail Tukhachevsky, were proclaimed geniuses after 1956. Under one variant, Stalin did it because of a provocation organised by the German military intelligence.

In fact, just several hundred army officers were shot.[7] This was not a result of a German provocation. Incidentally, the provocation story is so full of obvious holes that it is incredible it has been taken seriously for so long. (For example, it contains an episode where the Germans supposedly melt gold Soviet coins when in fact the type of money mentioned was actually paper banknotes. In another episode, German intelligence battles a Soviet security service which didn't exist at the time.)[8] Those executed were unruly, incompetent, and the army was better off without them. Moreover, most of those shot were not actually military officers but commissars and magistrates or belonged to the secret police.[9] Incidentally, it was not claimed that Stalin had decapitated the secret police yet it suffered far more extensive purges during the late 1930s.[10] Although several hundred still feels like a significant number, it was modest for the time. The USSR exterminated people by tens of millions during the 1930s. The officer corps was over 200,000 strong so, in percentage terms, it suffered less than the general population.[11]

Turning Corpses into Tanks

To understand how the Germans reached Moscow in 1941, we must remember that the staggering technological superiority the Soviets enjoyed on 22 June 1941 was achieved at the expense of the Soviet people. They were exterminated, terrorised, made to work long hours with no choice of job or pay (see the "Freeing the Workers Enslaved Them" chapter), lived in misery, and sometimes were driven to cannibalism. The USSR was converting human corpses into modern weaponry in the 1930s (exporting the grain of the starving peasants brought some of the currency for the heavy industry imported from the West[12]). About seven million people, most of them Ukrainians, were purposefully starved to death between 1932–1933 alone.[13] A comparable number were sent to concentration camps and few of them returned. The following extract shows how this worked in practice:

There were people who cut up and cooked corpses, who killed their own children and ate them. I saw one. She had been brought to the district centre under convoy. Her face was human, but her eyes were those of a wolf. These are cannibals, they said, and must be shot. But they themselves, who drove the mother to the madness of eating her own children, are evidently not guilty at all!... Just go and ask, and they will all tell you that they did it for the sake of virtue, for everybody's good. That's why they drove mothers to cannibalism.[14]

There were so many incidents of cannibalism that the secret police had to distribute a special instruction on what is to be done in such cases. Some people were eating members of their own families while others were ambushing strangers. Searches resulted in the discovery of children's corpses being cooked. Sometimes the parents ate their children. A mother instructed her children to eat her if she died. Human corpses were being sold for food.[15] In other cases mothers would kill their weakest children to feed the rest.[16] Given all that, several women gathered a group of children together to protect them only for them to end up eating the smallest child alive, some drinking the blood of his wounds.[17]

To put the number of seven million in perspective, the Communists exterminated more Ukrainians in a single year than the National Socialists exterminated Jews during the entire war.[18] As Professor Rafael Lemkin who drafted the (Genocide) Convention pointed out: "[The] Ukrainian famine was a deliberate act of genocide of roughly the same order of magnitude as the Jewish Holocaust of the Second World War, both in the number of its victims and in the human suffering it produced."[19]

The surviving Ukrainians did not like the USSR any more than the surviving Jews liked Nazi Germany. The same went for the Balts, the Chechens, the Kazakhs, and even the Russians, who also suffered during the 1930s.

A few years after this came the Great Terror, when millions more were exterminated for all manner of reasons. For example, the NKVD was even shooting "mothers and wives who appeared at NKVD headquarters for information about their arrested loved ones".[20] The most grotesque example has to be the murder of several hundred blind folksingers as part of the socialist policy to destroy the Ukrainian culture.[21]

It is not surprising that Soviet citizens preferred to fight their own government instead of the Germans when the latter invaded a decade later. Unlike in the rest of Europe, Hitler was met as a liberator in the USSR.[22]

The Second Russian Civil War

It is widely assumed that the first uprisings against Soviet rule were in East Germany in 1953, in Hungary in 1956, and in Czechoslovakia in 1968. However, recent studies have demonstrated that the first one took place as early as 1941 and was in the USSR itself. Even some of the symbols that are associated with these uprisings in Eastern Europe (like putting an equals sign between the swastika and hammer and sickle, thus equating Soviet socialism to the National Socialism) originated in the USSR.[23]

The uprising erupted against Soviet authority in the chaos caused by the German invasion in 1941.[24] It affected both civil and military authorities. The disintegration of a military detachment usually started with the loss of the commanding officers who sometimes fled or were shot by their subordinates.[25] The secret police were overwhelmed. An official remembers:

> There were numerous cases when formation commanders and privates left positions without an order, ran away in panic, and left all military equipment behind. The most dangerous is... that some special departments [how the secret police was known in the army] did not even investigate such cases and did not arrest the guilty servicemen, and they were not tried.[26]

The majority of Soviet citizens expected the arrival of German forces would mean a return to the pre-1917 way of life.[27] The authorities could no longer control the situation when the Germans neared a particular town.[28] The anarchic wave of insurgency among the civil population usually preceded the arrival of the German troops by two to three days. It began with the fleeing of the Soviet party and secret police (the forerunner of KGB) cadres.

> In many Soviet regions, especially Ukraine, in 1941 the local population greeted the German troops as liberators from the Soviet regime. The head of a partisan staff in Belarus reported that the day before the Germans came "the unstrained anti-Soviet individuals whistled at and unequivocally threatened the evacuating Soviet and Party activists and their families, while some Soviet administrators used every reason to escape the evacuation".[29]

A senior military prosecutor reported on 5 July 1941 that not a single institution functioned in the city of Vitebsk. All were closed and "self-liquidated", as he put it. People said that the Communists were fleeing and the NKVD and party cadres were indeed secretly evacuating.[30] Roughly the same was witnessed by Konstantin Simonov, one of the most famous Soviet writers, who was searching in vain for some government authority in Minsk, the capital of Belarus, on 26 June 1941.[31]

In both cases this was happening before the arrival of the German forces. Although the initial German invasion triggered the process (putting the Soviet command structure into disarray), it was the uprising that caused the German advance rather than the German advance causing the uprising.[32]

The fleeing Soviet cadres were afraid of their own population rather than of the Germans as the German authorities used the former Soviet cadres who stayed in their own administration.[33] (This makes sense when we think about how similar the two totalitarian brands of socialism were.)

The fleeing Soviet Party members and secret police officials were accompanied by open threats coming from the local population. On the other hand, the lower ranks, who were not threatened, found excuses not to evacuate to the Soviet rear; they preferred to be under German occupation.[34]

Meanwhile, the peasants disbanded the government farms and began dividing the land among themselves, arming themselves with the weapons abandoned by the fleeing troops and self-organising in order to protect their villages.[35] The deserters often sought civilian clothes to hide among the local population.[36]

The Red Army lost most of its soldiers due to mass surrenders and desertion.[37] This explains why the Soviet air force was bombing camps with Soviet POWs, an unprecedented fact in the history of the world.[38] Most of the KV tanks were ditched by their crews at the roadside just like the T-34s and the amphibious models, and the rifles and field guns, while the aeroplanes were abandoned on the airfields.[39]

Some of these weapons were used by the Germans against the Soviets until the end of the war.[40] The excellent Soviet 76 mm anti-tank gun was modified and used by the Wehrmacht on the Eastern front and in North Africa. There were German tankmen who fought on T-34s, and so on.

Stalin had built the most powerful arms industry in the world and stocked gigantic quantities of ammunition. Germany, by comparison, did not have enough ammunition but then, as Viktor Suvorov observed: "Hitler invaded the Soviet Union. Here, he had tremendous luck – at the very border he was able to take huge quantities of Soviet supplies. Without these supplies he would not have been able to reach Moscow."[41]

The Germans were mostly advancing unopposed in 1941 and the technical characteristics of the Soviet tanks are enough to prove that. Take the instances where German infantry divisions were successfully advancing against Soviet tank divisions.[42] This would have been impossible if there was any resistance given that the German anti-tank gun shells did not have enough energy to penetrate the T-34 let alone the heavy KV-1.[43] As a German soldier colourfully put it, the shells were bouncing off the Soviet armour like "rubber balls".[44]

The issue was the same when the Soviet tanks faced German tanks in 1941. Even the PZ-3s, let alone the other German models, had little chance of destroying T-34 from point blank range while T-34 could annihilate any German machine from over a kilometre away with its powerful 76 mm gun.[45] Worse than that, there were no PZ-3s in most places – the German 3rd Tank Group, for example, did not have a single one. As for the KV-1s, the German tanks had no chance of destroying them, with or without PZ-3s at hand. In other words, even if the Soviet tankmen were so inept that they could not fire a single shot (which clearly was not the case), it was still impossible for the Germans to defeat them in battle.[46]

So how did the Germans reach Moscow? The explanation is simple: they did not have to defeat anybody during the summer of 1941, they could just outflank the few Soviet units that fought because most Soviet tank crews simply abandoned their vehicles. Many Red Army soldiers and officers were surrendering en masse (sometimes in whole units)[47] and fully equipped (airmen along with their aircraft among them),[48] hoping to fight Stalin instead of Hitler. Even those who did not surrender turned against their own government:

> The memoirs of Soviet POWs mention an important psychological detail of being taken prisoner: "In a few days all imprisoned Red Army commanders suddenly turned into strong enemies of their own country, the country where they were born, and of the government which they had sworn allegiance to.... Those who continued to address 'comrade Commander' were punched in their faces or were even beaten up more seriously, and saying 'Gospodinofiser'

('Sir officer', the address used in the Czar's Army) became common"... These three generals soon became among the most enthusiastic supporters of General Andrei Vlasov and his army. These examples show that many servicemen hated the Soviet regime so much that they were ready to fight against it, even on the enemy's side.[49]

Sixty-three Soviet generals alone were in German captivity by the end of 1941.[50] It was not just the privates who were surrendering but the highest-ranking officers, those who were close to the regime and enjoyed tremendous power and privileges.

The uprising reached Moscow on 16 October. (Communists were destroying their party membership cards even before that.[51]) There was mass panic, looting of shops, and chaotic fleeing. What happened in Moscow mirrored what went on in all Soviet cities that had fallen into German hands already. It looked like Moscow would fall as well.[52] A Communist living in the capital at the time observed that "if the Germans had known what was going on in Moscow, 500 of their paratroopers could have taken over Moscow". The German intelligence services were not doing their job and Berlin only learned about the chaos in Moscow much later.[53]

By October 1941 a number of workers refused to work and even expressed anti-Soviet "moods" (as the Soviet jargon used in a report went) deep at the Soviet rear, far from the front. Some workers threatened to kill their bosses who were running away and hiding. There were those who shouted on the streets of a Soviet city, a city that was an important industrial centre: "Down with the Soviet government, long live father Hitler."[54]

The Russians proclaimed "independent states" on part of the Soviet territory.[55] The Lokot Republic was a self-governing region governed by Soviet citizens in the German occupied

Central Russia. The peasants got their land back, the government farms were mostly dissolved, industry was working and so were the schools, hospitals, and social services.[56] The order was kept, commerce flourished, the theatres opened and so on. While it seemed like normality was returning, the local militia was fighting the Soviet terrorists (partisans).[57] Their self-governance went as far as to sentence to death two German soldiers caught committing a murder and the sentence was carried out.[58]

The uprising developed into a civil war in many places.[59] Notably, more Soviet citizens fought against the Communists during WWII than during the Civil War that followed the 1917 coup.

> The scale of Russian collaboration with the Germans was astonishing. Approximately 10 percent of the whole population in the occupied territory supported the Germans, about 700,000 former Soviet servicemen became "hiwis" (non-combatant volunteers) and 1.4 million participated in the Nazi-controlled military units.[60]

These numbers could have been higher if Hitler did not forbid his generals to use the surrendering Soviet soldiers and those Soviet civilians who wanted to be drafted within the German army. They would have been even higher if the National Socialists did not commit the atrocities they committed in the USSR.

After WWII ended, the Soviet authorities put these events down to "panic" in order to hide the embarrassing fact that the people had risen up against it. Naturally, this approach required the myth of the German invincibility to be propagated. I remember both being repeated over and over in documentaries and feature films under socialism. We were taught from an early age that the Nazis were armed to the teeth while all the Soviet soldiers had was heroism.

Of this uprising little is known because the Communist propaganda hid it well.[61] Many Western scholars uncritically repeated its assertions as facts. Soviet historians fulfilled their orders to hide the uprising by painting the Red Army as being unprepared for war. For example, it depicted Soviet tanks as badly serviced and needing an overhaul, thus explaining the German success. These sources were then used by Western scholars who did not get their orders from USSR but also could not check their credibility.[62] The same went for the lie that the Soviet tanks were easier to set on fire. In fact, the majority of them were fitted with diesel engines and therefore were harder to set on fire than the tanks of Germany, the USA, Great Britain and all other combatant countries.[63] The reasonable question of how it was possible for the Germans to reach Moscow would have been asked if the truth that the Soviets had excellent weaponry had surfaced.

Ending the Uprising Ended Germany

Two factors re-established the socialist order in 1942–1943: on the one hand were Hitler's policies, on the other were Stalin's.

Hitler ordered the Soviet soldiers to be kept in overcrowded POW camps, where most of them died needlessly from starvation, disease, and exposure to the elements,[64] instead of being used against the Soviet state, which many of them were eager to do[65] or at least freeing them so that they could work the land in the German rear. Less than one tenth of these soldiers were released and almost none were used against Stalin.[66] (Vlasov's Army was to be created much later in the war.) The news of that spread fast.[67] Four out of the six million POWs were dead by the end of the war.[68] On top of this, the National Socialists by and large preserved the dreaded Soviet government farms[69] (the local population expected these to be abolished)[70] and committed atrocities against the civil population. As Vadim Birstein explains: "Soon the German atrocities against Soviet POWs and

Jews and later the whole population (with the German attitude toward Slavs as inferior Untermenschen) turned most of the people against the occupiers."[71]

This made some of the Soviet citizens, who volunteered to fight against Stalin, rebel against the Germans and the latter had to disband some of their detachments.[72] Overall, the Germans refused to use the numerous men who were not mobilised in the Red Army and who volunteered to fight under their command. The National Socialists would eventually try to correct this mistake when they saw the tide of war turning against them. After the defeat at Stalingrad, the Germans conceded that every nationality on Soviet territory was Aryan except for the Jews, the Gypsies, and the Poles. Consequently, the locals were allowed to govern themselves and to have their own detachments within the SS troops.[73] But that was too little too late.

Meanwhile, Stalin issued the draconian Order 227 popularly known as "Not a Step Back".[74] He ordered the families of the captured soldiers in the rear not to be provided with food by the state.[75] This, essentially, amounted to starving them to death.[76] The Soviet soldiers knew from this point on that not only would they die if they surrendered but that their families would die as well.

Still, 217,000 more Soviet soldiers had to be shot after being investigated by Soviet military counterintelligence alone.[77] That is a number equal to 15 full divisions. More were killed during interrogations.[78] Others were shot after being investigated by other institutions, and even more were shot by the blocking troops or by their own commanders. To put this into perspective, these numbers are comparable to the number of American servicemen killed on all fronts during WWII: 416,000.[79] As for those sentenced to death by the US military tribunals – a mere 146.[80] Lastly, there were the Soviet soldiers sentenced to serve in the so-called penal battalions which often amounted to a death sentence.

The Soviet soldiers had a clear choice: fight for Stalin, which may result in their deaths, or not fight for Stalin, which would mean certain death plus the death of their families. Stalin expressed this cynically when he said that great bravery was needed in order to retreat when you were in the Red Army.[81] He was telling the truth, judging by what veterans such as Professor Nikoulin remembers.[82] Advancing against the German machine guns meant probable death. Not advancing meant certain death.

The uprising was suppressed between 1942–1943, but at what cost? The USSR had lost its army, almost all its tanks and planes, most of its guns and small arms, vast stocks of fuel, metals, spare parts, clothing, shoes. Eighty-five per cent of its armaments industry[83] was gone along with the majority of its other industries, including almost 100 per cent of its aluminium production capabilities, its richest agricultural lands, and 40 per cent of its population.[84] Some industries were re-located deep into Soviet territory, far from the advancing Germans, but most could not. After all, one cannot possibly re-locate a hydroelectric power plant along with the dam or a blast furnace. Yet, despite all these losses, the German military successes were over as soon as the uprising was extinguished. Even a fraction of the Soviet pre-war capability was enough to break the Wehrmacht's back.

It is commonly accepted in the West that WWII was fought between Germany and the Anglo-Americans. However, the decisive struggle was between Germany and the Soviet Union. It appears now that the most important part of this conflict was between Russians and Russians because the outcome of the war in Europe was pre-destined by 1943, as soon as the Russo-Russian conflict was extinguished.

Endnotes

1 "Reytch Stalina Na Stantsee Mayakovskaya 6 Nayabreeya 1941, polnaya vyerseeya" (Stalin's speech given in the Mayakovskaya underground Metro station on 6 November 1941, Full Version), History Lab YouTube channel, published on May 1, 2020, consulted on May 6, 2021, https://www.youtube.com/watch?v=BIc18YqgyiE. (The speech is part of the film "For The Complete Vanquishing of German Invaders", directed by L. Varlamova, produced by the Central Newsreel Studio.)

2 Vladimir Beshanov, *Tankaviy Pagrom: Kuda Ischesley 28 Teysciatch Soviestskyekh Tankov (The 1941 Tank Rout: How 28 Thousand Soviet Tanks Disappeared),* (Minsk, Harvest, 2004), page 106.

3 Viktor Suvorov, Samohubeastvoh: Zechem Gitlyer Napal na Savietski Syooz? (Suicide: Why Hitler Invaded the Soviet Union?), (Moscow, AST publishing, 2003), page 235.

4 Viktor Suvorov, *Ochishcheniye: Zachem Stalin Obyisglaville Svyoo Armyoo? (Cleansing: Why Stalin Decapitated his Army?),* (Moscow, AST Moscow Publishing, 2007) page 161.

5 The relevant documents and other evidence are given by Viktor Suvorov, *Ochishcheniye: Zachem Stalin Obyisglaville Svyoo Armyoo? (Cleansing: Why Stalin Decapitated his Army?),* (Moscow, AST Moscow Publishing, 2007). pages 45–50.

6 Viktor Suvorov, *Ochishcheniye: Zachem Stalin Obyisglaville Svyoo Armyoo? (Cleansing: Why Stalin Decapitated his Army?),* (Moscow, AST Moscow Publishing, 2007) pages 45–49) quotes the newly published documents on the subject (RGVA, Fond 37837, List 10, Case 142, Sheet 93, first published in the Military-Historical Journal in 1993, Issue 1, page 56).

7 Only 412 according to Vadim J. Birstein, *SMERSH – Stalin's Secret Weapon,* (London, Biteback Publishing, 2011), page 24.

That figure is about a hundred times smaller than the one most sources used to quote.

8 Viktor Suvorov, *Ochishcheniye: Zachem Stalin Obyisglaville Svyoo Armyoo? (Cleansing: Why Stalin Decapitated his Army?)*, (Moscow, AST Moscow Publishing, 2007), pages 251–266.

9 Viktor Suvorov, *Ochishcheniye: Zachem Stalin Obyisglaville Svyoo Armyoo? (Cleansing: Why Stalin Decapitated his Army?)*, (Moscow, AST Moscow Publishing, 2007), pages 55–63 about the commissars and magistrates and 35–39, 66–71 about the secret police purges.

10 More than 20,000 NKVD personnel were wiped out on Stalin's orders during the 1930s: Roy Medvedev, *Let History Judge: The Origins and Consequences of Stalinism*, revised and expanded edition, (Columbia University Press, 1989), page 11.

11 Viktor Suvorov, *Ochishcheniye: Zachem Stalin Obyisglaville Svyoo Armyoo? (Cleansing: Why Stalin Decapitated his Army?)*, (Moscow, AST Moscow Publishing, 1998), Page 37.

12 Marina Svanidze, *Estoricheskiye Hroniki si Nikolaim Svanidze, (Historical Chronicles with Nikolai Svanidze*), Volume two, (Amphora Publishers, Saint Petersburg, 2007), page 103.

13 R. J. Rummel, *Never Again: Ending War, Democide, & Famine Through Democratic Freedom*, (nonfiction supplement), (The United States of America, Llumina Press, 2005), pages 98–100.

14 Robert Conquest, *The Harvest of Sorrow: Soviet Collectivization and the Terror – Famine*, (New York, Oxford University Press Inc., 1986), page 257.

15 Robert Conquest, *The Harvest of Sorrow: Soviet Collectivization and the Terror – Famine*, (New York, Oxford University Press Inc., 1986), pages 257, 258, 285, 326.

16 Askold Krushelnycky, "Ukraine: Famine – Survivors Recall The Horrors Of 1933 (Part 2)", Radio Free Europe, Liberty

Radio website, published on May 8, 2003, consulted on May 9, 2021, https://www.rferl.org/a/1103170.html.

17 Ron Rosenbaum, "Stalin's Cannibals: What the new book Bloodlands tells us about the nature of evil", published on February 7, 2011, consulted on May 9, 2021, https://slate.com/human-interest/2011/02/stalin-cannibalism-and-the-true-nature-of-evil.html.

18 R. J. Rummel, *Death by Government*, (New Jersey, Transaction Publishers, 1995), pages 98–100, 112.

19 R. J. Rummel, *Death by Government*, (New Jersey, Transaction Publishers, 1995), Page 88.

20 R. J. Rummel, *Death by Government*, (New Jersey, Transaction Publishers, 1995), Page 81.

21 R. J. Rummel, *Never Again: Ending War, Democide, & Famine Through Democratic Freedom*, (nonfiction supplement), (The United States of America, Llumina Press, 2005, page 172.

22 Mark Solonin, *22 Yunya: Anatomya Catastrophyee, (June 22: Anatomy of the Catastrophe)*, (Moscow, Yauza-Press, Eksmo, 2009).

23 The footage can be seen in "1941. Feelm Treeyeti 'Aglushitilnoiyeh Malchaneyay'-Polneey Voipoosk, (1941. Third film 'Deafening Silence'-full length documentary), Serialyee Ookraniee Premiere (Ukrainian Series Premiere) YouTube channel, published on April 29, 2015, consulted on August 5, 2022, https://www.youtube.com/watch?v=B9N3Zri--Cc.

24 For details see Mark Solonin, *22 Yunya: Anatomya Catastrophyee, (June 22: Anatomy of the Catastrophe)*, (Moscow, Yauza-Press, Eksmo, 2009).; Abdurakhman Avtorhanov, Zagadkata Okolo Sm'rtah Na Stalin. (The Mystery of Stalin's Death), (Interprint publishing, Sofia, 1991), pages 56, 57.

25 Mark Solonin, *22 Yunya: Anatomya Catastrophyee, (June 22: Anatomy of the Catastrophe)*, (Moscow, Yauza-Press, Eksmo, 2009), page 355.

26 Vadim J. Birstein, *SMERSH—Stalin's Secret Weapon*, (London, Biteback Publishing, 2011), page 102.

27 Igor Ermolov: *Ruskoyeh Gosudarstvoh v Nymetskom Taylieu: Estoria Lokotskovo Samo-oopravleniya 1941–1943 (A Russian State in the German Rear: History of the Lokot Autonomy 1941–1943)*, (Moscow 2009, Centrepoligraph), page 28.

28 Igor Ermolov: *Ruskoyeh Gosudarstvoh v Nymetskom Taylieu: Estoria Lokotskovo Samo-oopravleniya 1941–1943 (A Russian State in the German Rear: History of the Lokot Autonomy 1941–1943)*, (Moscow 2009, Centrepoligraph), page 30.

29 Vadim J. Birstein, *SMERSH – Stalin's Secret Weapon*, (London, Biteback Publishing, 2011), page 174.

30 "Doclatniya zapiska vayenava procurora vitiepskava garnizona o riezutatah pravierki pravavoy e abaronyee daeyaltelnasti v garnizonyeh" (Report by the Military Prosecutor of the Vietiebsk Garrison about the result of the inspection of the legal and defence activity in the garrison), from 5 July 1941, RKKA website, consulted on July 13, 2023, http://rkka.ru/docs/spv/SPV7.htm.

31 Marina Svanidze, *Estoricheskiye Hroniki si Nikolaim Svanidze, (Historical Chronicles with Nikolai Svanidze)*, Volume two, (Amphora Publishers, Saint Petersburg, 2007), page 136.

32 For example, the Red Army was under strict orders not to respond with force to German "provocations" and this order was not countermanded after the Germans attacked while its war plans, which were distributed throughout the chain of command, were never used; the Red Army got conflicting and unclear orders from its General Staff instead (Viktor Suvorov, *V Syankata Na Pobedata (Shadow of Victory)*, (Sofia, Fakel Express publishing, 2003), pages 145–162).

33 Boris Sokolov, *Accupatzia: Pravda e Mifoye (The Occupation: Truth and Myths)*, "Squabble for Lebensraum" chapter, Military Literature website, consulted on November 5, 2021, http://militera.lib.ru/research/sokolov3/01.html.

34 Igor Ermolov: *Ruskoyeh Gosudarstvoh v Nymetskom Taylieu: Estoria Lokotskovo Samo-oopravleniya 1941–1943 (A Russian State in the German Rear: History of the Lokot Autonomy 1941–1943)*, (Moscow, 2009, Centrepoligraph), page 30.

35 Sergei Chuev, *Prakliatiye Soldatiy: Praydatilee Na Staranyeh III Raykha, (The Damned Soldiers: Traitors Siding with the Third Reich)*, (Moscow, Yauza-Press, Eksmo, 2004), page 109.

36 Igor Ermolov: *Ruskoyeh Gosudarstvoh v Nymetskom Taylieu: Estoria Lokotskovo Samo-oopravleniya 1941–1943 (A Russian State in the German Rear: History of the Lokot Autonomy 1941–1943)*, (Moscow 2009, Centrepoligraph), page 32.

37 Mark Solonin, *22 Yunya: Anatomya Catastrophyee, (June 22: Anatomy of the Catastrophe)*, (Moscow, Yauza-Press, Eksmo, 2009), page 361.

38 Mark Solonin, *22 Yunya: Anatomya Catastrophyee, (June 22: Anatomy of the Catastrophe)*, (Moscow, Yauza-Press, Eksmo, 2009), page 363.

39 Mark Solonin, *22 Yunya: Anatomya Catastrophyee, (June 22: Anatomy of the Catastrophe)*, (Moscow, Yauza-Press, Eksmo, 2009), pages 350–353.

40 Viktor Suvorov, *The Chief Culprit: Stalin's Grand Design to Start World War II*, (Annapolis, Maryland, Naval Institute Press, 2013), pages 234–235.

41 Viktor Suvorov, *The Chief Culprit: Stalin's Grand Design to Start World War II*, (Annapolis, Maryland, Naval Institute Press, 2013), page 133.

42 See, for example, the so called "battle" of Grodno: Mark Solonin, *22 Yunya: Anatomya Catastrophyee, (June 22: Anatomy of the Catastrophe)*, (Moscow, Yauza-Press, Eksmo, 2009), page 91.

43 Mark Solonin, *22 Yunya: Anatomya Catastrophyee, (June 22: Anatomy of the Catastrophe)*, (Moscow, Yauza-Press, Eksmo, 2009), pages 39–41.

44 Mark Solonin, 22 *Yunya: Anatomya Catastrophyee, (June 22: Anatomy of the Catastrophe)*, (Moscow, Yauza-Press, Eksmo, 2009), page 96.
45 Mark Solonin, 22 *Yunya: Anatomya Catastrophyee, (June 22: Anatomy of the Catastrophe)*, (Moscow, Yauza-Press, Eksmo, 2009), page 201.
46 Mark Solonin, 22 *Yunya: Anatomya Catastrophyee, (June 22: Anatomy of the Catastrophe)*, (Moscow, Yauza-Press, Eksmo, 2009), pages 60–62.
47 Mark Solonin, 22 *Yunya: Anatomya Catastrophyee, (June 22: Anatomy of the Catastrophe)*, (Moscow, Yauza-Press, Eksmo, 2009), page 365.
48 Mark Solonin, 22 *Yunya: Anatomya Catastrophyee, (June 22: Anatomy of the Catastrophe)*, (Moscow, Yauza-Press, Eksmo, 2009), page 365.
49 Vadim J. Birstein, *SMERSH—Stalin's Secret Weapon*, (London, Biteback Publishing, 2011), pages 173, 174.
50 Mark Solonin, 22 *Yunya: Anatomya Catastrophyee, (June 22: Anatomy of the Catastrophe)*, (Moscow, Yauza-Press, Eksmo, 2009), page 50.
51 Vadim J. Birstein, *SMERSH – Stalin's Secret Weapon*, (London, Biteback Publishing, 2011), page 109.
52 Mark Solonin, *Niet Blaga na Voyne (Nothing Good Comes from War)*, (Moscow, Yauza-Press, 2012), pages 73–77.
53 Vadim J. Birstein, *SMERSH – Stalin's Secret Weapon*, (London, Biteback Publishing, 2011), pages 110, 111.
54 Mark Solonin, *Niet Blaga na Voyne (Nothing Good Comes from War)*, (Moscow, Yauza-Press, 2012), pages 73–77.
55 Mark Solonin, 22 *Yunya: Anatomya Catastrophyee, (June 22: Anatomy of the Catastrophe)*, (Moscow, Yauza-Press, Eksmo, 2009), page 441.
56 Sergei Chuev, *Prakliatiye Soldatiy: Praydatilee Na Staranyeh III Raykha, (The Damned Soldiers. Traitors Siding with the*

Third Reich), (Moscow, Yauza-Press, Eksmo, 2004), pages 114, 113, 117.

57 Boris Sokolov, *Accupatzia: Pravda e Mifoye (The Occupation: Truth and Myths)*, "The Lokot Republic" chapter, Military Literature website, consulted on November 5, 2021, http://militera.lib.ru/research/sokolov3/03.html.

58 Sergei Chuev, *Prakliatiye Soldatiy: Praydatilee Na Staranyeh III Raykha, (The Damned Soldiers. Traitors Siding with the Third Reich)*, (Moscow, Yauza-Press, Eksmo, 2004), page 116.

59 See, for example, Mark Solonin, *22 Yunya: Anatomya Catastrophyee, (June 22: Anatomy of the Catastrophe)*, (Moscow, Yauza-Press, Eksmo, 2009), page 415; Viktor Suvorov, Mark Solonin, Andrei Burovsky, Why They Fear Viktor Suvorov, (Moscow, Yauza-Press, 2012), page 104.

60 Vadim J. Birstein, *SMERSH – Stalin's Secret Weapon*, (London, Biteback Publishing, 2011), page 173.

61 Vadim J. Birstein, *SMERSH – Stalin's Secret Weapon*, (London, Biteback Publishing, 2011), page 111.

62 Mark Solonin, *22 Yunya: Anatomya Catastrophyee, (June 22: Anatomy of the Catastrophe)*, (Moscow, Yauza-Press, Eksmo, 2009), pages 329–335.

63 Viktor Suvorov, *Poslednata Republika: Zashto Savetskiyat Sayooz Zagoobi Vtorata Svetovna Voina? (The Last Republic: Why the Soviet Union Lost World War II?)*, (Fakel Express publishing, Sofia, 1996), pages 178–187.

64 Mark Solonin, *22 Yunya: Anatomya Catastrophyee, (June 22: Anatomy of the Catastrophe)*, (Moscow, Yauza-Press, Eksmo, 2009), page 442; Vadim J. Birstein, *SMERSH – Stalin's Secret Weapon*, (London, Biteback Publishing, 2011), page 104.

65 Mark Solonin, *22 Yunya: Anatomya Catastrophyee, (June 22: Anatomy of the Catastrophe)*, (Moscow, Yauza-Press, Eksmo, 2009), page 366; also, Boris Sokolov, *Accupatzia: Pravda e Mifoye (The Occupation: Truth and Myths)*, "Squabble for Lebensraum" chapter, Military Literature website, consulted

on November 5, 2021, http://militera.lib.ru/research/sokolov3/01.html.

66 318,770 out of 3.8 million. Mark Solonin, *22 Yunya: Anatomya Catastrophyee, (June 22: Anatomy of the Catastrophe)*, (Moscow, Yauza-Press, Eksmo, 2009), pages 361, 362, 370.

67 Boris Sokolov, *Accupatzia: Pravda e Mifoye (The Occupation: Truth and Myths)*, "Squabble for Lebensraum" chapter, Military Literature website, consulted on November 5, 2021, http://militera.lib.ru/research/sokolov3/01.html.

68 Boris Sokolov, *Accupatzia: Pravda e Mifoye (The Occupation: Truth and Myths)*, "POWs–Enemies" chapter, Military Literature website, consulted on November 5, 2021, http://militera.lib.ru/research/sokolov3/01.html.

69 Boris Sokolov, *Accupatzia: Pravda e Mifoye (The Occupation: Truth and Myths)*, "Way of Life under the Occupation" chapter, Military Literature website, consulted on November 5, 2021, http://militera.lib.ru/research/sokolov3/01.html; Peter Kenez, *A History of the Soviet Union from the Beginning to the End*, (Cambridge, Cambridge University Press, 2006), pages 153, 154.

70 Boris Sokolov, *Accupatzia: Pravda e Mifoye (The Occupation: Truth and Myths)*, "Squabble for Lebensraum" chapter, Military Literature website, consulted on November 5, 2021, http://militera.lib.ru/research/sokolov3/01.html.

71 Vadim J. Birstein, *SMERSH – Stalin's Secret Weapon*, (London, Biteback Publishing, 2011), page 174.

72 Boris Sokolov, *Accupatzia: Pravda e Mifoye (The Occupation: Truth and Myths)*, "Squabble for Lebensraum" chapter, Military Literature website, consulted on November 5, 2021, http://militera.lib.ru/research/sokolov3/01.html.

73 Boris Sokolov, *Accupatzia: Pravda e Mifoye (The Occupation: Truth and Myths)*, "Squabble for Lebensraum" chapter, Military Literature website, consulted on November 5, 2021, http://militera.lib.ru/research/sokolov3/01.html.

74 The other infamous order was 270. The deserter's family members were subjected to arrest. (Vadim J. Birstein, *SMERSH – Stalin's Secret Weapon*, (London, Biteback Publishing, 2011), page 105)

75 Mark Solonin, *22 Yunya: Anatomya Catastrophyee, (June 22: Anatomy of the Catastrophe)*, (Moscow, Yauza-Press, Eksmo, 2009), page 363.

76 Mark Solonin, *Kak Sovietskee Sayooz Pabedil v Voyne, (How The Soviet Union Won The War)*, (Moscow, Yauza-Press, 2019), page 230.

77 Vadim J. Birstein, *SMERSH – Stalin's Secret Weapon*, (London, Biteback Publishing, 2011), page 2.

78 Vadim J. Birstein, *SMERSH – Stalin's Secret Weapon*, (London, Biteback Publishing, 2011), pages 27, 28.

79 Vadim J. Birstein, *SMERSH – Stalin's Secret Weapon*, (London, Biteback Publishing, 2011), page 9.

80 Vadim J. Birstein, *SMERSH – Stalin's Secret Weapon*, (London, Biteback Publishing, 2011), page 63.

81 Boris Sokolov, *Pravda o Velikoi Otechestvennoi Voinye: Sbornik Statei (The Truth of the Great Patriotic War: Collection of Articles)*, (St. Petersburg, Aleteiia Publishing, 1998), page 240.

82 Nikoulin N. N., Vospomenania O Vineyneh (Memoirs About the War), (St. Petersburg, The State Hermitage, 2008), pages 29, 30.

83 Viktor Suvorov, *Dien M: Kakda nachalas vtayara meeroviya voyna? (M-Day: When Did World War II Begin?)*, (Moscow, AST Publishing, 2000), pages 126, 127; Viktor Suvorov, *The Chief Culprit: Stalin's Grand Design to Start World War II*, (Annapolis, Maryland, Naval Institute Press, 2013), page 132; Mark Solonin, *22 Yunya: Anatomya Catastrophyee, (June 22: Anatomy of the Catastrophe)*, (Moscow, Yauza-Press, Eksmo, 2009), page 33.

84 Alter Litvin and John Keep, *Stalinism: Russian and Western Views at the Turn of the Millennium*, (United Kingdom, USA, Canada, Routledge an imprint of Taylor & Francis, 2005), page 81.

Chapter 5

Hitler Ended Racism

Professor Thomas Sowell wrote: "Racism is not dead. But it is on life-support, kept alive mainly by the people who use it for an excuse or to keep minority communities fearful or resentful enough to turn out as a voting bloc on Election Day."

Yet racism used to be alive and well prior to WWII. In fact, it was so mainstream that Hitler's own racial laws – the Nuremberg Laws – were inspired by the widely accepted American Jim Crow laws.[1] Hitler noted: "I have studied with great interest the laws of several American states concerning prevention of reproduction by people whose progeny would in all probability be of no value or be injurious to the racial stock."[2]

He expressed his admiration of immigration law. It matched his own racial prejudices: whites are better than black, yellow, and brown people, Nordic whites are better than Southern and Eastern European whites.[3] The US Immigration Act of 1924 made it virtually impossible for people from Asia and Africa to immigrate to the USA and made it hard for those from Southern and Eastern Europe. It favoured Western Europeans.[4] To illustrate, the 1929 immigration quotas gave 51,227 of the overall 150,000 annual slots to Germans, 100 to Greeks, and zero to Chinese.[5]

Racist beliefs that these days are associated with Nazism were common before WWII. For example, *The Passing of the Great Race* was a best-selling book in the USA, translated into French, Norwegian, and German. It expressed the fear that the whites (and the Nordic whites in particular) were going to lose their dominance because of unrestricted emigration and higher birth rates of lesser races. Hitler called it his "bible".[6]

The last was part of a trend. National Socialism is considered a uniquely evil ideology nowadays, an exotic cult if you will, but it may be argued that it was mundane. As the name suggests, it was a mixture of the two most fashionable ideas at the time: nationalism and socialism.[7] Hitler took the national and racial prejudices from the West and the mass extermination of people using concentration camps from the East (from the USSR). The difference with Soviet Socialism was that Hitler's socialists exterminated some nationalities more than others (Jews more than Poles, Poles more than Ukrainians and so on) while the socialists in the Soviet Union were internationalists, they preached racial equality and supposedly exterminated all equally. At least that was the theory. The difference between the two was blurred in practice, as we will see in the next few pages.

So, Nazism was just a remix of what was trendy – and not even an original remix at that. Mussolini was there first, blending socialism with nationalism.[8] The rest was a hodgepodge of symbols and causes of the day. Hitler took the colours of the National Socialist flag – red, white, and black – from the flag of the German Empire. (That corresponded with the trendy idea that the Weimar Republic, whose flag had different colours, is a failure.) Being the leader of a workers' party, he was particularly impressed by the way the workers' movement used the red.[9] Fittingly, the red became the domineering colour in Hitler's own design. The swastika was a symbol used by many ancient cultures and contemporary movements (for example, by the Volkisch movement).[10] It was adopted by some Soviet institutions before the Nazis appropriated it. (The Soviets stopped using the swastika after a Soviet minister, Anatoly Lunacharsky, forbade its use because it was adopted by the fascists.)[11] The Nazi salute was used by many movements before, including the Italian Fascists and the Soviet Socialists.[12] Before the "Work Will Set You Free" sign was placed at the gates of Auschwitz, it was used at the gates of the Solovetsky concentration camp in the USSR.[13] Before the Nazi death camps came into being, their Soviet prototypes were operational.

The Soviet Union began experimenting on living people, treating them as lab rats, ultimately killing them in the process, long before the Nazis in Germany ever did. Both totalitarian regimes conducted these experiments in the most logical place: where prisoners were kept.[14]

The Gestapo was modelled after the Soviet State Security (usually translated into English as "secret police"). Goering first intended to name it the Secret Police Office, but he changed his mind because the German initials GPA sounded too much like the Soviet GPU, the initials of the Soviet State Security at the time.[15] Enslaving people and working them to death was inspired by the Soviet concentration camps. (This is covered in the "Freeing the Workers Enslaved Them" chapter.) The dehumanisation of the victims prior to their physical extermination was also borrowed from the USSR. The Kulaks, the wealthy Soviet peasants who were exterminated in the 1930s, were first portrayed as evil sub-humans.[16] The same went for the Jews who had to be hated by the population under National socialist rule so that it would co-operate with the authorities in exterminating them. The Kulaks and Jews were both drawn with crooked facial features and big noses. As Georgi Markov observed, terror needed hate to function and hate was instilled by the propaganda under socialism.[17] He spoke of the Soviet socialism as he had to live under it, but the same applied to its cousin, German National Socialism. The National Socialists' public trials were modelled after Andrei Vyshinsky's public trials and Hitler himself acknowledged this.[18]

The basic architecture of the National Socialist government was copied from the Soviet Socialist government. Apart from the state security, this included the party-state, the total propaganda, the monopoly on communication, the state-run trade-unions and youth organisations (Leninist Young Communist League in the USSR, Hitler Youth in Germany, both named after the founders of their respective states, Lenin and Hitler), the closed borders, the puppet parliaments, and the planned economy (5-year plans under Soviet socialism and 4-year plan under National Socialism).

The Nazi phraseology that stereotyped nations (Germans being heroic idealists, Britons being small-minded merchants who lacked spirituality, etc.)[19] was in circulation ever since WWI when nobody had heard of Hitler.[20] Moreover, one can argue that it was in circulation even before that, given that the German monarch, Kaiser Wilhelm II, called the British a "nation of shop-keepers".[21] Incidentally, not only Hitler, but German society itself was not unique here, given that such self-centred superiority myths were present in every country that took part in WWI. What these all had in common was to portray "our nation" as good and the others as bad. The British viewed the Germans as mindless fanatical militarists who were crazy about discipline and lacked humanity (in a word: "the Hun"), a stereotype mocked so brilliantly in the *Blackadder* TV series.

The Turning Point

The story of a prominent USA senator Theodore G. Bilbo of Mississippi illustrates how attitudes towards racism began to change. His racist statements were ignored in the 1920s and 1930s. The shift started during WWII. *The Nation*, "the leading liberal magazine of its kind",[22] wrote in 1943: "We cannot fight fascism abroad while turning a blind eye to fascism at home... We cannot liberate oppressed peoples while maintaining the right to oppress our own minorities."[23]

The Washington Post commented on one of Bilbo's speeches in 1944 that "Dr Goebbels himself could not have hewed more faithfully to Nazi racial doctrines".

When Bilbo gave a speech that contained racial remarks in 1945, *The Nation* wrote: "Senator Bilbo's exhibition last Thursday made it appear that at the cost of hundreds of thousands of lives we had destroyed Hitler's racial obscenity in Europe only to have it parade in all its shameless arrogance at the very center of our democracy."[24]

That same narrative was adopted by the black community, who continued to fight for equality after risking their lives during the war: "I spent four years in the army to free a bunch of Dutchmen and Frenchmen, and I'm hanged if I'm going to let the Alabama version of the Germans kick me around when I get home. No siree bob! I went into the army a nigger; I'm coming out a man."[25]

African American WWII veterans often appeared in uniforms while testifying about the intimidation campaigns they faced when they attempted to vote.[26] They wanted their rights to be associated with the defeat of Nazism.

Eventually, even a magazine that supported immigration restrictions on racial grounds before the war turned against Bilbo.[27] Condemning racism was becoming mainstream.

Bilbo lost his seat in 1947 after calling "on every red-blooded white man to use any means to keep the niggers away from the polls" in 1946.[28] He was compared to Hitler in the senate debates.[29]

That story was the forerunner of what the Civil Rights movement achieved in the 1950s through the actions of Rosa Parks and Martin Luther King Jr. One thing led to another and one argument proved irrefutable at every turn: Hitler.

Hitler the Boogeyman

Hitler exterminated about 2.5 times fewer people than Stalin (21 million compared to about 50 million),[30] but Soviet propaganda said all the right things that the politically correct would approve of today: racial equality, inclusion, social justice. The USSR is to blame for starting WWII just as much as Germany. (In fact, a case can be made that the USSR was the chief culprit – for more on this see the "Attempts to Prevent WWII Made It Happen" chapter.)

However, this was not widely known at the time and is still not widely known today. British and American soldiers died fighting Hitler and being aided by the Soviet soldiers. Moreover, it was the German and not the Soviet concentration camps that were liberated, filmed, and shown to the Western public. Everybody has heard of Auschwitz but not many of Kolyma although the latter was every bit as bad.[31] Everybody knows of Anne Frank's house in Amsterdam. The houses of the Ukrainian girls who perished in the Soviet concentration camps don't get any tourists. Therefore, German National Socialism and not the Soviet Socialism fitted the bill of being the ultimate evil. As recently as 2018, long after all the above facts became known, an article in *The New Yorker* stated that "the Holocaust is the greatest crime in history".[32]

How can this be when the Nazis exterminated 21 million people while the Soviets exterminated 62 million?[33] Such questions are not asked partly because Hitler was a proud racist and Stalin, supposedly, was not.

In practice, Soviet socialism was as racist as National Socialism:

> Even race and ethnicity were grounds for arrest. Greeks were arrested throughout USSR in 1937. Chinese were arrested en bloc. National minorities in Russian towns were all but eliminated. All Koreans from the Far East were arrested; all those with Estonian family names were arrested in Leningrad; all Latvian Riflemen and Chekists were arrested.[34]

Stalin accused whole nations of being "traitors" and punished them collectively.[35] As Thomas de Waal puts it:

> The execution of this policy virtually amounted to genocide. Soviet secret police troops closed off an entire region, rounded up hundreds of thousands of people – women and children as well as men, Red Army soldiers included – evicted them from their homes, crammed them into disease-ridden cattle-trucks, and sent them into permanent exile in Kazakhstan or Siberia. Their homelands were abolished, their cemeteries dug up, and their culture erased from the official record. As many as a quarter of the deportees died en route or never returned.[36]

One can fill a whole chapter with examples of the USSR's racial policies that were no less cruel than those of the Nazis, including the mass extermination of millions simply because they belonged to certain ethnicities. However, while Soviet Socialism was a wolf in sheep's clothing, German National Socialism was proudly racist. History remembers that Hitler was a racist while Stalin was not, although Stalin exterminated about as many Ukrainians as Hitler did Jews.

Still, numbers don't matter when perception is reality. History teaches but has no pupils.[37] The perception was that racism and not socialism was to blame for the German concentration camps and the war. Since the Germans were white and Westerners happened to be white too, the West began to be associated with war and mass murder. It did not matter that those who defeated National Socialism in war were white as well, nor that those exterminated in the concentration camps were also white.

Unlike Rosenberg and Goebbels (who inspired the National Socialists), Marx and Sartre (who inspired the Soviet Socialists and the Khmer Rouge) are still revered today. The tens of millions who were shot, starved, or tortured to death because of Marx and Sartre are just nameless statistics.

People seem to be okay with the Wikipedia entry on Hitler, which gives National Socialism a bad name, but they want the entry on victims of Stalin, Pol Pot and Mao to be deleted, because it gives "communism" a bad name. In the words of Cambridge historian Professor Robert Tombs, this attempt to change Wikipedia is like "holocaust denial". Yet most people are not outraged by it, the way they would be outraged if neo-Nazis asked that a Wikipedia page about the Nazi atrocities be deleted.[38]

Apple online bookstore forbids the use of Nazi symbolism or Nazi propaganda by would-be authors hoping to publish with them. Yet there is no mention of Communist symbolism or propaganda being banned.[39]

Then there's white guilt. Mao and Stalin do not make Westerners ashamed of their past. The modern social engineers blame the West for the world's ills and therefore they need the ultimate evil to be associated with white Westerners. Soviet Communists may have been white as well, but they were non-Westerners and came from countries that are neither Catholic nor Protestant.

Everybody Is a Nazi

Both the National Socialists (Nazis) and the communists exterminated tens of millions of people in concentration camps, both caused WWII, and yet the Nazis pass for mass murderers while the communists are supposedly fighting for free education.

The word Nazi began to be thrown around to silence opponents. If you falsely accused someone of being a Nazi, it usually won the argument. Even Jews began to be called Nazis if they dared to have conservative views.[40] A Jewish university professor was not only branded a Nazi, he was also called "anti-Semitic" and "a white supremacist" although he was brown-skinned and came from Lebanon.[41] The *Los Angeles Times* printed an article referring to Larry Elder, a well-known black politician, as the "black face of white supremacy".[42] A prominent black intellectual was compared to a Nazi collaborator.[43] A famous black radio-show host was accused of "white privilege".[44] If this happens to black people and Jews, imagine how easy it is to brand a white person a Nazi. Not surprisingly, when Putin invaded Ukraine in 2022, he claimed that he was fighting Nazism. The Ukrainian response? They called the Russians fascists, of course.

"Denier", like "Nazi" or "Fascist", is another overused word to shut down opponents. It started as "holocaust denier", somebody who denies the holocaust has taken place, and then began to be applied to anybody whose image was to be tarnished by associating them with Neo Nazism. Thus, we have "climate change deniers", people who deny that global warming is caused by humans. Richard Dawkins introduced the term "evolution denier".[45] "Covid deniers" followed. What's next, a "Big Bang theory denier"? A "bad cholesterol denier"?

The leader of Insulate Britain implied that opposing his views would amount to genocide, a word that in the minds of most people is associated with Hitler.[46]

The same goes for the word "racist". It is the ultimate accusation because the media, corporations, and governments have zero tolerance towards anybody who is considered to be racist. Its application widens all the time because campaigners want to reach different goals by using Hitler's political legacy. Incredibly, even mathematics was once branded "racist": "According to Seattle educators, math instruction in the United States is an example of 'Western Math', which apparently is the appropriation of mathematical knowledge by Western cultures."[47]

This may seem ridiculous to outsiders, but it is not a laughing matter for those on the receiving end. They know it works because it is backed by intimidation campaigns and intrigues. It has transformed the social sciences departments in Western universities to the point where "diverse" (meaning non-white or non-heterosexual) credentials matter more than scientific merit for somebody's career and that ideology then replaces science.[48] Bad science makes for good politics.

The National Socialists also presented their ideology as science. They practised identity politics given that one's ethnic origins, skin colour or sexual orientation mattered more than one's scientific abilities. This is why the Nazis got rid of Jewish physicists.[49]

Immigration Coming to a Neighbourhood Near You

The changing attitudes towards racism after WWII eventually affected US immigration policies. The Civil Rights movement wanted equal treatment of immigrants, regardless of race or nationality.[50] There were international pressures as well. For example: "Radio Moscow's broadcasts to Asia argued that the US immigration system was based on ideas about racial hierarchies that were similar to Nazism."[51]

Evidently, aspects of the argument stemmed directly from Hitler's legacy.

> In 1965, Congress passed the Immigration and Nationality Act (INA), which replaced restrictive immigration policies giving preference to Western and Northern European countries with quotas for countries in both hemispheres, allowing entry of more immigrants from non-Western countries. Consequently, between 1970 and 2010 the number of foreign-born residents of the United States grew from 9.6 to 40.0 million, an increase from 4.7 to 12.9 percent of the total population.[52]

The "demographic makeup of the American population" was changed because "immigrants entering the United States under the new legislation came increasingly from countries in Asia, Africa and Latin America, as opposed to Europe ... other major

Anglophone countries later followed suit in removing their race-based policies – Canada in the 1960s, Australia in 1973, Britain in 1981, and New Zealand in 1986".[53]

Eventually, the process gathered momentum to the point of not only allowing legal immigration from Asia, Africa, and Latin America, but illegal immigration as well. Migrants who had destroyed their identity papers (and therefore made it impossible to check whether they were refugees or not) or who came from safe countries (like Turkey) were allowed into Europe in 2015. The doors were widely opened by Germany, the country burdened by guilt because of Hitler. Moreover, this move opened the doors of the other European countries.[54] Fittingly, those who wanted to stop illegal immigrants or erect a wall between Mexico and USA were called Nazis, although a wall was meant to stop illegal immigration only; there are checkpoints for the legal emigrants. Congresswoman Alexandria Ocasio-Cortez went as far as to compare the detention centres for illegal immigrants in USA to "concentration camps" and referring to the Trump administration she said: "A presidency that creates concentration camps is fascist."[55]

Hitler the Islamist?

This story has an unexpected twist. As was shown, Hitler's efforts to engineer a racially pure society backfired. However, he may be successful in turning one of his other wishes into reality.

> "It's been our misfortune to have the wrong religion," Hitler complained to his pet architect Albert Speer. "Why did it have to be Christianity, with its meekness and flabbiness?" Islam was a Mannerreligion – a "religion of men" – and hygienic too. The "soldiers of Islam" received a warrior's heaven, "a real earthly paradise" with "houris" and "wine

flowing." This, Hitler argued, was much more suited to the "Germanic temperament."[56]

With the current spread of Islam across Europe, Germany and Austria will likely become Islamic countries before the end of this century because of the different birth rates between Muslims and non-Muslims. (The statistics are quoted in the "Feminism to End Female Rights" chapter.) Therefore, Hitler may get his wish after all.

Ironically, this could happen precisely because his plans to keep Europe white were so counter-productive. Hitler was a racist and wanted to keep Europe white. Yet his legacy made racism unacceptable. It also opened the floodgates of non-white immigration to the West which could make the white population a minority by the end of this century.

Endnotes

1 See James Q. Whitman, "Hitler's American Model: The United States and the Making of Nazi Race Law", consulted on January 5, 2020, https://press.princeton.edu/books/hardcover/9780691172422/hitlers-american-model.

2 Dinesh D'Souza, *The Big Lie: Exposing the Nazi Roots of the American Left*, (USA, Regnery Publishing, 2017), page 158.

3 Dinesh D'Souza, *The Big Lie: Exposing the Nazi Roots of the American Left*, (USA, Regnery Publishing, 2017), page 157.

4 Elizabeth Fussell, "Warmth of the Welcome: Attitudes toward Immigrants and Immigration Policy", https://www.ncbi.nlm.nih.gov/pmc/articles/PMC4782982/, published on April 14, 2014, consulted on January 4, 2020.

5 David S. FitzGerald and David Cook-Martín, "The Geopolitical Origins of the U.S. Immigration Act of 1965", published on February 5, 2015, consulted on January 5, 2020, https://www.migrationpolicy.org/article/geopolitical-origins-us-immigration-act-1965.

6 Thomas Sowell, *Intellectuals and Society*, (Basic Books – a member of the Perseus Books Group, New York, 2011), page 387.

7 On whether National Socialism was socialism see George Reisman, *Why Nazism Was Socialism and Why Socialism Is Totalitarian*, (The Jefferson School of Philosophy, Economics and Psychology, CA, USA, 2014).

8 Thomas Sowell, *Intellectuals and Society*, (Basic Books – a member of the Perseus Books Group, New York, 2011), page 99.

9 Bob Carruthers, *Hitler's Violent Youth: How Trench Warfare and Street Fighting Moulded Hitler* (England, Pen & Sword Military, 2015, e-book edition), page 111.

10 Bob Carruthers, *Hitler's Violent Youth: How Trench Warfare and Street Fighting Moulded Hitler* (England, Pen & Sword Military, 2015, e-book edition), page 112.

11 "Predoopreschdeyniyeh o svastikay" (*Warning about the swastika*) from 11.11.1922, Naslediyeh A V Lunacharskava (The Heritage of A. V. Lunacharsky) website, consulted on February 11, 2021, http://lunacharsky.newgod.su/articles/preduprezhdenie/.

12 See footage of communists saluting like that in the 1920s in the documentary Paslednyee Meef (The Last Myth), part 2, Vladimir Sinelnikov YouTube channel, published on July 11, 2012, consulted on June 15, 2022, https://www.youtube.com/watch?v=kl4vVYgLnds&list=PL8E5DC8F66DFF2CB2&index=2

13 Niall Ferguson, *War of the World: Twentieth-Century Conflict and the Descent of the West*, (New York, The Penguin Press, 2006), page 220.

14 Pavel Sudoplatov, *Spiyetzaparatsii: Lubyanka e Kremil 1930–1950s (Special Operations: Lubyanka and Kremlin 1930s–1950s)*, (Moscow, Olma-Press, 1998), page 441.

15 William L. Shirer, *The Rise and Fall of the Third Reich: A History of Nazi Germany,* (New York, London, Toronto, Sydney, Simon and Schuster Paperbacks, 1990), page 270.

16 Video footage of these placards and the rallies can be seen in the Soviet Story documentary, "The Soviet Story 2008–English subtitles", The Ben Tame YouTube channel, published on August 30, 2019, consulted on June 15, 2022, https://www.youtube.com/watch?v=v7IrB_6mX4k.; Video footage of caricatures of kulaks may also be seen in the Russian documentary *"Dyela" Yusefa Stalina* (2012), (*The "Lifelong Achievement" of Joseph Stalin*) (2012), directed by Viktor Pravdyuk, Evgeniy Chelpanov YouTube channel, published on March 25, 2020, consulted on June 15, 2022, https://www.youtube.com/watch?v=nuLT2nBe3JI.

17 Georgi Markov, *Zadochnee Reportagee za Bulgaria, (In Absentia Reports About Bulgaria),* (Sofia, Profizdat Publishing, 1990), page 27.

18 Marina Svanidze, *Estoricheskiye Hroniki si Nikolaim Svanidze, (Historical Chronicles with Nikolai Svanidze*), Volume two, (Saint Petersburg, Amphora Publishers, 2007), page 60.

19 Vanessa Ther, "Stereotypes", 1914–1918-online International Encyclopedia of the First World War website, published on September 24, 2015, consulted on February 4, 2024, https://encyclopedia.1914-1918-online.net/article/stereotypes.

20 See, for example, Werner Sombart, *Torgashi e Geroyy: Razdoomeyah Patriota, (Merchants and Heroes: Thoughts of a Patriot),* (Complete Works, Volume 2), (Saint Petersburg, Vladimir Dal Publishing, 2005).

21 Niall Ferguson, *The Pity of War,* (London, The Penguin Press London, 1998), page 170.

22 "The Nation American journal", published on July 20, 1998, consulted on May 6, 2021, https://www.britannica.com/topic/The-Nation-American-journal.

23 Robert L. Fleegler, "*Theodore G. Bilbo and the Decline of Public Racism, 1938–1947*", The Journal of Mississippi History, Volume *68:1* (2006), page 13.

24 Robert L. Fleegler, "*Theodore G. Bilbo and the Decline of Public Racism, 1938*–1947", The Journal of Mississippi History, Volume *68:1* (2006), page 16.

25 James T. Patterson. *Grand Expectations: The United States, 1945–1974,* (Oxford University Press, New York, Oxford, 1996), page 23.

26 Robert L. Fleegler, "*Theodore G. Bilbo and the Decline of Public Racism, 1938*–1947", The Journal of Mississippi History, Volume *68:1* (2006), page 22.

27 Robert L. Fleegler, "*Theodore G. Bilbo and the Decline of Public Racism, 1938*–1947", The Journal of Mississippi History, Volume *68:1* (2006), page 19.

28 Martha M. Hamilton and Aaron Wiener, "The Roots of the 'Great Replacement Theory' Believed to Fuel Buffalo Suspect", The Washington Post website, published on May 15, 2022, consulted on July 9, 2022, https://www.washingtonpost.com/history/2022/05/15/great-replacement-theory-buffalo-bilbo/.

29 Robert L. Fleegler, "Theodore G. Bilbo and the Decline of Public Racism, 1938–1947", *The Journal of Mississippi History,* Volume 68:1 (2006), page 24.

30 R. J. Rummel, *Death by Government,* (New Brunswick, USA, London, UK, Transaction Publishers, 2009), pages V and 83.

31 Shalamov, Varlam, *Kalimskiyeh Raskazee (Kolyma Stories),* Completed Works in Four Volumes, (Moscow, Vagrius, 1998).

32 Alex Ross, "How American Racism Influenced Hitler", published on April 30, 2018 issue, consulted on January 4, 2020, https://www.newyorker.com/magazine/2018/04/30/how-american-racism-influenced-hitler.

33 R. J. Rummel, *Death by Government*, (New Jersey, Transaction Publishers, 1995), page V.

34 R. J. Rummel, *Never Again: Ending War, Democide, & Famine Through Democratic Freedom*, (nonfiction supplement), (The United States of America, Llumina Press, 2005, page 176.

35 Peter Kenez, *A History of the Soviet Union from the Beginning to the End*, (Cambridge, Cambridge University Press, 2006), page 296.

36 Thomas de Waal, *The Caucasus: An Introduction*, (Oxford University Press, New York, 2010), page 85.

37 Words said by Antonio Gramsci, quoted by Alex Ross, "How American Racism Influenced Hitler", published on April 30, 2018, consulted on January 4, 2020, https://www.newyorker.com/magazine/2018/04/30/how-american-racism-influenced-hitler.

38 Craig Simpson, "Wikipedia may delete entry on 'mass killings' under Communism due to claims of bias", published on November 27, 2021, consulted on November 28, 2021, https://uk.news.yahoo.com/wikipedia-may-delete-entry-mass-203714321.html.

39 Apple Books Formatting Guidelines, Apple website, consulted on June 21, 2023, https://help.apple.com/itc/applebooksstoreformatting/en.lproj/static.html#itcb1219ee5c.

40 Referring to Dennis Prager and Ben Shapiro. John Gage, "Crenshaw calls Google 'disturbing' after employee calls Ben Shapiro a 'Nazi'", June 26, 2019, consulted on March 4, 2020, https://www.washingtonexaminer.com/news/crenshaw-calls-google-disturbing-after-employee-calls-ben-shapiro-a-nazi.

41 Professor Gad Saad, "A Tsunami of Maladies Afflicting the Soul of Our Universities (THE SAAD TRUTH_676)", Gad Saad YouTube channel, published on June 19 2018, consulted on May 13 2020, https://www.youtube.com/watch?v=GXjzYh6p4WE&t=2601s.

42 Erika D. Smith, "Column: Larry Elder is the Black face of white supremacy. You've been warned", published on August 20, 2021, consulted on August 22, 2021, https://www.latimes.com/california/story/2021-08-20/recall-candidate-larry-elder-is-a-threat-to-black-californians.

43 Thomas Sowell was compared to Vidkun Quisling: Henry Allen, "Hot Disputes", published October 1, 1981, consulted on September 26, 2019, https://www.washingtonpost.com/archive/lifestyle/1981/10/01/hot-disputes-38/6621d792-a922-4093-858d-aa056663eeee/.

44 "David Webb accused of 'white privilege' by CNN legal analyst", Fox News YouTube channel, published on January 16, 2019, consulted on February 8, 2022, https://www.youtube.com/watch?v=BAlig2jW7SA

45 Joe-Rojas Burke, "Darwin's Pitbull: Richard Dawkins on evolution and unintelligent design", Oregon Live website, published on October 9, 2009, consulted on June 16, 2022, https://www.oregonlive.com/news/2009/10/darwins_pitbull_richard_dawkin.html.

46 GB News, "Inaya launches brutal takedown of Insulate Britain", GB News YouTube channel, published on October 15 2021, consulted on October 30, 2021, https://www.youtube.com/watch?v=g0BM5ri-s-k.

47 Lee Ohanian, "Seattle Schools Propose To Teach That Math Education Is Racist – Will California Be Far Behind?", Stanford University website, published on October 29, 2019, consulted on May 7, 2021, https://www.hoover.org/research/seattle-schools-propose-teach-math-education-racist-will-california-be-far-behindseattle.

48 Professor Gad Saad is one of many who talk about it: "A Tsunami of Maladies Afflicting the Soul of Our Universities (THE SAAD TRUTH_676)", Gad Saad YouTube channel, published on June 19, 2018, consulted on May 13, 2020, https://

www.youtube.com/watch?v=GXjzYh6p4WE&t=2601s. https://www.youtube.com/watch?v=GXjzYh6p4WE&t=2601s.

49 Andrew Grant, "The scientific exodus from Nazi Germany", published on September 26, 2018, consulted on February 16, 2021, https://physicstoday.scitation.org/do/10.1063/PT.6.4.20180926a/full/.

50 U.S. Immigration Since 1965, website of the History tv channel, published on June 7, 2019, consulted on January 5, 2020, https://www.history.com/topics/immigration/us-immigration-since-1965.

51 David S. FitzGerald and David Cook-Martín, "The Geopolitical Origins of the U.S. Immigration Act of 1965", published on February 5, 2015, consulted on January 5, 2020, https://www.migrationpolicy.org/article/geopolitical-origins-us-immigration-act-1965.

52 Elizabeth Fussell, "Warmth of the Welcome: Attitudes toward Immigrants and Immigration Policy", published on April 14, 2014, consulted on January 4, 2020, https://www.ncbi.nlm.nih.gov/pmc/articles/PMC4782982/.

53 David S. FitzGerald and David Cook-Martín, "The Geopolitical Origins of the U.S. Immigration Act of 1965", published on February 5, 2015, consulted on January 5, 2020, https://www.migrationpolicy.org/article/geopolitical-origins-us-immigration-act-1965.

54 Douglas Murray, *The Strange Death of Europe,* (London, Bloomsbury Continuum, 2017), pages 159–162.

55 Caroline Kelly, "Ocasio-Cortez compares migrant detention facilities to concentration camps", CNN website, published on June 18, 2019, consulted on August 6, 2021, https://edition.cnn.com/2019/06/18/politics/alexandria-ocasio-cortez-concentration-camps-migrants-detention/index.html.

56 Dominic Green, "Why Hitler Wished He Was Muslim", Wall Street Journal website, published on January 16, 2015,

consulted on March 18, 2020, https://www.wsj.com/amp/articles/book-review-ataturk-in-the-nazi-imagination-by-stefan-ihrig-and-islam-and-nazi-germanys-war-by-david-motadel-1421441724.

Chapter 6

Raising the Minimum Wage Lowers the Income

Minimum wage laws have existed for a long time, but they really became widespread throughout the Western world during the second part of the twentieth century.

The conundrum is this: will workers receive £2 more per hour if the government raises the minimum wage from £7 to £9? No, they won't. On the contrary, they will get less than £7 per hour.

This counter-intuitive result has been backed by unequivocal statistics and explained in many textbooks on economics.[1] The mechanism behind it is simple, easy to grasp, and is not disputed by anybody in the know. Yet the public is still convinced that raising the minimum wage by law will somehow raise the wages of workers, and some politicians still make careers by promising such laws.

The inability of the public to grasp this is down to the fact that people are not used to the idea that their labour is a commodity. Finding a job is just a way to say you have found a buyer for your labour. The employer is that buyer. The price of this commodity that you, the worker, sell is governed by supply and demand just like all other prices: from the price of rice to property prices, from the cost of sexual services to the cost of TV subscriptions.

Now, imagine that the government wants to help not the workers by raising their wages, but the house sellers by raising the property prices. The house prices in, say, Glasgow are low – you can buy one for as little as £50,000. The government enacts a law according to which a buyer cannot pay less than £500,000 to a house seller in Glasgow. What will happen? Will the house sellers get £500,000 or will their properties stay unsold? To put it another way, will the house buyers buy in Glasgow or go to Edinburgh or Newcastle? Believe it or not, this is the gist of the whole minimum wage issue. It is that simple.

To begin with, the very name of the minimum wage laws is misleading because it implies that they compel the employers to pay it. (We should keep in mind that the names of all such laws are a kind of advertisement, a PR trick, invented by their authors.) What such laws actually do is forbid workers to work for less than the minimum wage. They give the employers a choice: to pay the minimum wage or not hire. But, as we will further see, they take away the choice of the worker to work for less than the minimum wage or stay unemployed. Therefore, the title of this law should be something like: *Forbidding Workers to Work for Less Than a Certain Wage Act*. Laws like this don't give rights, they take rights away.

There's a joke about a worker who asks his boss to pay him what he deserves. The boss tells him that he cannot possibly do that because there's a minimum wage law. This punchline goes to the core of the problem: the legislator says what a worker is worth and the business owner has no say even though he is the one who pays.

There's just one thing that the joke, being a joke, does not get right. The boss implies that he pays more than the worker is worth by paying him the minimum wage. This doesn't happen. If employing an additional worker will bring the employer's business an extra £8 per hour in revenue, the employer will not hire someone and pay him £9. If the employer hires him, his business will lose money (at the rate of £1 per hour). That means that the employer will be better off if he doesn't employ this worker. The worker will be, as the economists put it, priced out of the market.[2] The same worker can still have a job if he is paid, say, £7 per hour. However, the minimum wage law makes this impossible. It says that a worker can be paid no less than £9 per hour. Thus, it turns out, the people harmed by the minimum wage rules are precisely those who are supposedly benefiting from it – the low-paid workers – because it is only they who are affected by the minimum wage law.[3] (Affected by being sacked or not hired, that is.) The higher paid, those who earn £9 or more per hour, neither benefit from nor lose out because they will be paid what they are paid anyway, with or without the law.

The higher the minimum wage, the greater the number of the workers affected by it. If the minimum wage is £5, it will concern only those who are paid, say, £4 per hour. Obviously, minimum wage law will be irrelevant if it says everybody must be paid at least £2. It will be practically the same as if there's no minimum wage law. If it is raised to £5, whoever is paid £5 or more per hour will be paid the same with or without such a law. If the minimum becomes £9, it will affect not only them, but also those paid 5, 6, 7, or 8 pounds. If it is increased to £20, it will practically affect everybody because very few are paid £20 or more per hour. In other words, almost everybody's labour will be too expensive to buy, and almost every worker will be priced out of the market.

This explains why countries with no minimum wage laws (like Switzerland) have low unemployment. Employers won't hire people in order to lose money. Therefore, the higher the minimum wage, the harder it becomes for those who are protected by it to find a job.[4]

Supporters of the minimum wage law would say that the employer can actually afford to pay the minimum wage but will not do so because he is greedy. However, if the employers could indulge in their greed, who is to say they would even pay £7 per hour and not £1 or £2? That way they would maximise their profits. So, why wouldn't they? Because they would be left with no workers. Likewise, a worker would rather be paid £200 per hour, but there's no employer who would pay that. Clearly, the price of labour, as any other price, is not a matter of greed or generosity but of supply and demand. Therefore, the price of labour is not determined by the employer, it is determined by all employers and all workers combined. In much the same way, a house seller does not determine the price at which he sells. On one hand, he would like to sell it for a million, but nobody would buy it if a similar property next door may be bought for a hundred thousand. On the other hand, he would not sell it for a thousand because there are buyers willing to pay more. So, like it or not, he is forced to sell for a price that is determined by all property sellers and property buyers. All sellers and all buyers are the market. This is something economist Adam Smith explained in the eighteenth century when he coined the phrase "invisible hand of the market". Likewise, employers compete among themselves to hire workers, and this drives wages up to the point where employers cannot offer more. Therefore, with or without minimum wage laws, the wage paid is already the maximum that can be paid if the employer is to benefit from the hiring. In the same way, the price a house sells for is the maximum that can be paid for it because there's nobody willing to pay more.

Some think that the employer will not really lose money under a minimum wage law because the latter forces all employers to raise the wage and thus the cost will be passed on to the consumer. According to this idea, employers will still be able to sell their product because the consumer will have no choice since he won't be able to find the same product for less elsewhere. In other words, a single employer cannot increase the price of his product since he will be outcompeted by other employers who pay less to their workers and whose product is therefore cheaper. The minimum wage law supposedly takes care of this problem as all employers will increase their product price simultaneously.

Even if it was true that the consumer has no choice, there's one problem with this reasoning: the worker is also a consumer. Since the minimum wage law affects not just the worker's job but all jobs throughout the economy, all prices of all products will rise to compensate for the higher wages. The workers will get more per hour, but they will now have to pay more for food, accommodation, clothing, and transportation. They will not be better off or, as any economist would put it, they will not have "greater purchasing power". The effect of the minimum wage law will be nothing but inflation.

However, the consumer has a choice. The minimum wage law will not apply to all nations in the world but just to the nation that enacts it. Let's say we are talking about the minimum wage in the UK and shoes manufactured in the UK. The same shoes will be imported from China and will cost less than in the UK since the UK minimum wage law will raise only the wages in the UK and not in China. The UK shoes will not be competitive as a result and this means shoes will no longer be manufactured locally. The UK shoe manufacturers will go out of business or will take their business to China.

This is not just a theoretical possibility, it is already happening. All those blue-collar workers in the USA and Western Europe lost their jobs when their coal mines, steel mills, and machine shops closed. This is something to think about next time we call customer support in India or buy a computer made in China.

From Minimum Wage to Taking More Choices Away

Is the way out of this predicament to limit the imports so that the choice of the consumer is taken away? Will the problem go away if there are no Chinese shoes sold in the UK? This may be done either by banning foreign produce outright or by introducing import duties. The latter is known as protectionism because it supposedly protects the native national industry from foreign competition. If the native consumer can only buy shoes manufactured in his own country, he will (according to the protectionists) have to buy locally manufactured shoes or walk barefoot.

Let's say that steel producers in the USA cannot manufacture a tonne of steel for less than $600. (The actual prices are somewhat different and so are the import duties but let's simplify it all for the sake of argument because it is the principle that matters here and not the details.[5]) Their Chinese counterparts manufacture it for, say, $400. The cost to transport a tonne of steel from China to the USA is, say, $100. That means the US consumer will prefer Chinese steel. To prevent this, the US government imposes a duty on the Chinese steel at $100 per tonne. Now, the US steel manufacturers can compete with the Chinese. If the duty is more than that, say $200 per tonne, the US manufacturers will have a competitive advantage on US territory as their steel will be cheaper.

However, this comes at a price, literally. To begin with, the US consumer now pays more for steel. Domestically this translates into a lower standard of living because everything costs more: from the building made of steel to the infrastructure projects that now require more tax money to be spent in order to be constructed, to everything else which does not use steel directly (as all prices are affected by cost of transportation, by taxes, etc). For example, the cost of gasoline reflects the cost of extraction, transportation, and refinement of the crude oil. All these require large quantities of steel. An oil rig is made of it, so is the pipeline, and the refinery. Increasing the price of steel increases the price of gasoline.

Then there's the reduced competitiveness of the US economy on the international market. Obviously, the US steel manufacturers will not be able to sell their steel abroad as they will not be aided by the same import duty in, say, Europe. The European buyer can still choose between paying $500 per tonne for Chinese steel and $650 for American steel.

But steel is also used in many other industries and this means that the consequences do not end there. Now the US automobiles, machines, weapons, etc., are more expensive (because the steel used to make them is more expensive). More expensive means less competitive. This, in turn, will mean that the USA will export fewer of these automobiles, machines and weapons and this has other negative knock-on effects on the economy as a whole, which includes those US workers on minimum wage. They may get more per hour now, but this does not necessarily mean they are better off.

Worst of all, some manufacturing industries using steel are chased out of the country to places where steel is now cheaper.[6] Out of the country means that they will no longer employ American workers, which already means being paid zero per hour.

The effects of protectionism were well understood more than a century ago.[7] Yet even today protectionism has not lost its appeal as Trump's trade war with China in 2018 demonstrated. In much the same way, the minimum wage increases by law have still not lost their appeal given that they are still demanded by trades unions, labour movements, and socialist political parties, in other words by those who want to help the workers.

The economy is a system in which everything is interconnected. Altering any one element alters others. Tinkering with the minimum wage affects commerce and vice versa. As the supporters of the theory of complexity put it, you affect everything and control nothing. The arrogant assumption that it can all be predicted and therefore controlled has been proven wrong again and again.

The bottom line is that employers cannot freely increase their prices to compensate for the increased minimum wage. They will either outsource these jobs or replace them with automation or go bankrupt. We experience all three in present-day Western economies. Whichever of the three occurs, the consequence for the low paid Western worker is just one: they will be unemployed. In other words, they will be paid less, not more since, as Professor Thomas Sowell has observed, zero pounds per hour is less than any wage.[8]

Endnotes

1 See, for example, Thomas Sowell, *Basic Economics: A Common Sense Guide to the Economy*, (New York, Basic Books, 2011), chapter 10.

2 Thomas Sowell, *Basic Economics: A Common Sense Guide to the Economy*, (New York, Basic Books, 2011), page 121.

3 Thomas Sowell, *Basic Economics: A Common Sense Guide to the Economy*, (New York, Basic Books, 2011), page 123.

4 Thomas Sowell, *Basic Economics: A Common Sense Guide to the Economy*, (New York, Basic Books, 2011), page 121.

5 World Steel Prices, MEPS website, consulted on 19 March 19, 2020, https://mepsinternational.com/gb/en.; Reuters staff, "U.S. imposes duties on structural steel from China, Mexico", Reuters website, published September 4, 2019, consulted on March 19, 2020, https://www.reuters.com/article/us-usa-trade-steel/us-imposes-duties-on-structural-steel-from-china-mexico-idUSKCN1VP2R7.

6 Jim Tankersley, "Trump's Metals Tariffs Added Some Jobs and Raised Consumer Prices", New York Times website, published on May 30, 2019, consulted on March 19, 2020, https://www.nytimes.com/2019/05/30/us/politics/norway-trump-aluminum-tariffs.html.

7 William Graham Sumner, Protectionism: the-ism Which Teaches that Waste Makes Wealth, (New York, Henry Holt and Company, 1888).

8 Thomas Sowell, *Basic Economics: A Citizen's Guide to the Economy*, Chapter 10 Controlled Labour Markets, Minimum Wage Laws, (United States of America, Basic Books, 2004).

Chapter 7

The More You Give Them, the Less They Have

Foreign aid took off after the success of the Marshall Plan (a US-sponsored programme designed to rehabilitate the economies of Western and Southern European countries in order to create stable conditions in which democratic institutions could survive.)[1] The evidence suggests that this plan was not really successful,[2] but that is immaterial here since the perception was that it revived the European economy devastated during WWII. The policy makers assumed that if aid worked in Europe, it would surely work for Africa.[3]

Here's a question. Johnny has 10 apples and Billy has 2. If Johnny gives an apple to Billy, how many apples will Billy have? The answer is 3 in a maths textbook, but less than 2 when we talk of foreign aid. Such aid was meant to make poor nations richer. It turned out that it has made them poorer. There have been plenty of authors demonstrating this during the last few decades. The most recent person who achieved notoriety, Dambisa Moyo, summarised the story like this: "What is it about Africa that holds it back, that seems to render it incapable of joining the rest of the globe in the twenty-first century? The answer has its roots in aid."[4]

Bruce Bueno De Mesquita and Alistair Smith went further by calling foreign aid "a force for evil".[5]

The arguments made in these and other books make sense, the facts they are based on are not disputed, and yet people still feel good when they give to charities that collect money for Africa or support their governments in donating aid.

Thanks for Nothing

The following may explain why that is. Whenever British people learn that I was born in Bulgaria, they want to be nice by telling me that they've been there and that it is a beautiful country. (By "Bulgaria" they usually mean Sunny Beach, a seaside resort built for Western tourists that has little to do with the actual Bulgaria.) A lady went a step further recently by telling me how she gave money to the "poor beggars" there. She was unpleasantly surprised by my response: "It is such a good thing that you helped organised crime. It needs all the money it can get."

The poor beggars she helped are in fact not poor. I witnessed many beggars, spoke with some of them, and I sometimes watched and counted in my head the money they were given per hour. They earn more than the average Bulgarian and sometimes more than the average Briton. The same experiment was done by others and the observations tie up. The rags are props. The same goes for the crutches some of them use: they are able to run, but pretended to limp. One of them used to commute to Sofia on the same train as me while putting on his beggar's outfit in front of me. All those who lived in his town knew that he owned a three-storey house and had a Mercedes in his garage. But those who gave him money didn't.

So, it is a lucrative job, but there's a catch: one cannot simply sit on a street corner and beg. A beggar (just like a prostitute or a drug dealer) must pay the gang whose turf the street belongs to. This goes especially for the most sought-after places (around hotels for foreigners). There are three things that matter in this business: location, location, and location.

Thus, each time a well-meaning Westerner gives, they are supporting organised crime, mainly the people who use violence to settle scores and bribe the police, and all the associated detrimental effects that violent crime and corruption have on the country. What for them is an insignificant sum of money (say, a couple of pounds), combines into a steady trickle for those begging and then into a torrent downstream when it reaches the thugs and their police buddies.

However, most tourists don't care to know any of this just like they are not interested in what goes on in the restaurant kitchen where all their delicious meals come from or what the personal life of their local guide is. They want to be righteous at affordable prices.

Similar mechanisms are at work when money is given by governments and international institutions. This explains a paradoxical fact: EU approval ratings in Bulgaria rose each time the EU withheld funds intended for the country due to fraud committed by Bulgarian recipients. The less the EU gave, the more popular it was among ordinary Bulgarians. The Bulgarians were meant to benefit from the money and yet they didn't like it when the EU was giving. The following suggests why that might be. Prominent local businessmen were arrested and accused of fraud involving EU funds in 2007. EU payments were frozen.[6] Then the EU resumed the payments, the businessmen were freed, and eventually nobody was convicted.

We saw the fruits of these policies years later. A leading expert recently demonstrated how EU money created the Bulgarian Mafia.[7] Bribes were given, documents were forged, thugs were used, landowners whose land had been taken over were threatened, and some of those who were not cowed disappeared. This was the EU taxpayers' money at work.

Bulgaria is not an isolated example. A connection between EU funds on one hand and organised crime, fraud, and corruption on the other has been established in other European countries like Italy, Greece, Spain, and Slovakia. Some cases even involve Western countries that are not known for corruption like Germany, Belgium, and the United Kingdom.[8]

These are not African countries; the EU is not the World Bank and yet there are similarities, as Dambisa Moyo explores in *Dead Aid*:

> The World Bank has participated (mostly passively) in the corruption of roughly US$100 billion of its loan funds intended for development. When the corruption associated with loans from other multilateral-development banks is included, the figure roughly doubles to US$200 billion. Others estimate that of the US$525 billion that the World Bank has lent to developing countries since 1946, at least 25 percent (US$130 billion) has been misused. Vast sums of aid not only foster corruption – they breed it.[9]

That's bad enough, but the percentages in some African countries could get much worse. Moyo describes the aid-fuelled corruption in Uganda throughout the 1990s, where "only 20 cents of every US$1 dollar of government spending on education reached the targeted local primary school."

So, what where these projects for which the money was not intended? Perhaps the governments themselves had decided to use the money elsewhere for greater benefit? That does not appear to be the case, says Moyo:

> As much as 85 percent of aid flows were used for purposes other than that for which they were initially intended, very often diverted to unproductive, if not grotesque ventures. Even as far back as the 1940s, international donors were well aware of this diversion risk. In 1947, Paul Rosenstein-Rodin, the Deputy Director of the World Bank Economics Department, remarked that "when the World Bank thinks it is financing an electric power station, it is really financing a brothel".[10]

The Business of Putting Business Out of Business

Aid damages the economy of the recipient nation not just through increased corruption. Supplying "free stuff" puts those who produce it out of business. A mosquito net manufacturer in Africa cannot sell his nets if the Western donors supply mosquito nets for free.[11] Local clothing manufacturers cannot compete with Western charities who dump their second-hand clothes in Africa.[12] Western food aid makes it impossible for local farmers to sell their produce and they are ruined. Next year they will also queue up for donated food instead of producing it.

A rock star raises money to relieve the starving in Africa. This is good public relations for him, but the result for the "beneficiaries" is that there will be more starving people in the future. Still, the PR works in the long run even if the relief doesn't because TV viewers in the West don't connect these dots. They attribute the people fed today to the rock star and the Africans starving tomorrow to Africa. Incidentally, this immoral behaviour (doing PR at the expense of human lives) parades as a moral crusade (saving lives). This reminds us of other pseudo-moral stances like raising the minimum wage laws (see the "Raising the Minimum Wage Lowers the Income" chapter) or imposing political correctness (see the "Less Rape Jokes, More Rape" chapter) that were meant to help the disadvantaged but ended up hurting them.

On top of it all, there's something known as the Dutch Disease, which makes Africa get poorer the more aid it gets. It is not in the water supply (where the public expects all African diseases to be) but is a matter of economics. It turns out that aid starts a vicious circle: it stifles development which increases the need for more aid. (The details are given in Appendix 2.) However, no number of technical arguments can beat a single pair of large, sad eyes belonging to a starving child.

Foreign Aid Works Like Welfare Benefits

Aid causes aid-dependency. African governments relied on aid to be given forever and therefore did not plan adequately for the future or seek alternatives.[13] This reminds us of the Western benefits system, which has created a scenario where people are less motivated to seek out permanent employment, feeling that there's no real need to find it, and that obtaining work will take away their welfare benefits. The official development aid to Liberia made up 73 per cent of its gross national income in 2011[14] and thus this country was, for all practical purposes, on welfare benefits. Nations, just like individuals, respond to incentives and they tend to fail when they are paid for being a failure. The consequences are occasionally grotesque. "Aid incentivises autocratic leaders to fail to fix problems" and this includes preparedness for natural disasters that result in a high death toll because a high death toll translates into more aid, which gives an opportunity to embezzle more aid.[15]

As Professor Thomas Sowell has observed, foreign aid punishes those who have done the right thing and rewards those who have been irresponsible. The countries whose policies led to starvation receive aid while the ones whose policies led to prosperity do not.[16]

The more you give, the more they will need it in the future.

Demodernisation

The effects of aid look even uglier if we zoom out in order to see the wider historical context. This requires grasping the numerous links between the economic, social, and legal developments in a country.

To begin with, aid increases government bureaucracy because it is distributed by the recipient government. More aid equals less free market.

Then it shifts the attention from what makes economic sense (say, producing something the consumer would want to buy) to politicking (as aid is being distributed by those currently in power).

Needless to say, neither favours economic progress. Instead of entrepreneurs, the country ends up with sly players who are good with under-the-counter dealings, bribing, and organising coalitions, but not with real, productive work. Those who benefit in such a country have not developed new technology, they have not invented a new computer, or found a way to manufacture cars more cheaply. They have not come up with an ingenious marketing campaign and have not found new markets. All they have achieved is to use public resources for personal gain, which is the very definition of corruption.

Aid distribution is a zero-sum game. The focus is on how to share the pie rather than how to enlarge it. A market economy grows and therefore somebody's gain is not somebody else's loss. In contrast, the size of an aid-dependent economy is determined by the size of the aid: a bigger slice of the aid for one faction means a lesser slice for another. Instead of creating wealth, the players squabble about how to share it.

Rule of law is undermined by under-the-counter dealing and the rule of law is one of the prerequisites of economic growth. Donors may say that their aid is conditional on holding elections, observing human rights, the rule of law and other modern niceties, but what happens in practice is the opposite: the recipient country is being de-modernised.

The Real Achievement

Given everything explored in this chapter so far, it is not hard to explain why, for example, South Korea began its incredible transformation from one of the poorest countries in the world to one of the richest only after the aid it received was drastically reduced in the 1960s.[17]

If aid is not good for development, what it is good for? After making the case that aid keeps corrupt governments in power,

Bruce Bueno De Mesquita and Alistair Smith say that: "What aid does well is help dictators cling to power." When aid money substitutes government spending, dictators have spare cash to "shore up their political positions".[18]

Compassion, even sincere compassion, causes suffering.

Endnotes

1 Marshall Plan European-United States history, Britannica website, published on January 14, 1999, consulted on May 6, 2021, https://www.britannica.com/event/Marshall-Plan.

2 Thomas E. Woods Jnr, PhD, lecture "The History of Foreign Aid Programs (Lecture 13 of 15) Thomas E Woods, Jnr." LibertyInOurTime YouTube channel, published on June 10, 2012, consulted on June 28, 2022, https://www.youtube.com/watch?v=fft3l-sao6c&list=PLpmOMu_Jxhdnq2A2Ug-3ETXsOs-eqWzrn&index=13.

3 Dambisa Moyo, *Dead Aid: Why Aid Is not Working and How There Is a Better Way for Africa*, (New York, Farrar, Straus and Giroux, 2009), page 26.

4 Dambisa Moyo, *Dead Aid: Why Aid Is not Working and How There Is a Better Way for Africa*, (New York, Farrar, Straus and Giroux, 2009), page 22.

5 Bruce Bueno De Mesquita and Alistair Smith, *The Dictator's Handbook: Why Bad Behavior Is Almost Always Good Politics*, (New York, Public Affairs, 2012), page 166.

6 Doreen Carvajal and Stephen Castle, "Bulgarian corruption troubling EU", New York Times website, published on October 15, 2008, consulted on March 28, 2020, https://www.nytimes.com/2008/10/15/world/europe/15iht-bulgaria.4.16989483.html.

7 A Nova TV interview with Tihomir Bezlov from The Center for the Study of Democracy: "Expert: Kak si Paree ot ES be sizdadina Bulgarska Mafia", (Expert: How A Bulgarian Mafia was Created with EU Money), Vesti website,

published on August 9, 2018, consulted on November 16, 2019, https://www.vesti.bg/bulgaria/ekspert-kak-s-pari-ot-es-be-syzdadena-bylgarska-mafiia-6085329; New York Times puts the story into its European context on November 3, 2019, consulted on November 16, 2019, https://www.nytimes.com/2019/11/03/world/europe/eu-farm-subsidy-hungary.html

8 PriceWaterhouseCoopers, Belgium PriceWaterhouseCoopers Netherlands, Directorate General For Internal Policies Policy Department D: Budgetary Affairs, "How does organised crime misuse EU funds?", consulted on April 8, 2021, https://www.europarl.europa.eu/document/activities/cont/201106/20110616ATT21560/20110616ATT21560EN.pdf, Brussels, © European Parliament, 2011.

9 Dambisa Moyo, *Dead Aid: Why Aid Is not Working and How There Is a Better Way for Africa*, (New York, Farrar, Straus and Giroux, 2009), page 59.

10 Dambisa Moyo, *Dead Aid: Why Aid Is not Working and How There Is a Better Way for Africa*, (New York, Farrar, Straus and Giroux, 2009), page 48.

11 Dambisa Moyo, *Dead Aid: Why Aid Is not Working and How There Is a Better Way for Africa*, (New York, Farrar, Straus and Giroux, 2009), page 52.

12 Linton Besser, "Dead white man's clothes", Australian Broadcasting Corporation website, updated on October 21, 2021, consulted on June 29, 2022, https://www.abc.net.au/news/2021-08-12/fast-fashion-turning-parts-ghana-into-toxic-landfill/100358702.

13 Dambisa Moyo, *Dead Aid: Why Aid Is not Working and How There Is a Better Way for Africa*, (New York, Farrar, Straus and Giroux, 2009), pages 46, 47.

14 Daron Acemoglu and James A. Robinson, "Why foreign aid fails – and how to really help Africa", The Spectator website, published on January 25, 2014, consulted on

February 26, 2020, https://www.spectator.co.uk/2014/01/why-aid-fails/.

15 Bruce Bueno De Mesquita and Alistair Smith, *The Dictator's Handbook: Why Bad Behavior Is Almost Always Good Politics*, (New York, Public Affairs, 2012), page 189.

16 "This is why foreign aid is bad for less developed countries", Thomas Sowell TV YouTube Channel, published on March 13, 2021, consulted on April 5, 2021, https://www.youtube.com/watch?v=ZPxjquGHlyU.

17 Thomas Sowell, *Applied Economics: Thinking Beyond Stage One*, (The United States of America, Basic Books – a member of the Perseus Books Group, 2009), page 266.

18 Bruce Bueno De Mesquita and Alistair Smith, *The Dictator's Handbook: Why Bad Behavior Is Almost Always Good Politics*, (New York, Public Affairs, 2012), page 183.

Chapter 8

Restricting Nuclear Weapons Spreads Them

The efforts to curb the spread of nuclear weapons began immediately after the bombing of Hiroshima and Nagasaki in 1945. The enlargement of the "Nuclear Club" started with another superpower, the USSR (1949), continued with the not so powerful and yet technologically advanced countries of the UK (1952) and France (1960). It proceeded with the not so technologically advanced (at the time) nations of Israel (1967), China (1964) and India (1974). The "Club" was eventually joined by the small nation of South Africa (1980) and later included the poor and technologically inferior countries of Pakistan (1998) and North Korea (2006), Iran seemingly destined to be next. The trend is clear: the "Nuclear Club" is not only growing, it is becoming accessible to ever lesser powers.

Apart from several former Soviet republics (Ukraine, Belarus, and Kazakhstan) which inherited their nuclear weapons from the USSR, only one nation voluntarily gave up its nuclear arsenal – that of South Africa. The former Soviet republics had neither the money nor the industrial facilities to maintain the weapons (the factories remained on Russian territory).[1] Still, they could have found a way to keep them by replacing the electronics and the means for delivering the weapons given that they already had the components that were hardest to obtain: the plutonium cores and the other parts that undergo nuclear reactions during the blast. That applied in particular to Ukraine where the Soviet nuclear bombs and missiles were partially designed and produced. However, Ukraine, Belarus, and Kazakhstan did not see why they would need their weapons at the time. That is why they easily yielded to international pressure and bribery to hand over their nuclear weapons to Russia.

As for South Africa, its president considered them useless given that his country was engaged in what he called a "bush war", with no cities to bomb, and that the Soviet and Cuban menace had disappeared with the end of the Cold War.[2] Additionally, with the collapse of the Soviet Union in the early 1990s, South Africa's regional enemies posed no threat anymore as it was the USSR that was backing them up.

The "Axis of Evil"

Iraq was invaded in order to stop the production of weapons of mass destruction. (President Bush talked of a nuclear mushroom cloud at the time.) However, as senator Robert Byrd observed, this invasion was likely to cause "unintended consequences which might make the world a vastly more dangerous place as countries scrambled to acquire nuclear weapons and long-range missiles to deter the new trigger-happy United States from unprovoked attacks".[3]

This opinion ties up with Putin's. When Tokayev, the president of Kazakhstan, said that nuclear weapons do not guarantee safety in the modern world, Putin retorted: "This is what Saddam used to think."[4]

Of the three countries constituting the "Axis of Evil" President Bush talked about (Iraq, Iran, and North Korea) the only one which was invaded was the one that gave up its nuclear ambitions: Iraq. Its leader ended up humiliated and executed, and the country was devastated. Iran resisted giving up its nuclear programme but was slow and sly in manufacturing nuclear weapons; its invasion was on the table, but was not carried out. The one country that could not be invaded was the one which went farthest with its nuclear programme: North Korea. There was a clear pattern emerging: more weapons, more security (for those developing the weapons, that is).

In the case of North Korea, the West not only motivated it to acquire nuclear weapons, but economically helped it to do so. Western countries perform an impossible juggling act: on one hand they try to show goodwill towards the regime and its people and on the other hand they pressure the same regime. While the West sanctioned North Korea, presumably to hurt it economically, it also kept its economy afloat by providing free food and other essentials.[5] An author aptly summed it up: "The United States became North Korea's largest aid donor while remaining its most demonized enemy."[6]

South Korea was another helpful enemy: it supplied the North with fertiliser and food.[7] Much Western aid directly ended up in military depots, with Western aid organisations unable to confirm that it went to those in need.[8] The North Korean government insisted on being the sole authority for transporting donated food.[9]

However, even if every sack of grain went to the hungry and not to the military, the food aid still supported the military economy of North Korea. (Incidentally, while the food aid is the one usually mentioned, it is not the only one. For example, the North is helped with fuel.) If the West fed part of the population, this gave the regime the opportunity to divert resources to other projects, say to the army or to the nuclear weapons programme. Supplying "butter" allowed for more "guns". It gave the Korean Communists the opportunity to divert other resources away from the food-production effort. We should keep in mind the most widely accepted definition of economics, the one proposed by Lionel Robbins: the allocation of scarce resources between competing ends.[10] In other words, feeding the population and arming the military compete for scarce resources. If a government is freed of taking care of the butter, it can allocate its scarce resources on producing guns.

This seems to be a lesson that the West struggles to learn. The American Relief Administration was providing free food to the USSR a century ago. This allowed Lenin to sell food abroad so that the Russian Communist Party could buy armaments or armament industries from the same West in order to attack... the West![11] Later, under Brezhnev, the USSR had to pay for the American grain and, what is even more important, to pay for it with hard currency (or its equivalent: gold). Not only was this a drain on the anaemic Soviet economy but it was a factor in forming Gorbachev's political views and in helping him to power. Alas, this experience is not put to good use when it comes to North Korea.

Beyond the "Axis"

The same correlation is evident beyond the "Axis of Evil". Those regimes that acquired nuclear weapons (like that of Pakistan) were not attacked while those regimes that gave up their nuclear programmes or actual weapons (like Libya and Ukraine) became victims of aggression. In particular, Libya was pressured by the USA to abandon its nuclear programme and then, when it yielded, the USA aided the enemies of the Libyan regime. The Libyan leader ended up being murdered in a humiliating way. North Korea repeatedly said it was aware of these facts.[12]

Unlike the North Korean government, the Ukrainian government is democratic; it does not breed slaves in concentration camps (inmates are imprisoned for three generations in North Korea and this is how their children are born slaves[13]), and it does not deal in counterfeit currency, etc. Yet it was Ukraine that was bombed, not North Korea. Conclusion: having nuclear weapons matters more than being a good member of the international community.

Ukraine is the best example that compliance with the international community does not pay. It ended up with a gigantic arsenal of nuclear weapons after the dissolution of the USSR (far larger than that of the UK, France, or even China), but was persuaded to give them up by being guaranteed territorial integrity. That was the gist of the 1994 Budapest Memorandum. The West wanted less countries to possess nuclear weapons in order to reduce the chance of them falling into the wrong hands. True, Ukraine lacked the technological capability to maintain the missiles and even the ability to launch them and was in dire financial straits on top of that in the early 1990s. Still, it could have kept the weapons and eventually adapted them since it had experts in the field.

The result of Ukraine giving up its nuclear weapons can be summarised in two points. First, it was invaded (in 2014, and then in 2022) something that arguably would not have occurred had it kept its arsenal of nuclear bombs and ballistic missiles. Second, it was invaded by one of the very parties that signed the Memorandum (Russia) and the other two parties (the USA and UK) did not come to its defence. Ukrainian politician Pavlo Rizanenko conceded that: "We gave up nuclear weapons because of this agreement. Now there's a strong sentiment in Ukraine that we made a big mistake."[14]

In 2023, President Clinton showed remorse for pushing Ukraine to surrender its nuclear weapons.[15] This would seem to suggest that nuclear weapons work better than international treaties.

In the fourth or fifth century AD, Roman author Vegetius wrote: "If you want peace, prepare for war."[16]

To bring that into the world today, we would need to say: "Acquire nuclear weapons if you want your borders intact." This is why Russia can afford to be a failure and yet defy the international community all it wants. (A subject covered in "The West Encouraged Putin by Discouraging Him" chapter.) It will not be bombed by NATO, the way Yugoslavia was, no matter how much it antagonises the West.

Endnotes

1 Interview of the former Ukrainian president Leonid M Kravchuk: "Kravchuk o Tom, Pacheymoo Ookrania Atkazalas ot Yadreynava Aruszhia", (Kravchuk on why Ukraine gave up their nuclear weapons), V Gasteeach oo Gardona YouTube channel (At Gordon's YouTube channel), published on October 10, 2016, consulted on June 29, 2022, https://www.youtube.com/watch?v=LGEALnD8Haw.

2 F. W. De Klerk giving interview to The Atlantic, published on September 9, 2017, consulted on March 29, 2021, https://www.theatlantic.com/international/archive/2017/09/north-korea-south-africa/539265/.

3 William A. Sherden, *Best Laid Plans: The Tyranny of Unintended Consequences and How to Avoid Them*, (California, Colorado, England, Praeger, 2011), Chapter 6, section "The Balance of Power".

4 RIA Novosti, Putin Pashuteel O Saddamye Husseinye E Yadrehynom Arujhee (Putin Joked About Saddam Hussein and Nuclear Weapons), published on October 3, 2019, consulted on December 9, 2022, https://ria.ru/20191003/1559415828.html.

5 Barbara Demick, *Nothing to Envy: Real Lives in North Korea*, (Granta Publications, 2010), page 145.

6 Blaine Harden, *Escape from Camp 14: One Man's Remarkable Odyssey from North Korea to Freedom in the West*, (London, Pan Books an imprint of Pan Macmillan, 2015), page 29.

7 Blaine Harden, *Escape from Camp 14: One Man's Remarkable Odyssey from North Korea to Freedom in the West*, (London, Pan Books an imprint of Pan Macmillan, 2015), pages 29, 92.

8 Barbara Demick, *Nothing to Envy: Real Lives in North Korea*, (Granta Publications, 2010), page 146.

9 Blaine Harden, *Escape from Camp 14: One Man's Remarkable Odyssey from North Korea to Freedom in the West*, (London, Pan Books an imprint of Pan Macmillan, 2015), page 100.

10 Thiago Dumont Oliveira and Carlos Eduardo Suprinyak, "The nature and significance of Lionel Robbins' methodological individualism", Science Direct website, published on October 19, 2017, consulted on November 4, 2020, https://www.sciencedirect.com/science/article/pii/S1517758016301436#!.

11 R. J. Rummel, *Never Again: Ending War, Democide, & Famine Through Democratic Freedom*, (nonfiction supplement), (The United States of America, Llumina Press, 2005, pages 93, 94.

12 Evans J.R. Revere, "Endgame: A Reflection on U.S. Strategic Choices and the North Korean Threat", consulted on June 30, 2022, page 15, https://www.brookings.edu/wp-content/uploads/2018/02/fp_20180202_endgame_strategic_choices_north_korean_threat.pdf.

13 Blaine Harden, *Escape from Camp 14: One Man's Remarkable Odyssey from North Korea to Freedom in the West*, (London, Pan Books an imprint of Pan Macmillan, 2015).

14 Anthony Zurcher, Echo Chambers, BBC News website, published on March 20, 2014, consulted on November 19, 2019, https://www.bbc.co.uk/news/blogs-echochambers-26676051.

15 Ben Wolfgang, "Bill Clinton expresses 'terrible' regret for pushing Ukraine to give up its nuclear weapons", Washington Times website, published on April 5, 2023, consulted on April 5, 2023, https://www.washingtontimes.com/news/2023/apr/5/bill-clinton-expresses-terrible-regret-for-pushing/.

16 Vegetius fl. ad 379–395 Roman military writer, Oxford Reference website, no publish date, consulted on 7 May 2021, https://www.oxfordreference.com/view/10.1093/acref/9780191866692.001.0001/q-oro-ed6-00011152.

Chapter 9

The West Encouraged Putin by Discouraging Him

Russia came under sanctions for the first time when it snatched Crimea and began its creeping invasion of the Donbas in 2014, not when it openly invaded Ukraine in 2022. More sanctions were introduced after the attempted assassination of Sergei and Yulia Skripal, and still more after the poisoning of Alexei Navalny.

Since 2014, freedom of speech was further curtailed in Russia and its aggressiveness only grew. If anything, less people spoke publicly against Putin in 2021 than prior to 2014.

Much has been written about the inefficiency of sanctions. The USSR, Nazi Germany, Cuba, North Korea, Iran and other countries have all been under sanctions and yet none of these rogue regimes have been toppled as a result, and their aggressive policies (like waging wars or developing nuclear weapons) were not curbed. But this chapter is not about the ineffectiveness of sanctions, it is about sanctions making things worse.

Some odd facts about these attempted assassinations may give us a clue about what is really going on. Russia has been leaving a trail of breadcrumbs for a long time because the chemical substances it uses to poison people can be traced back to them. Alexander Litvinenko was poisoned by a radioactive material which is available only to some governments. The Skripals and Navalny were poisoned by a nerve agent that is not only impossible to find on the black market but is Soviet in origin. Moreover, Novichok is a weapon of mass destruction; it is designed to kill a very large number of people indiscriminately. Using it to murder a specific individual makes its use unnecessarily complicated. Why, then, was it chosen?

The Russian government has the means to be undetected when assassinating people. The USSR has had an advanced laboratory developing untraceable poisons ever since Stalin was in power. It was none other than Lavrentiy Beria who clearly formulated its task: to develop poisons which cause death resembling that of natural causes, traces of which cannot be found by an autopsy. This goal was accomplished as early as the 1950s.[1]

If the USSR had these capabilities, then the Russian Federation had them, just like it had Novichok, because the USSR developed it. That is to be expected. Russian ICBMs (Intercontinental Ballistic Missiles) were Soviet ICBMs, Russian space rockets were Soviet space rockets, Russian rifles were the Soviet AKs, Russian fighters over Syria were Soviet Su-27s and so on.

British investigators in the Litvinenko and Skripal cases didn't have to go to great lengths to find the perpetrators as the Russians were not hiding. It is as though the assassins were leaving a "calling card". If Russia wanted these to be anonymous assassinations, they could have used untraceable substances. Even a gun would have been preferable because it would have been harder to trace it back to Russia. A gun could have been bought anywhere and manufactured by anybody. It is hard to imagine that this was sloppiness. Was the point of these two assassinations to be caught red-handed so that the voters in Russia would know that their president was punishing traitors?

This suggests that Vladimir Putin wanted to be vilified by the West. Yet in June 2019, Theresa May warned Putin that Russia must end its hostility to the West if it was to have normal relations with the UK.[2] Apparently, she assumed Putin was interested in normal relations. The subsequent invasion of Ukraine has proved unequivocally that he is not.

In order to make sense of this strange story, we must go way back to Brezhnev's times and remember how the Russian relationship with the West became what it was in 2022.

The Russians Used to Like the West

Socialism, the way we who lived under it in the Soviet empire remember it in the 1980s, was dull. It wasn't just the tedious queues for shoes and meat, cars and TV sets. The programmes one had to watch after buying the cherished TV set were tedious too.

There was nothing new in the news. A newspaper or a magazine would typically be structured according to a formula: On the first page there was a new declaration adopted by a subsequent Party congress. On the second page there was a photo of the comrade General Secretary of the Party greeting the people. Although the word "comrade" implies equality, the very fact that he was addressed as "comrade" reminded us that he was no comrade to us, that we were not his equals. Again, nothing newsworthy there, he was greeting the people in much the same way 10 years ago. Then an article on the workers of factory such-and-such who had over-fulfilled their quota (they always over-fulfilled it). Then there were the imperialists, Reagan and Thatcher, threatening world peace again, but "we" ("progressive humankind" as the propaganda formula went) would not let their aggressive plans come to fruition.

All these pages were ritualistic. Those of us living under socialism did not bother to read them; they were just white noise to us. Then, towards the end, there may have been something interesting, which had been translated from the Western press or explained how bad capitalism is (thus revealing something real about "rotting capitalism" as another formula went). It would all still be vetted, of course, but it could allow us to guess what must be going on out there, in the larger world.

Then the same news would be broadcasted for us to watch on our low quality, Soviet-made TV sets, which were not much better than the newspaper in terms of colour. Then a meeting would be organised in our local school, factory, or farm and a local activist would repeat the same "news": from the comrade General Secretary to the war-mongers Thatcher and Reagan.

I remember how desperate we, the people living under socialism, were to experience anything that was not state-run: be it unofficial music or charlatans who supposedly were psychics. The system was designed in a way that there would not be such a thing. This craving made all things Western cool: from adverts to chewing gum, from cigarettes to philosophical ideas. Youngsters were eagerly copying recordings of Western songs onto music cassette tapes from each other, no matter how loud the crackling (after many duplicate recordings) was. A pair of smuggled jeans in the Soviet Union could easily exceed a monthly wage. Worse than that, a retail catalogue of the type which in the West was given away for free, like Neckermann, could cost around 80 rubles – the monthly wage for most people in the Soviet Union. (Moreover, having the money was not enough: one needed to find it on the black market.)[3] Things in the People's Republic of Bulgaria, where I lived, were a bit better (we could buy smuggled Neckermanns cheaply), but the adoration of all things Western was the same. We craved everything coming from the Western world, even if it was considered rubbish or junk-mail over there. What to a Westerner was a tedious commercial, was entertainment to us. This was not just a longing for the electronics, food, clothing, and all the other material things we did not have, it was psychological, a kind of escapism. Colourful, glossy catalogues were a welcome and exotic relief after slowly turning over the dull, grey pages of last week's political news and national "triumphs" that nobody believed in during the 1980s. Opening a department store catalogue was like Dorothy stepping out from a dreary black and white Kansas house into the fabulous technicolour of Oz.

Western movies were exciting (such as *Towering Inferno* or *Jaws*, the 1970s movies we watched in the 1980s). Soviet films were usually blunt and predictable: there were issues (usually in a factory), but they were eventually resolved in an ideological happy ending. The rules for scriptwriting were as simple and formulaic as a children's moral tale: One character believes in socialism, another does not – both believe in the end. Both believe but are not believed by the others – all believe in the end. All believe, but there are objective difficulties – a struggle follows and all is well in the end.[4] We typically enquired about a new movie in my hometown by asking, 'is it Soviet or a good one?'

The West did not have to do anything to achieve this: socialism did all the work for it. Capitalism came to signify everything socialism was not. We deeply respected politicians like Reagan and Thatcher precisely because they were against our own governments. Incidentally, Thatcher was liked so much that Professor Nicolai Svanidze, a prominent Russian author, placed her, a foreigner, among the significant **Soviet** personalities in his popular book and TV series.[5] Contrast this with the attitudes in Russia in 2022, where Western politicians are disliked for the same reason: being against the Russian government.

A Self-Defeated Country

How did the West squander its popularity? The Soviet Union and the West became friendly under perestroika. This warming in relations finished with the Soviets ending the Cold War, surrendering Eastern Europe without firing a shot, and eventually letting their own country disintegrate. When the dust settled, the "great motherland" was gone, along with Gorbachev; he was presumably living abroad and wealthy for having betrayed and sold the Soviet Union. (He actually lived in Moscow.) The interest of the West and the respect of Eastern Europe was gone as well. Many countries in Eastern Europe were accepted into NATO and then the EU while Russia was not. (Incidentally, Russia hoped to be a NATO member as well, even

Putin himself expressed this.[6]) All Russia got was to become a signatory of the European Convention on Human Rights and the privilege of being often and successfully sued in Strasbourg. While the Soviet Union abandoned its overseas military bases with the end of the Cold War, the United States kept its own. Russia's new president, Boris Yeltsin, was perceived by the people as a drunk clown. The Russians were left to pick up the pieces enduring poverty, corruption, crime, and chaos. Ordinary people felt seduced and betrayed by the West. Russia was democratic, weak, and humiliated. Democracy and friendship with the West began to be associated with failure, betrayal, and disgrace.

To understand what this meant to an average Russian citizen, you should know how society functioned during the "Dashing 1990s", as the time period came to be known.[7] Might became right. It was not the law, but having private thugs and public officials in your pocket was what mattered. Most ordinary Russians, of course, had neither. The role assigned to them was to be impoverished and frightened victims. The kind ones were humiliated while the powerful were emulated.

A Sausage-Giving American

The material and moral collapse of the early 1990s was captured by one of the pop bands at the time, Combination. The female pop singers sang of sausages, where an apparently hungry girl is being wooed with common food in a situation she doesn't find romantic. The sausage here was not a code for something, it was actual food that was in short supply.

He is offering a swap: he will feed her an actual sausage if she accepts his man-sausage. The second song is called "American Boy" and the text is a witty mixture of Russian and English. It is about a local girl hoping to meet her American Prince Charming so that she may leave Russia.[9] (What she is charmed by is his passport.) To make it even more disrespectful, the pop music was intertwined with folk music themes associated with traditional values. The way the singers danced was also reminiscent of traditional folk dances. This can be perceived as funny, but to many in Russia it was trashing the motherland.

You don't need to speak Russian to grasp the cultural U-turn these songs represented. Just compare Combination's songs to the music that was aired only a few years earlier. The beautiful song "My Bright Future" would be an apt illustration here.[10] Incidentally, the phrase that is its title was a propaganda line that we, those in the Soviet empire, were raised with. It referred to the idyllic time when communism would finally come. But the post-socialist dystopia replaced the expected utopia in the early 1990s. This, along with the poverty and lack of law and order, explained the nostalgia towards socialism many began to feel. Russia used to have a bright future, now it had a bright past.

There were even more striking examples which demonstrate the chaos, lawlessness and emptiness that followed. In 2001, a porn movie was shot in the centre of Saint Petersburg in full view of passers-by. (You can see startled mothers with prams in some of the scenes; they are not extras.) It was called *Saint Petersburg's White Nights* and the title is mocking a famous Soviet movie drama based on Dostoevsky's short story. (It was also structured in the same way: First Night, Second Night, and so on.) Therefore, it perfectly illustrates the transition from Dostoevsky to porn. Many of the porn scenes were filmed at night, however, some were shot in broad daylight. Unbelievably, the third "night" (which actually takes place during the day) was shot in front of the monument of Peter the Great, the founder of the city. To grasp how scandalous this was, imagine this happening in front of Nelson's Column in London or the Lincoln Memorial in Washington. To add insult to injury, the fourth "night" (daylight again) ended with a girl masturbating at an exhibition of guns from WWII, a conflict that is held sacred in Russia and is known as the Great Patriotic War.[11] The credits gave useful tips on the amount one has to pay in bribes and the other practicalities involved in shooting porn around some of the famous sites where the action takes place. The creator of the movie explained in interviews how the crew had to bribe policemen in order to film in public places. He was prosecuted, but unsuccessfully. Thus, this porn movie can also be evaluated as a social experiment or as a documentary.

A popular mainstream movie reflected the public moods at roughly the same time: *Voroshilov Sharpshooter* (1999).[12] The plot begins with a plausible premise: a girl is raped and the perpetrators are not prosecuted due to widespread corruption. Nobody, not even her mother who is interested only in chasing material things, cares about what happened and the girl sinks into depression. Her grandfather, a decorated WWII veteran (played by the same actor who played Zhukov, the most celebrated Soviet general, in the 1971 epic film series *Liberation*) buys himself a rifle on the black market and begins to execute the rapists in satisfying ways. Eventually he is caught by a policeman who doesn't report the old man because he approves of what he has done. Unlike the afore-mentioned porn movie, this film is superb in terms of acting and directing. The Russian public, tired of the widespread crime, corruption, and government impotence in the "Gangsters' 1990s" (as the period was often referred to), was thirsty for brutal vigilante justice. This was mixed with Soviet nostalgia because the Soviet authorities used to act swiftly and decisively. The Soviet past was already romanticized by the time the movie was made because it was perceived as the opposite of everything that was wrong with the present. The name of the movie itself represents a well-known phrase coined by Stalinist propaganda that signifies military prowess and owning problems instead of passing the buck. It was released just a year before the former anthem of the USSR was adopted as the new anthem of the Russian Federation in

2000. This is something to remember when one reads that the so-called "separatist" regions of Ukraine (in reality captured by the Russian military) call themselves "peoples' republics" or when one sees Russian tankmen in Ukraine in 2022 waving the Soviet flag rather than the flag of the Russian Federation.

Incidentally, the *Voroshilov Sharpshooter* was not the first film where criminality was fought by military rather than legal means. In *To Love the Way Russians Do* (1995) war veterans stop the organised crime using a WWII field gun.[13]

The notion that brute military force is the solution to the lawlessness was common in 1990s Eastern European countries where the statehood had collapsed after the fall of socialism. For example, it was expressed by many in Bulgaria, including a poet who became popular when he called for a coup in 2000.[14]

Porn shot in the centre of one of the two largest cities in Russia and glorifying extra-judicial violence represents just part of the process. The other part may be harder to grasp to a Westerner. A TV documentary made in 1999 was no less scandalous than the porn movie *The Last Myth*.[15] It refers to debunking the last Soviet myth and is about an author who is both popular and hated in Russia and who is quoted in this book as well: Viktor Suvorov. He was the first to make the case that the USSR prepared to take over Europe in 1941 when it was stopped by Hitler's pre-emptive invasion of the Soviet Union. (The literature on the subject has grown since the 1990s and there are other authors now, but the trend is still associated with Suvorov.) The Russians reluctantly accepted the idea that their brand of socialism had been evil ever since perestroika, but that their role in WWII may have been unholy was too much for them. While Suvorov's books sold like hot cakes as millions were anxious to know all about it, millions more were scandalised and perceived this as another low blow against their country. In their eyes, democracy began to be viewed not merely as chaos and lawlessness but as being anti-Russian.

New words were coined that reflected the shift in popular perceptions some Russians had of their compatriots who wanted Russia to be democratic and Western-like. The word "dyermokrat" is a composite of the Russian words for "excrement" and "democrat". Another one is "dyermocrast": a combination between "democrat" and the local word for a male homosexual, the latter being an insult in Russia. "Liberast" has the same meaning, only it combines "liberal" and "homosexual".

All this happened in the 1990s, but it must be remembered in 2022. The shooting war in Ukraine, like many wars and many civil wars throughout history, began as a culture war decades earlier. Ukraine was the country where the Ukrainian "liberasts" took power while Russia was the country where the Russian "liberasts" lost. Just like the culture war in the West is not limited to the USA or to Britain, the culture war in the post-socialist world raged throughout all post-socialist countries. The 2022 war, therefore, is not so much a conflict between two nations as it is just the military stage of the culture war between those who want to follow the Western ways in this part of the world and those who don't.

Back to the 1990s. It was against the post-socialist culture war background that the West attacked first Serbia and then Iraq, not bothering to obtain a UN Security Council decision for either. The aggression against Serbia was particularly humiliating and painful to Russia because the first was its traditional ally. The bombing of Yugoslavia and the invasion of Iraq constituted aggression according to the Definition of Aggression, United Nations General Assembly Resolution 3314 (XXIX), Article 1. (Note that the presence of weapons of mass destruction, even if true, is irrelevant under Article 5, Paragraph 1.) There are only two instances when use of military force does not constitute an act of aggression: first when the state using it has been attacked (and therefore acts in self-defence) and second when there is a decision of the Security Council of UN (as per Charter of the

United Nations, Chapter VII, action with respect to threats to the peace, breaches of the peace, and acts of aggression). The USA did not commit aggression against Afghanistan although there was no Security Council decision authorising it to bomb and occupy it because Afghanistan was sheltering the organizers of 9/11 and this is equated to aggression under Article 3G. Therefore, the USA was acting in self-defence in Afghanistan. However, the same cannot be said of Yugoslavia or Iraq.

A popular song at the time was dedicated to this event, where Yugoslavia was called "sister" (sister of Russia, that is).[16] The bitterness of this memory shows in the comments section under some of the YouTube videos with the same song.[17] (The caption in one reads in Russian: "Fifteen years since the NATO atrocities in Yugoslavia."[18]) One of the videos is edited in a way that illustrates how Russians connected the dots: footage of a laughing President Clinton aside a drunk President Yeltsin is mixed with graphic footage of the NATO bombings in Yugoslavia: bridges being blown up, residential buildings burning, corpses of people, blood on the streets. The title below the video is in both Russian and Serbian. The public comments underneath it are in agreement with this message: the Russians apologise to the Serbs for Yeltsin and for letting this happen.[19]

The bombing of Yugoslavia by NATO led to the altering of international borders. Five years later, after invading Crimea, Putin reminded the West of this violation of international law. Unfortunately, he had a point: why should Russia be bound by the UN Charter in Crimea if NATO was not bound by the Charter in Kosovo?[20] Putin went on to use a Roman quotation, saying in another interview: "what is allowed to Jupiter is not allowed to the bull."[21] His message was clear: we are allowed to do it if the USA and Britain are, we are not second-class players.

Whatever the West won in "little Kosovo", it lost in big Russia. Some streets in Kosovo were named after US presidents. If pleasing the Muslim world has been the goal (as most Albanians in Kosovo were Muslims and the Serbs were Orthodox Christians), it was not achieved. That NATO protected Muslims is not remembered in Muslim countries today, but Western aggression is still remembered in Orthodox Russia and is milked by Putin's propaganda machine.

After NATO bombed Serbia, it moved its borders closer to Russia by accepting most Eastern European countries as members, along with some former Soviet republics. Georgia and Ukraine were queueing up. Popular politicians in Russia did not expect their country to be the next NATO member but the next NATO victim.[22]

To make things worse, NATO's expansion was perceived as treacherous because James Baker, the Western negotiator, had promised Gorbachev that this would not happen.[23] One may argue that no treaty was signed or that this promise was superseded by later agreements, but this is not how things are perceived in Russia because this is a country where deals are usually struck verbally, and lack of a document is no excuse for not following them.

To add insult to injury, prominent Western politicians said all the wrong things. The US Secretary of State John Kerry said to the Russians in 2014: "You lost the Cold War."[24]

Hillary Clinton, another Secretary of State, said about the Soviet Union in 2013:

> They invaded Afghanistan... and we did not want to see them control Central Asia and we went to work... And guess what ... they (Soviets) retreated ... they lost billions of dollars and it led to the collapse of the Soviet Union.[25]

President Trump continued the trend, saying that the USA put communism on its knees.[26]

Even if it was true that the Cold War was won (and it was not – something that is covered in Appendix 3) this was the last thing that should have been said. It increased the bitterness Russian voters felt and made them support Putin even more. Whether the Cold War was won matters because Russians don't think that they lost it, just like the Germans didn't think that they were defeated after WWI (which fuelled their desire to get even).

Additionally, the USA and Europe lost respect within Russia due to the rise of political correctness. The West was associated with freedom and "cool" culture back in the 1980s. It was adored by those living under socialism because it was a counterpoint to everything that was wrong with their way of life. The Russians liked the clear-cut "manliness" of 1980s movies like *Top Gun*: there are good guys and there are bad guys, heroes and villains; it is black and white. The good guy wins and gets the girl at the end. This is not the case today when political correctness makes Westerners walk on eggshells. Present-day Western culture of transgenderism and multi-culturalism is confusing and unappealing to the Russians. In some respects, the Russian psyche is closer to the Vikings than it is to the modern world. This is a country where brute force is respected and emulated while weakness is despised, and where the social elite consists of violent organised criminals. "Homosexual" is the worst insult a man can receive, as it implies he is not a man but a failure.

Given all this, it is not surprising that Russians find today's modern Western culture alien. Watch, for example, how RT (Russia Today TV network) covers the political aspect of grooming gangs to see the resentment felt towards modern Western culture.[27] Keep in mind that RT is in English; it is meant to appeal to Western viewers and therefore is moderate. What the Russians have to say in Russian about all things postmodern is not toned down on their domestic TV channels or in the websites for domestic consumption, going as far as to use photos from horror movies to illustrate the point how horrible the West is.[28] The West is presented as decadent, degenerate, and deranged.

This is the real reason conservatism and Orthodox Christianity are back in vogue; they are presented as the counterpoint to everything wrong with the West today. This is also the reason why the likes of Putin, former KGB officers who did their best to uproot Christianity under socialism, became churchgoers in our times.

Incidentally, that is something Russians and East Europeans have in common. Poles, Hungarians, and Czechs are passionately anti-Russian. Eastern Europeans squarely embrace Western culture, but not when it comes to Western Europe allowing Islamic emigration and political correctness. The same can be said of the opponents to Putin and his propaganda in Russia itself. For example, Yevgeni Ponasenkov, a popular Russian historian who frequents the Russian TV channels, has only harsh words to say about Putin and Russia.[29] He adores the West. Yet the same Ponasenkov finds himself in Putin's camp when it comes to Western liberal policies like the welcoming of migrants.[30] He is convinced his beloved West is committing suicide by allowing "the savages" (as he calls them) in. Ironically, people like Ponasenkov share the message of Putin's anti-Western propaganda precisely because they find this message to be pro-Western. Putin, a politician who has made a career out of bashing the West, turns out to have a pro-Western message when it suits him.[31]

A promotional clip illustrates how Putin wants to be associated with traditional values. It goes like this: A boy is being adopted from an orphanage. His new father arrives. The child asks: "Where's my mother?" It turns out that the mother is another man who exhibits all the stereotypical features and gestures of a homosexual. The "mother" has brought a dress as a gift for the boy. The child is sad, the carers from the orphanage are horrified, one spits in disgust. Caption appears: "Amendment in Article 72 of the Constitution of the Russian Federation defines marriage as a union between a man and a woman."[32] (Therefore, two men cannot marry and hence the orphans are safe.)

The Need for a Strongman

Few remember now that most of these anti-Western attitudes were in place before Putin appeared on the scene. Even fewer remember that Putin began his political career posing as a modernizer. He learned from experience that no popularity will come out of it, that there's a demand for a different message. The Russians did not want Western niceties, they wanted somebody to impose order in a harsh way. So, it was Putin who followed the voters rather than leading them. Like a good opportunist, he made good use of what was already available. Putin was riding the crest of a wave, becoming the face of a process which would have developed with or without him. In this sense, Putinism preceded Putin.

Russia may be unique in some respects, but not here. People all over the world tend to crave a strong leader when times are chaotic and unsafe. The proverbial example is Hitler being elected in the dysfunctional Weimar Republic, but the American voters were not that different during the Great Depression. "Millions of Germans worshipped Hitler; millions of Americans worshipped Roosevelt. Both nations wanted strong, dynamic leadership and responded to it."[33]

The Russian Great Depression was in the 1990s. What was peculiar for Russia at the time was that not just the economy was privatised, but government functions went into private hands as well. Westerners call this "corruption", but it was more than that. In effect, the state existed on paper only. To use Weber's definition of what a government is, it no longer had the monopoly on violence and therefore was no longer a real government.[34] It is no accident that organised crime bosses at the time were actually called "authorities". (Sometimes the absurd phrase "criminal authority" was used, which may not make sense to a Westerner, but made sense in the local context.) Criminal bosses even resolved civil disputes and dispensed justice. The police were mostly useless if your life or property was in danger, but a criminal boss could help to keep other criminals at bay. Russian society after the fall of the Soviet empire resembled European society after the fall of the Roman Empire. There was no effective central authority (kings were mostly rulers in name only during the early Middle Ages) and it was the local warlord who mattered.

Taking that into account, it is not hard to understand why the Russians looked for somebody like Putin. A public opinion poll was conducted in 1999, at the time he came to power. It showed that the Russian people wanted a brutal and decisive officer (military, police, or from the security services) for president.[35] This is how the people who used to be terrorised by the KGB ended up voting for a KGB man. In the words of Professor Yuri Maltsev, the meat voted for the meat-grinder.[36] Ironically, they also voted for organised crime (which was an extension of the former socialist security services) hoping to get rid of organised crime.

Russia was not unique even among the former socialist countries. Bulgaria is in the EU and NATO while Russia is not, it is submissive while Russia is a bad boy, it is small while Russia is big. However, Bulgaria is the same where it counts: it is also an Orthodox Christian country (not Catholic or Protestant like most former socialist countries in Eastern Europe), and it also had its "Great Depression" in the 1990s in the same way and for the same reason. Fittingly, its longest-ruling prime minister, Boyko Borisov, was remarkably similar to Putin in his career and manner. Both Borisov and Putin were officers (Borisov in the police, Putin in the KGB) under socialism, switched to organised crime after its fall (Borisov turned to racketeering, Putin to corruption), both were showing off their martial arts prowess (Boyko practised karate, Putin practised judo), both played tough and talked like convicts during their subsequent political careers, and both became popular because of all this. To illustrate, Putin said that he would drown terrorists in a pit latrine using convict jargon.[37] The difference between the two leaders was the difference between Russia and Bulgaria. While Russia wanted to be an empire, Bulgaria wanted to be part of an empire; while Russia wanted to be strong, Bulgaria wanted to be with whoever was strong at that moment.

So, there was demand for a strong leader in 1990s Russia. However, the corruption of the Russian government presented a problem for any would-be strong leader. Being such a leader anywhere in the world is not so much about personal character, it is about having well-oiled bureaucratic machinery to lean on. There was not much of this in a country like Russia where one could bribe the police to shoot a porn movie in the centre of a major city or where you need a sniper rifle to get justice.

Phoney Strength

Whoever came to fill the "strongman" niche in Russia had one option left: faking it. He couldn't do much about the bad infrastructure or the corrupt police; he wouldn't look so strong if he were to be judged by that. No amount of propaganda can convince a driver that he rides on a smooth road if it is full of potholes[38] or a patient that he is not in a crumbling hospital if the plaster is falling off the ceiling.[39] Putin could dazzle his constituency in the international arena only. This was how Russian foreign policy became a continuation of Russia's domestic politics by other means: a show for domestic consumption. In other words, it was not aiming to achieve anything abroad. Putin wanted to win elections, not take over the world, when he behaved like a nuclear-armed hooligan who wanted to pick a fight.

Putin has the reputation of a dictator in the West but, unlike how it used to be under socialism, the people in Russia were able to vote freely when sanctions were imposed in 2014. Yes, the main TV channels were controlled by the government and there were occasional political assassinations that removed some contenders (such as Boris Nemtsov), but the election results were not falsified as they were in Belarus. Apparently, Putin gave the Russians what they wanted because they kept on electing him. He was genuinely popular (and independent studies confirmed this).[40]

This cannot be explained away as Putin's influence on the mass media because present day propaganda cannot possibly be more efficient than the Soviet one. Whereas Russian TV channels must compete with a relatively free flow of information via the internet, the Soviet propaganda machine enjoyed a monopoly on news, education, and entertainment. Moreover, whereas people could by and large speak their mind in Russia prior to 2022, they were afraid to do so in Soviet times for fear of being reported to the KGB.

The ability to speak freely in Russia might come as a surprise to those who assume Putin is an all-powerful dictator who kills everybody who dares oppose him. Don't take my word for it. Just watch Russian TV from before 2022 (there are plenty of clips on YouTube) and you will see that many like Victor Shenderovich, Yevgeny Ponasenkov, Dmitry Gordon, Irina Khakamada, Nikolai Svanidze, and others regularly spoke out against Putin on the already mentioned Echo of Moscow and sometimes even on the official TV channels. As for YouTube, there were hardly any restrictions there. The people mentioned were sometimes criticised or shouted at, but they were still given the opportunity to appear in front of the cameras and, no, they were neither locked up nor killed. Alexei Navalny spoke out against Putin for many years before he was poisoned. (Many more spoke and continue to speak against Putin on Navalny's YouTube channel.) He was arrested numerous times, but his YouTube channel remained active. Moreover, there were opposition members in the Parliament of Moscow who spoke out against Putin as well.[41] The same went for the Parliament of Saint Petersburg.[42] Those MPs might have been heckled and obstructed by the parliamentary speakers, but they were still able to give speeches without being imprisoned.

There is no denying that Russia was gradually moving away from Europe. It disobeyed the European Court of Human Rights by refusing to free Navalny and eventually ceased to be a party to the European Convention of Human Rights. Some opposition figures like Solonin and Shenderovich felt threatened enough to leave Russia. Navalny's Anti-Corruption Foundation along with Memorial, the most prominent human rights organisation, were harassed by the authorities. The number of the political prisoners was rising. The opposition stations of Echo or Moscow and Dozhd were eventually taken off air when the war began in 2022. Still, to compare Russia to the USSR would be like comparing a common cold to Ebola simply because both are contagious diseases.

Because there were real elections in Russia, Putin needed suitable propaganda to get re-elected and the role assigned to the West was to be the boogey-man. He needed to manufacture an enemy that supposedly only he could keep at bay. Putin did not have to work hard to make the West look like an enemy as the West did most of the work for him. He needed confrontation in order to present himself as a defender of Russian sovereignty against the encroachment of NATO. His message was: we must unite to withstand. Fittingly, his party is called United Russia. This is the oldest trick in the book for authoritarian leaders: united we stand.

Poking the West in the eye was Putin's only source of legitimacy. Apart from that, his rule was a dismal failure. The Russian government was so notoriously corrupt that Serguei Cheloukhine and M. R. Haberfeld assert it is the same entity as the organised corrupt networks themselves.[43] To put it simply, the government and mafia are the same thing in Russia. Putin poses as a strongman and yet he has achieved nothing to solve this issue. He cannot achieve anything because, to do so, he would have to fight himself and his own associates. Putin has done nothing to solve the other everyday problems of the Russian people either. For example, the pension age was raised in 2019 so much that it will exceed the life expectancy of 43 per cent of men and 17.5 per cent of women.[44]

Putin was not always a liar. Back in the 1990s, he used to do the right thing by saying the wrong thing. He told the Russians to own the problems, that the West must not be blamed for the Russian domestic issues.[45]

However, as politicians all over the world know, most people don't like to hear that they are responsible for their misfortunes. Fat people want to blame their genes, hormones, or the food industry for being fat and the poor want to blame the privileged for being poor. Blaming your lifestyle or laziness is good if you are determined to lose weight or to gain wealth, but most people lack such determination. Hearing that they are greedy or lazy is not productive to them, it just makes them miserable. Likewise, the ordinary Russian, who would not complicate his own life by refusing to bribe the traffic cops, needed to believe that it is not up to him to fight corruption. All people need self-respect. If self-respect cannot be obtained by being successful, they need a convenient explanation of why they are not successful. Politicians who ignore what their voters want to hear don't stay popular for long.

So Putin, like a good politician, changed his tune and began blaming the West for the Russians' shortcomings. This choice was forced on him if he wanted to stay in politics just like a toy manufacturer has no choice but to supply the toys that the market demands or else he will go out of business.

The Russian public, therefore, was not an innocent victim fooled by Putin, they demanded to be fooled. The life of an ordinary Russian was grim, but the list of consolations was growing: the West fears Russia; it has a big nuclear stick, and Putin is putting the traitors (like Skripal) in their place; Russians are not living in the humiliating 1990s under Yeltsin anymore. With Putin in charge, they might still be suckers but at least their country will not be. Frustrated Americans have Superman, frustrated Russians have Putin. It is for the psychologists to determine whether voting for him was a compensatory mechanism. It may seem strange that Russians voted for somebody from the KGB, the institution that used to oppress them. But as a Russian saying goes: "Whoever is born in a prison does not dream of being free but of being the warden."

This context addresses a question that the Russian and Ukrainian observers posed after the Russian invasion in 2022: how the "thief" (meaning the corrupt Putin) became a warmonger. On the surface, corruption is associated with a pragmatic, down to earth approach to life while wars are associated with fanaticism. However, the two are just sides of the same coin in the Russian context. Because the thief steals and the country is impoverished as a result, he has to seek legitimacy in some phoney heroism. There is a saying in Russia (usually attributed to the eminent nineteenth-century author Saltykov-Shchedrin[46]): "When they begin to talk about patriotism in Russia, know: somewhere they stole something."

It was against this background that Putin portrayed himself as a restorer of Soviet glory. Whereas the former rulers were weak, Putin was strong; whereas Yeltsin was a drunk, he was sober; where the former was sick, he was healthy (hence the Judo and the topless photos); whereas former rulers were losing positions, Putin regained them; whereas Russia was being betrayed before, the traitors (like Skripal or the Ukrainians who wanted to bring NATO to Crimea) were being punished now. In particular, whereas his predecessors were friendly with the West, he was not. Under this version of events, having good relations with the West was associated with weakness and betrayal.

Military Showmanship

A sense of pride, nationalism, and longing for the Soviet past was already evident in the public mood of the early 2000s, around the time Putin came to power. "Udarnaya Sila"[47] (A Striking Force) was a documentary series on the history of the Soviet weaponry. (It is notoriously well known that the USSR was not good at producing cars or refrigerators, but it did well in developing tanks and guns.) Each successive episode brought home the same message: "We, the Russians, are exceptionally talented; the Americans feared us once and they will fear us again; Gorbachev and Yeltsin scrapped our weapons, however, we have the means to manufacture them again."

It was as though Putin's military policies followed the script of this documentary. They were designed to look formidable but were just for show – and a domestically consumed show at that. Moreover, since they involved Soviet weapons and tactics, these policies satisfied domestic nostalgia for everything Soviet. The Soviet Union was not famous with its TV sets and refrigerators so that, too, narrowed the choice of what could be used to stir up pride.

It all started when the flights of the Soviet long-range "Bear" bomber (Tu-95), capable of carrying nuclear weapons, were resumed in 2007.[48] (Incidentally, most military aeroplanes, fighter jets included, have been capable of delivering nuclear weapons ever since the last were miniaturised in the 1950s and therefore the only thing that set Tu-95 apart was that it can carry somewhat bigger weapons.) This seemed significant in the press releases, although the Tu-95 was just one of many nuclear bomb delivering systems – and an outdated one at that. The Russian Federation had land-based ballistic missiles that were not visible, but which in themselves were enough to devastate the

West. There were no effective countermeasures against them. The same went for Russian nuclear submarines. These too, just like the Bear, could come close to Western shores, but, unlike the Bear, could not all be destroyed. In contrast, the Tu-95 could easily be shot down by Western fighter planes and, on top of that, it did not even carry nuclear weapons at the time.[49]

Given that, why did the Russian Air Force bother to obtain several Bears from Ukraine, saving them from the scrap yard?[50] That made no military sense, but it worked as good PR. It was all form and no substance. There is a word in Russian for this: *pokazuha*. It means something like "for show" or "not practical, not for real use". The Tu-95 was chosen perfectly in terms of a nickname: journalists all over the world repeated the word Bear each time they mentioned it, a word which has become synonymous with Russia.

Roughly the same analysis may be made for the Russian campaign in Syria. What exactly was it intended to achieve except poking America in the eye? Did saving Assad's regime show potential client regimes that they can count on Russian help if they do not want to be in the USA's pocket? The USSR tried this and it did not work well. It exported military hardware for free or cheaply to any dictator who was willing to pay lip service to the socialist phraseology in Africa, Asia or Latin America. The USSR succeeded in achieving tactical successes like Vietnam, but strategically it was stuck in a blind alley; it was contained. It spread socialism in many third world countries, however, this brought little more than additional expenses. The Soviets established an outpost in Nicaragua in the 1980s, but this hardly meant they could ever take over the USA by way of Mexico. They also had allies in Africa and Asia, but this could not translate into taking over the world's oil supplies. All these scattered successes may have looked good as propaganda, as they satisfied a vague claim that socialism was still spreading, however, they did not correspond to a practical plan of how to get rid of the main obstacle: the West. Therefore, the bottom line of the Soviet policies was: lots of expenses, no solid results. Why would the Russian Federation, which has fewer resources than the USSR once did, do any better playing this game?

Military involvement is costly. It is too costly even for the biggest economy of the world, that of the USA, which must be struggling judging by its increasing government debt that has risen to over 30 trillion dollars as of 2023. Therefore, as much as the Russian involvement in Syria was generating noise, that was as far as it could go. Moreover, Syria was one of the last countries where Russia had a military base and therefore one of the last where Russian involvement was possible.[51] (Apart from several bases in former USSR countries, Russia had bases in Vietnam and Syria.) In contrast, the USA has nearly 800 bases all over the world.[52]

Apart from bases, the USA has carrier groups which can act like bases anywhere in the world; Russia has nuclear submarines and these are suitable for a doomsday scenario, but not for measured conventional airstrikes. The Russian Navy announced in 2007 that it was to receive six new nuclear-propelled aircraft carriers over the next 20 years. This did not happen due to the global economic crisis.[53]

Just like Russia had no money to modernise its navy, it had none for its air force and ground forces. The new fighter Su-57 dazzled with its aerobatics[54] and the tank T-14 Armata supposedly had incredible characteristics,[55] but neither ended up in mass production. Would-be military experts argued about whether the first was a great plane and whether the second was a good tank, but in actuality there was nothing to argue about as there was no such plane and no such tank; it was just Russian politicians staging a show in order to convince their voting public that they could fill the big Soviet shoes.

What they actually did was the opposite of what the USSR used to do. The latter would first develop a weapon, mass produce it in secret, re-arm their forces with it, and only then display it to the world. For example, this is what was done with the AK-47 assault rifle or the T-64 tank. In contrast, the only place the new Russian fighters and tanks could be found was in air shows and military parades. The field troops still used the old Su-27s and T-72s.

The same can be said of the weapons Putin spoke of on 1 March 2018.[56] They range from the irrelevant to the imaginary.

A hypersonic missile was presented as innovative although all ballistic missiles have been hypersonic since the 1940s. Putin claimed that the new one could manoeuvre and therefore would be impossible to intercept. (Ballistic missiles, unlike aeroplanes, are like bullets: their trajectory is governed by purely physical forces such as gravity and air-resistance, once they have been accelerated; their trajectories are therefore predictable and can be calculated, which theoretically makes it possible to shoot them down.) There are two problems with what Putin claimed. To begin with, lack of manoeuvrability may have been true of Wernher von Braun's V-2 during WWII, but the sophisticated missiles developed during the Cold War could manoeuvre in flight, albeit not extensively. They may still be called "ballistic", but strictly speaking they are not. Moreover, even if they could not manoeuvre, they are next to impossible to intercept. That is because any object flying with speeds exceeding seven kilometres per second is hard to shoot down, whether you can calculate its trajectory or not. (The speed is reduced close to the surface, but it is still supersonic and, what's worse, there is almost no time left before the nuclear blast.) This has been compared to stopping a bullet with another bullet. While this comparison is colourful, it is an understatement because an ICBM re-enters the atmosphere 25 times faster than a bullet exits the muzzle of a gun (assuming the average speed of a handgun bullet is around the speed of sound). At the time of writing, new intercepting missiles are being developed that could hopefully intercept a few primitive North Korean rockets in a large number of cases (but not always). These defensive missiles would be hopelessly overwhelmed if they had to deal with hundreds of Russian (Soviet-made) ICBMs launched against the USA at the same time. In summary: the weapon Putin claims Russia has developed would add nothing to its ability to wage a nuclear war against the USA.

The same can be said of the second type of hypersonic missile Putin bragged about, the one which is carried by a MIG-31 interceptor. In fact, there's nothing new with this missile, it is just the same old Iskander ballistic missile (Cold War Soviet technology again) modified to be launched by an aeroplane. Sure, it is hypersonic, but hypersonic in the same way the Soviet Scuds from the 1960s, and even the German V-2 developed during WWII, were. Given its high price and other characteristics, its military usefulness is doubtful. It is not even certain it cannot be intercepted.[57] Putin also announced the deployment of a new ICBM, which is supposedly an improvement on the Soviet SS-18 "Satan". Even if true, it again changed nothing because, as was pointed out, Western powers were still incapable of intercepting the old Soviet version. The problem was the same: ICBMs fly too fast. Russia may as well have saved the expense for new developments.

Putin talked of a 100 megaton nuclear torpedo capable of causing a tsunami that could wipe out the North American or Western European coastlines. However, Russia has had this capability ever since Khrushchev detonated the so-called "Tsar Bomb" in 1961. Its yield was around 56 megatons but only because some components were removed to decrease the blast range (as it was too large even for the largest country in the world); the actual yield would have been 100 megatons otherwise. So, the USSR could have used such a torpedo as early as the early 1960s and, in fact, its creation was contemplated at the time. (Incidentally, the idea was proposed by Andrei

Sakharov who was also one of the creators of the Tsar Bomb, and yes, that is the same Sakharov who was awarded the Nobel **Peace** Prize in 1975. So, the scientist who came up with the idea of a single weapon which could kill more people in one hour than had been killed in WWII was also honoured for his contributions to world peace.[58])

Since 1961, there has been no limit to how powerful nuclear weapons can be and creating more powerful ones does not change the MAD (Mutually Assured Destruction) doctrine. MAD is just what its name suggests: that mutual destruction is assured whatever the scenarios, thus making a total nuclear war unwinnable. That is why the USA and USSR stopped making more powerful bombs: it was pointless. 100 megatons, 200, 2000… what's the difference?

It was considerations like these that led to Edward Teller, the father of the thermonuclear bomb, to come up with the concept of the "backyard bomb". That is a bomb so powerful (the device had a yield of no less than 10,000 megatons) that you don't need to drop it on your enemy in order to destroy him. You can detonate it on your own territory – in your backyard, so to speak – and the effect would be the same as delivering it to the enemy since it would kill all humans on all continents anyway. Now, that is MAD. As you can imagine, the US government was not interested to build it.[59]

Then Putin spoke of something exciting for a change: a cruise missile with a nuclear engine. Alas, it probably does not exist due to a list of reasons too numerous to discuss here.[60] (It is this project that is associated with the nuclear accident in August 2019.[61]) Yet, even if it does exist, it would be a great technical achievement, but not a game changer because of, you've guessed it, the prevailing MAD. Its supposed advantage – to be capable of flying for months at a time (as it does not need refuelling) – is irrelevant during a missile exchange that would be over within an hour in a total nuclear war. Such a missile would be equally impractical in a conventional war as hitting the target would result in radioactive fallout. (One may as well use a tactical nuke since it would be cheaper, more effective, and the contamination would be smaller.) In short, it would be a marvellous machine but militarily useless.

Putin made this all sound patriotic and milked it to the last by asking the public to propose names for some of these weapons that supposedly guaranteed Russia's independence. (That the West was poised to take over Russia was a recurring theme in many local TV shows and thus independence was a thing.)

The summary was the same: much noise and nothing revolutionary. The world was and remains a dangerous place with or without Putin and his gadgets, whether they are new or are non-existent. The experts cannot be impressed by his gimmicks. (But the voters can. He won the election after this speech.) What Putin did, therefore, was for domestic consumption. He had no chance of being able to intimidate the West and was not trying to. Let's not forget that weapons not only have military uses. Unlike roads, hospitals, wages, law, order and all the other things that are visible and therefore visibly lacking, weapons are secret. The more incredible they are, the more secret they must be. Therefore, it is the only area where a politician can lie with impunity.

Here we again encountered something that was mentioned before: Putin did the only thing he could. Just like he had to oppose the Americans in Syria (as there was no other place with a Russian base left) and he had to use military build-up to build up his popularity (as he could do nothing about the corruption, the infrastructure, or the pensions), he had to focus on what is secret (because otherwise it would be too obvious to his constituency that he was lying).

Roughly the same analysis can be made of Russia's non-military foreign policy. Take its involvement in the 2016 USA presidential elections. The evidence suggests that it did not alter the results.[62] What Western observers miss here is that it achieved a great deal in the Russian elections. The noise generated about it in the West convinced Russian voters that their country was meddling in somebody else's affairs just like the USA meddles in everybody else's affairs. Russia looked significant in their eyes because, it seemed, it was competing with the Americans; it was not a second-class player anymore. By making noise, the Democrats in the USA thought they were harming Trump, but they were actually helping Putin.

Bread or Circuses

The Russian government could not afford bread and circuses, it could only afford circuses. The phoney war with the West aimed to hide the real war that Putin waged. In Russia it was known as the war of the "TV set against the fridge": a metaphor of the conflict between propaganda and reality. The TV lifted the spirits by patriotic bravado, but the fridge was empty. A cartoonist captured this well by drawing a shocked Russian who opened his fridge to find nothing but the TV set inside.[63] The novelty of Crimea wore off; the euphoria was gone.[64]

The Russian military had an easy time when they went to Syria and Libya; they fought ragtag rebels who didn't have their own air force. But then they faced a modern and disciplined army, that of Turkey, and the tables turned.

Worse still, the Turks went on to challenge Russia in its own backyard by backing Azerbaijan in the 2020 war against Armenia, the only Russian friend in the Caucasus. Instead of helping his orthodox Armenian brethren, all Putin did was to issue toothless and vague statements. Armenia, and therefore Russia, lost this war as a result. The impression was left that Russia did not dare face Turkey. It looked weak and so did Putin.

The failed poisoning of Navalny added to this precisely because it failed. At least the secret services were supposed to be efficient, but it turned out that they were not working any better than the sloppy and corrupt traffic police.

In the absence of real military success, Putin tried to ratchet up the patriotism by organising domestic military parades dedicated to the Soviet victory in WWII. But not everybody in Russia was impressed, given one of the jokes circulating there: "What's the biggest success during Putin's reign?"

"Winning WWII."

Incidentally, Putin was respected so much after Crimea that Russians stopped inventing jokes about him. Over the next few years, they started to make jokes about him again.

Clausewitz used to say that war is a continuation of politics with other means. In Russia, a war would be a continuation of propaganda with other means. Putin needed to come up with some new foreign stunt or else he would lose the domestic war against the fridge. He needed to invade somewhere.

But where? The former socialist countries that became NATO members were out of the question: NATO was too strong. China was no less dangerous. Russian military backwardness would become apparent if Putin attempted something in these directions.

Logically, the only options left were the former Soviet countries. Still, even there Putin had to be careful because some, like Azerbaijan, had obtained modern weaponry and Russian hardware was what Armenia had when it lost to Azerbaijan in 2020. Russian voters will swallow a lot when it comes to economic hardship, they always have, but they were high on national pride, pumped-up with patriotic fever, and would be sensitive to their country losing militarily. Since this pride was the only joy most of them had in their lives, crushing their delusions of grandeur would be the surest way for Putin to lose popularity. This, and not sanctions, was the real danger to him.

Putin was a hostage to this reality. On the one hand, he was not interested in starting a war for real as this would expose how phoney Russia's military strength was. (The great Russian losses and modest gains during the subsequent invasion of Ukraine in 2022 demonstrated this.) On the other hand, he could not rest either, as the territorial acquisitions in Georgia (2008) and Ukraine (2014) became old news.

The problem with pumping up hysteria by military build-ups on somebody's border is that this approach could not go on indefinitely, either. The longer it was practised, the less threatening it would seem and, consequently, the less Russia's adversaries would take its bluffs seriously. Eventually, Putin had to walk the walk and thus risk exposing Russia's weakness – or continue to talk the talk and thus also expose Russia's weakness.

Worse, walking the walk, even if successful, would mean filling the TV at the expense of emptying the fridge. It is supposed to compensate for the empty fridge, not to empty it further. Besides, if there's a mobilisation of army reservists, civilians will have to cease watching TV from the comfort of their homes to go to the front. And this is the wrong type of circus, since the spectators must become gladiators. Moreover, a war effort, including the mobilisation of many people, would be inefficient in a corrupt and poorly organised country like Russia. Bottom line: Putin would be in a lose-lose situation unless he had a war that would be both successful and short. If it is unsuccessful, it would hurt the TV. If long, it would hurt the fridge.

Roughly the same model applied to the sanctions. Putin needed them to support Russia's TV-projected version of the world: we are surrounded by enemies, Russia is unique, the West hates us because we are better than them, and so on. Yet they must not be so extreme as to affect the fridge. The sanctions between 2014 and 2022 were perfect for Putin. Most Russians did not care about having the choice of many types of French cheese anyway, and as for essential things such as Western electronics, they could be supplied through third parties. At the same time, the West continued to buy Russian oil and gas, which mean that the Russian economy was not significantly affected.

Western Sanctions

What Britain did with the Skripal investigation fitted into this context. That is why the more successful Britain was in proving Russian involvement in the assassination, the better it was for Putin. If you were to have watched Russian TV around the time when the Skripals were in the news, you would have seen their story unfolding as a soap opera which distracted Russian public attention from the real issues. The same went for Ukraine and NATO, two subjects which Putin wants to merge into one. The accusations and the sanctions confirmed his belief that the West was involved, that it was hostile, that it wanted Russia on its knees. (Actually, the "on one's knees" phrase was used in a similar way as the National Socialists used the "stab in the back" phrase after WWI. Fittingly, "Getting Russia off its Knees" was an expression associated with retaliating against the West after the Cold War.)

Moreover, the sanctions and the other indecisive steps showed that the West was weak and weakness is despised in Russian society where "might is right". (Watch some road-rage videos on YouTube if you want to grasp how scores are settled over there.[65] While British motorists shout out driving advice at unruly drivers, Russian motorists casually pull out guns or hatchets to show who is boss.)

The expulsion of Russian diplomats, as the UK did, was an impotent gesture. The same went for the declarations and the sanctions. The only thing that would work was the one thing that would cause pain in the West: not buying Russian oil and gas. The Russian economy is based on oil and gas exports and so shutting the pipelines, all of them, could really lower the standard of living and hurt Putin. However, that would require the participation of the whole of the EU as British action alone would not do the trick. Putin did not believe this would happen and he was proven right.

If the West had no stomach to go all the way after 2014, it would have been better to do nothing. Doing something half-heartedly (imposing some sanctions, but not hitting where it hurts) did more harm than good. It was not enough to make life in Russia so miserable that Putin could be voted out of office, but it was enough to convince the voters that Putin must be doing something right if the West is against him.

This brings us to Ukraine again. Western policies until 2022 were too timid to give Ukraine any real help but they were enough to make Putin's propaganda believable. He wanted to associate the Ukrainians with the Americans in order to present the war against Ukraine that started in 2014 as being against NATO and not as aggression against their Russian speaking brethren (which is what it was). In reality, it was a conflict which resembled a civil war where, tragically, both opposing forces often spoke the same language: Russian. Moreover, some Ukrainian fighters identified themselves as Russian and yet they said they hate Russia.[66] However, because the West was trying to stop Putin, he was able to sell the conflict to the public as a war against the West; the more the West did to stop him, the more Putin was incentivised to continue.

Furthermore, measured, half-hearted sanctions portrayed the West as hostile but impotent: hostile because it imposed sanctions and impotent because those sanctions made little difference. To illustrate, the sanctions were mocked with a popular T-shirt saying: "Sanctions? Don't Make our Iskanders Laugh". (Iskander is the already mentioned "hypersonic" Russian missile, the one from Putin's 2018 speech.) Some cheeky women wore a "Don't Make My Iskanders Laugh" variant.[67] Hostile but impotent is the worst possible combination: hostile means that a retaliation is called for and impotent means that this retaliation will not be costly to Russia. In summary, the West encouraged anti-Western hostility.

Given all that has been said so far, it should be clear why Russia wanted to be accused of the Skripals' assassination. It would have been pointless to assassinate them otherwise.

That somebody might want to be caught red-handed sounds strange until we think of the terrorists. Unlike other criminals who claim they are innocent, terrorists brag about what they are doing to the point of filming it. It is a PR activity that generates free publicity. Coca Cola had to pay for its clips to be aired, the Islamic State didn't. Putin and his cronies came from the secret police of the former USSR, which had a long tradition of news-making by using terror. The Soviet show trials of the 1930s are the proverbial example here. (A show trial is a public trial where the outcome is predetermined and the only goal is to send a message to the local population or to the outside world.) The confessions of the accused were scripted by the secret police.[68] (This way the picture painted by Soviet propaganda could be substantiated.) The actors in this show died for real, yet it was still a show and the reality still followed a script. In the much-quoted words of the already mentioned Beria: "Let me have one night with him and I'll have him confessing he is the King of England."[69]

These invented plots had to convince the domestic public that the USSR was under siege, that great vigilance was needed, along with more weapons. Stalin could have executed those people without a trial, however, he needed the publicity.

But Russia denied involvement in both the Litvinenko and Skripal cases, didn't it? Well, sort of. Russia denied involvement in Ukraine after 2014, but it didn't really hide it and one can watch videos where YouTubers track the transportation of Russian tanks to separatist forces.[70] That is what we call a public secret: it is officially denied for legal reasons and yet is widely known in practice. Russia also denied it had soldiers in Crimea although everybody knew who the "little green men" were.[71] (Putin admitted it much later.) Russia denied involvement in the US election. In 2018, Russia denied that its private soldiers died in a skirmish with the American forces in Syria. (Then Russia downplayed it.)[72] The latest incident became a source of jokes within Russia itself where the deceased were known as *ihtamniety* which can be translated as "those who are (officially) not there". The same went for the Skripals' assassination. The assassins became characters in numerous Russian-language comedy shows because of their clumsy explanations of why they wanted to see Salisbury, which sounded like a recitation of the Wikipedia page on local landmarks.[73] The fact that they lied was the whole point of these jokes.

As unconvincing as the lie was, it gave Putin's regime the best of both worlds. On one hand, his voters had no doubt who fought in Ukraine or assassinated the Skripals (both made Russia significant in their eyes). On the other hand, the victims (Ukraine, UK) had a hard time proving who is legally responsible. Why would Putin need to convince anybody that Russia is innocent? That would defeat the purpose. The Russians needed to be convinced that Russia is behind the war in Ukraine and the assassinations. As for the Westerners, it didn't matter what they believed as they didn't vote in the Russian elections.

Just like with the Skripals, Russia gained nothing out of its involvement in Ukraine. But Putin did. While the country was wasting money on military hardware and was suffering sanctions, his approval ratings soared to 81 per cent after the Crimean annexation.[74] There is nothing unique in principle here; politicians tend to spend public funds and sacrifice the public interests in order to buy voters all over the world. (See the "Raising the Minimum Wage Lowers the Income" chapter.) The only difference is that while in the West they spend tax money on things like welfare benefits, in Russia the money is spent on illusions of grandeur. The attempted assassination of

Skripal was no more about him than the war in Donetsk was about territory. Skripal was not important and Russia did not need more territory. (In fact, it had so much of it that it was no longer capable of maintaining the infrastructure in vast parts of it.)

Russia had a choice in 1991: to join the West by becoming just another Eastern European country or to go back to its hollow exceptionality. It chose the second and became this large irritant of a country on the fringe of Europe. It was desperate to be noticed, feared, and to look more formidable than it was. Being sanctioned was part of this image prior to its brazen invasion of Ukraine in 2022.

The West imposes sanctions not because they work, but because this is what the West wants to do (given that it must do something). There is an old anecdote about a drunken man who is unsteady against a lamppost. A policeman asks him:

"What are you doing here?"
"Looking for my key."
"Where did you lose your key?"
"Over there." (The drunk indicates a place some hundred metres away.)
"Why are you not searching for it over there then?"
"It is too dark over there; I will never be able to see it."

Endnotes

1 You can find more details in Vadim J. Birstein's book *The Perversion of Knowledge: The True Story of Soviet Science*, (USA, Westview Press, 2001).

2 Henry Zeffman, "End your hostility to West, Theresa May tells President Putin of Russia", on June 29, 2019, consulted on March 4, 2020, https://www.thetimes.co.uk/article/irresponsible-russia-must-halt-hostilities-warns-may-frrrk7v2h.

3 "SSSR: Kakooyo Stranu Patayreealyee..." (USSR: What a Country we Lost...), published on the Samoy Sock 2 YouTube channel on June 18, 2018, consulted on June 23, 2022, https://www.youtube.com/watch?v=dS0cvQeTjFI&list=PL1E32Douoi6IINXhXWHbvyreWGCdwzj34&index=3.

4 Georgi Markov, *Zadochnee Reportagee za Bulgaria, (In Absentia Reports About Bulgaria)*, (Profizdat Publishing, Sofia 1990), page 131.

5 Marina Svanidzea and Nikolai Svanidze, *Estoricheskiye Hroniki (Historical Chronicles): 1981–1983*, (Amphora Publishers, Saint Petersburg, 2014).

6 Putin Doesn't Object to Russia Joining NATO, Kommersant Daily website, published on March 7, 2000, consulted on February 15, 2021, https://www.kommersant.ru/doc/142046.

7 Ekaterina Chertkovskaya, Alexander Paulsson, Stefania Barca, *Towards a Political Economy of Degrowth*, (London, Rowman & Littlefield International Ltd, 2019), Page 108.

8 "Combination – two small sausages", Gem Mediatheque YouTube Channel, published on February 11, 2018, consulted on June 23, 2019, https://www.youtube.com/watch?v=Zbgr6Hpqcpg.

9 "Combination – American Boy", Gem Mediatheque YouTube Channel, published on May 7, 2016, consulted on June 23, 2019, https://www.youtube.com/watch?v=W7hAo28NCXc.

10 "Praycrastnoyeh Dalehko" ("My Bright Future"), Lubimiyah Muzika YouTube channel, published on April 16, 2015, consulted on June 23, 2022, https://www.youtube.com/watch?v=m7A4uy6Nw0k. The name of the song is often translated as "My Fine and Distant Future" or as "The Voice of My Tomorrow", but these literate translations don't convey its propagandist aspect. Although the song appeared for the first time in a 1985 movie (*Guest from the Future*), the phrase used in its title blends in well with the decades old ideological Soviet universe where the future was to be

far better than the present. This future was known as the "bright future", a formula that was sanctified by the powers that be and repeated often in speeches, literature, etc.

11 Appropriately, the movie can be viewed on a porn site, Pornhub website, consulted on June 23, 2019, https://www.pornhub.com/view_video.php?viewkey=1910676746.

12 "Voroshilovskiy Strelok", (Voroshilov Sharpshooter) (1999), Veselin Strahilov YouTube channel, published on October 9, 2018, consulted on June 23, 2022, https://www.youtube.com/watch?v=wH-FkNGo9qU.

13 "Lyubit po-Russki", IMDb website, consulted on July 21, 2023, https://www.imdb.com/title/tt0178725/.

14 Za prozata na poetitay (About the prose of the poets), Capital BG website, consulted on June 13, 2023, https://www.capital.bg/biznes/media_i_reklama/2000/05/12/203074_za_prozata_na_poetite/.

15 "Posledny Miff", (The Last Myth), Vladimir Sinelnikov YouTube channel, published on July 11, 2012, consulted on June 23, 2022, https://www.youtube.com/watch?v=YtukSNdQ21s&list=PL8E5DC8F66DFF2CB2.

16 Tatu, "Yugoslavia", Viacheslav Sukhanov's YouTube channel, published on April 2, 2014, consulted on July 4, 2020, https://www.youtube.com/watch?v=BCTvMcSccNE.

17 See, for example, Tatu, "Yugoslavia", QuattroSol YouTube channel, published on December 10, 2011, consulted on July 4, 2020, https://www.youtube.com/watch?v=gjb93LrE8h4,; Lena Katina, "Yugoslavia", SinCity company YouTube channel, published on July 22, 2016, consulted on July 4, 2020, https://www.youtube.com/watch?v=7Jftw4VcTjI.

18 "Yugoslavia–ruska pesma, prevod na sribski", Serbskijkazak (Serbian Cossack) YouTube channel, published on March 1, 2014, consulted on July 4, 2020, https://www.youtube.com/watch?v=GYQJEEOKqWc&list=RDjGxRzx5DNLw&index=17.

19 Lena Katina, "Yugoslavia", Serbia-Russia-God-with-us YouTube channel, published on October 8, 2014, consulted on July 4, 2020, https://www.youtube.com/watch?v=NGMnojYvaVc.
20 Putin's speech after taking Crimea, RT in Russian YouTube Channel, streamed live on March 18, 2014, consulted on September 5, 2019, https://www.youtube.com/watch?v=mhrPXMQUNBA.
21 "Putin: raseeyeski myedved nee oo kavo sprasheevat nyeh budyet. Valdie, 24.10.2014", (Putin: the Russian bear is not going to ask for permission), MIR 24 YouTube channel, published on October 24, 2014, consulted on September 5, 2019, https://www.youtube.com/watch?v=EbHMIluLYmI.
22 Zhirinovsky about the bombing of Yugoslavia, video footage from 1999, LDPR TV YouTube channel, published on March 27, 2019, consulted on June 13, 2019; https://www.youtube.com/watch?v=LL5oi1IE2Us.
23 Michail Smotriaev, "Rassheeraynier NATO: Abmanool Lee Zapad Gorbachova? (NATO's Enlargement: Did The West Deceive Gorbachov?), Russian Service of BBC website, published on December 26, 2017, consulted on June 23, 2022, https://www.bbc.com/russian/features-42483896,
24 "John Kerry to Russia: You Lost the Cold War, Get Over It", ABC News website, published on March 18, 2014, consulted on May 15, 2017, http://abcnews.go.com/blogs/politics/2014/03/john-kerry-to-russia-you-lost-the-cold-war-get-over-it/.
25 Prof. Michel Chossudovsky, "Hillary Clinton: 'We Created Al Qaeda', The Protagonists of the 'Global War on Terrorism' are the Terrorists", Global Research website, published on June 1, 2013, consulted on May 15, 2017, http://www.globalresearch.ca/hillary-clinton-we-created-al-qaeda/5337222.

26 "Trump: The United States won two world wars and put communism on the knees", Weapon News website, published on December 9, 2017, consulted on December 9, 2017, http://weaponews.com/news/19816-trump-the-united-states-won-two-world-wars-and-put-communism-on-the-kn.html.

27 "Sex-gang's background must be acknowledged without fear of racism" – UK MP, https://www.youtube.com/watch?v=A57hnJx8kVE, RT YouTube channel, published on August 12, 2017, consulted on May 19, 2020.

28 Ksenia Jharava, "Beyeleeyeh Rabeenyih: Megrantee Godamee Naseelooyoot Britanskeeh Deyevachek. Palitizia Bayeetsyah Abvneeyneeyeh V Raseesmiyeh", (White Female Slaves: Migrants Rape Young British Girls. The Police Fears Racism Accusations), Lenta.RU website, published on January 6, 2018, consulted on August 5, 2022, https://lenta.ru/articles/2018/01/06/bri/.

29 See, for example, The Russian Civilization, Common Sense YouTube channel, published on December 9, 2013, consulted on July 4, 2020, https://www.youtube.com/watch?v=sizcDk0UZqo.

30 "Evgeniy Ponasenkov: Pro Adaptazieu Meegrantav v Evropay (S Naoochnoy Tochkee Zraynia), (Evgeniy Ponasenkov: About the Integration of Migrants in Europe (From a Scientific Point of View)", published on the Common Sense YouTube channel, published on June 6 2016, https://www.youtube.com/watch?v=SXOMp8W5Gug, consulted on July 4, 2020; "Gibel Evropayskoy Tvleezatseeyee, Mif o Padeynee Rojdaemostee v Evropay/Evgeniy Ponasenkov" (The European Civilisation is Doomed, The Myth of Dropping Birth Rates in Europe/Evgeniy Ponasenkov), Piervay Naoochni YouTube channel, published on September 15, 2021, consulted on June 23, 2022.

31 "Putin compares 'Western Woke' to Soviet Bolshevism (Marxism) via RT", Main Street Media YouTube channel,

published on November 1, 2021, consulted on June 23, 2022, https://www.youtube.com/watch?v=O0tNi5w3mo4.

32 "Your Children Will Be Given to the Gays if You Don't Vote: A Disgusting Agitation for Constitutional Amendment", published on June 2, 2020 on the Informational Family Policies Protal "Ivan - Chay" YouTube channel, https://www.youtube.com/watch?v=YqD_2G2bZTc, consulted on June 11, 2020.

33 Alonzo L. Hamby, (*For the survival of democracy: Franklin Roosevelt and the world crisis of the 1930s*), (New York, USA, Free Press, 2004), page 202.

34 Max Weber defines the state as a "human community that (successfully) claims the monopoly of the legitimate use of physical force within a given territory", Andre Munro, "State monopoly on violence", Britannica website, consulted on March 12, 2021, https://www.britannica.com/topic/state-monopoly-on-violence.

35 Stierlitz Forever, the All-Russia Centre for Study of the Public Opinion website, published on October 21,2019, consulted on June 24, 2020, https://wciom.ru/index.php?id=236&uid=9953.

36 "Inside the Kremlin: The Mind and Policies of Vladimir Putin", carthagecollege YouTube Channel, published on June 26, 2015, consulted on June 23, 2022, https://www.youtube.com/watch?v=s88pMN3qDRQ&t=339s.

37 "Mochit Terroristav v Sarteeriyeh! Starye Soviet ot Putina" (Dipping the Terrorists in the Pit Latrine, Putin Shares Old Wisdom), '5 Canal' YouTube channel, published on May 27, 2014, consulted on February 11, 2021, https://www.youtube.com/watch?v=-2f-Q4K_J70.

38 "Russia activists push state to fix potholes", Al Jazeera English YouTube channel, on August 19, 2013, https://www.youtube.com/watch?v=eQoeBUKZQBg, consulted on 8 January 2021; "Russia Finally Found a way to resolve

all Potholes on Road", Awesome Stuff YouTube channel, published on September 4, 2018, consulted on 9 January 2021, https://www.youtube.com/watch?v=-guO722mvH0,; "Bad roads in Russia. Terrible Russian roads, holes in the road", Vehicle Tuning YouTube channel, published on April 30, 2015, consulted on January 3, 2021, https://www.youtube.com/watch?v=9G3qmjO1Mu8.

39 "Neegayria v Snyegakh" Putinism kak on yest: Ad Raseeskeekh Balntiz ("A Snowy Nigeria" Putinism as it is: The Hell of the Russian Hospitals), Acute Angle YouTube channel, published on September 15, 2020, https://www.youtube.com/watch?v=L4VhuxrC3Is, consulted on January 8, 2021; "Eta Tresh! Chto Realnoh Proeezhodit v Raseeskeekh Balnitzsach" (This is Trash! What Really Goes on in the Russian Hospitals), published on Dnyevnik Dyeputata YouTube channel, on October 31, 2019, https://www.youtube.com/watch?v=MY9OhrMPn8U, consulted on January 3, 2021; Russkiya Balntiza, Katoroyou Prievrateelee v Ad! Plesen, Greebok, Gnieleyeh Matrasi! Oojhas e Shok! (A Russian hospital turned into hell! Fungus, Mould and Rotten Mattresses! Horror and Shock!), Cultura Dostoynstva YouTube channel, published on May 25, 2020, consulted on January 8, 2021, https://www.youtube.com/watch?v=59S_DvHBLQc&list=WL&index=1, "Balnitza v Rassee-Ujhas e Strah-Viy Takoyeh Vidilee? (Blog o Jhiznee), (A Hospital in Russia-Horror and Fear-Have You Seen Such a Thing? (Blog About Life), Vladik Fokin-Blog o Jhiznee YouTube channel, on January 2, 2018, consulted on January 8, 2021, https://www.youtube.com/watch?v=Hx-bq-WBEsQ&list=WL&index=2,; Raseeskiyeh Balnitzee-Papali v ad Pree Jhisnee (The Russian Hospitals-We Found Ourselves in Hell While Alive), hoffMAN YouTube channel, published on February 19, 2018, consulted on January 8, 2021, https://www.youtube.com/watch?v=j6E4uRnFeGU

&list=WL&index=3,; "Boodnee Sverhdejavay" | Putinism kak on yest: Ad Raseeskeekh Balntiz ("A Day in the Life of a Superpower" Putinism as it is: The Hell of the Russian Hospitals), Acute Angle YouTube channel, published on 20 May 2020, consulted on January 8, 2021, https://www.youtube.com/watch?v=GNLnLID5xHc&list=WL&index=4.

40 "Avgoostovskiyeh Ratinggee Adabrayneeyah" (August Approval Ratings), Levada Center website, published on August 6, 2014, consulted on June 23, 2022, https://web.archive.org/web/20140808235142/http://www.levada.ru/06-08-2014/avgustovskie-reitingi-odobreniya.

41 See, for example, Darya Besedina Demands Public Budget Hearings, Darya Besedina YouTube channel, published on October 31, 2019, consulted on June 10, 2020, https://www.youtube.com/watch?v=Qc8vjSCT1AA,; "Darya Besedina vs Mosgorduma. 'Veyaychnee Putin', 'Vashingtonskee Abcom' e Pratyestee Protiv Papravak", (Darya Besedina vs Moscow City Council. 'The Eternal Putin', 'Washington's Regional Committee' and the Protest Against the Amendments), RTVI Novastee YouTube channel, published on March 14, 2020, consulted on June 10, 2020, https://www.youtube.com/watch?v=Qlbp8NRNfj8.

42 A Deputy Said "No" to the Eternal Putin, Culture of Dignity YouTube Channel, published on June 10, 2020, consulted on June 10, 2020, https://www.youtube.com/watch?v=zCn9RNKRcJA.

43 Serguei Cheloukhine, M.R. Haberfeld, *Russian Organized Corruption Networks and their International Trajectories*, (New York, London, Springer, 2011), page 3.

44 The Pension Age Raised in Russia, http://www.ng.ru/itog/2018-12-28/1_7476_itog2.html, Nezavisimaia, published on December 28, 2018, consulted on June 1, 2020.

45 "Pragrama Sergeiya Darienka (31.10.1999). Gost: Vladimir Putin" (The programme of Sergei Darienko (31.10.1999).

Guest: Vladimir Putin), RVISION YouTube channel, published on September 26, 2016, consulted on July 14, 2023, https://www.youtube.com/watch?v=wVciK18nEeA&t=493s.

46 "Did Saltykov-Shchedrin: 'When they begin to talk about patriotism in Russia, know: somewhere they stole something'?", geospatialcollaborative website, consulted on January 8, 2023, https://geospatialcollaborative.com/did-saltykov-shchedrin-when-they-begin-to-talk/.

47 "Udarnaya Sila" (Striking Force) YouTube channel, consulted on June 23, 2022, https://www.youtube.com/channel/UCFxyaS_iXLK-MCLyu-fgQZg/featured.

48 Luke Harding and Ewen MacAskill, "Putin revives long-range bomber patrols", The Guardian website, published on August 18, 2007, consulted on June 8, 2019, https://www.theguardian.com/world/2007/aug/18/russia.ewenmacaskill.

49 "Russian Bombers Did Not Carry Nuclear Weapons to British Borders–Military Source", The Moscow Times website, February 2, 2015, consulted on October 29, 2016, https://themoscowtimes.com/articles/russian-bombers-did-not-carry-nuclear-weapons-to-british-borders-military-source-43463.

50 Yefim Gordon, *Tupolev Tu-95/-142*, (New York, Polygon Press, IP Media Inc, 2003), page 6.

51 Apart from several bases in former USSR countries, Russia has bases in Vietnam and Syria.

52 David Vine, "Where in the World Is the U.S. Military?'", Politico Magazine website, published on July/August 2015, consulted on February 1, 2022, https://www.politico.com/magazine/story/2015/06/us-military-bases-around-the-world-119321/.

53 David E. McNabb, *Vladimir Putin and Russia's Imperial Revival*, e-book, (London, New York, CRC Press, Taylor and Francis Group, 2016), page 54.

54 "Sukhoi Su-30MKM Dances in the Sky over Singapore with Thrust Vectoring Maneuvers – AINtv", Aviation International News YouTube channel, published on February 8, 2018, consulted on September 5, 2019, https://www.youtube.com/watch?v=gNx6DV8EcF8.

55 "Russia's T-14 Armata Tank Is Amazing (But There Is a Big Problem)", The National Interest website, published on April 6, 2019, consulted on September 5, 2019, https://nationalinterest.org/blog/buzz/russias-t-14-armata-tank-amazing-there-big-problem-51022.

56 "Putin's Speech before the Federal Assembly recorded from the Russia 1 TV Channel", Ilya Makrin YouTube channel, published on March 1, 2018, consulted on June 8, 2019, https://www.youtube.com/watch?v=_u1IKd9vgfo.

57 Mark Solonin, "Ceance Ahotneechay Magee" ("A Hunting Magic Seance"), published on March 7, 2018, personal website of Mark Solonin, consulted on June 16, 2022, https://www.solonin.org/article_seans-ohotnichey-magii.

58 Andrei Saharov, *Sabraniyeh Sacheenaynyee, Vaspamenania* (Complete Works, Memoirs) Volume 1, (Moscow, Vremya, 2006), pages 488, 489.

59 Peter Goodchild, *Edward Teller: The Real Dr Strangelove,* (Weidenfeld & Nicolson, 2004, Great Britain), page 259.

60 Jeffrey Lewis, "Russia's Nuclear Powered Cruise Missile", Arms Control Wonk website, published on March 24, 2018, consulted on June 12, 2019, https://www.armscontrolwonk.com/archive/1205006/russias-nuclear-powered-cruise-missile/.

61 "Russian nuclear accident: Medics fear 'radioactive patients'", BBC News website, published on August 23, 2019, consulted on September 3, 2019, https://www.bbc.co.uk/news/world-europe-49432681.

62 Alan I. Abramowitz, "Did Russian Interference Affect the 2016 Election Results", published on August 8, 2019,

consulted on June 23, 2022, https://centerforpolitics.org/crystalball/articles/did-russian-interference-affect-the-2016-election-results/.

63 The cartoon is used as a caption for a talk show discussing the said war on the Echo of Moscow radio station, vsegard1 YouTube channel, published on February 18, 2016, consulted on April 16, 2020, https://www.youtube.com/watch?v=H_rpPXBZ2ms&list=WL&index=3.

64 This is suggested by videos with titles like "Haladealnik Pabyeajzdyet Televizar" ("The Fridge winning over the TV-set"), Krasnaya Linia YouTube channel, published on December 4, 2018, consulted on April 16, 2020, https://www.youtube.com/watch?v=MoufV4C1Igg&list=WL&index=25).

65 "Armed and extremely dangerous Russian drivers | Road Rage in Russia", Epic Driving YouTube channel, published on March 17, 2016, consulted on February 11, 2021, https://www.youtube.com/watch?v=J2Dl2QLkKOs.

66 The witness testimonies can be seen in the video "Zaprayschenee Efeer Eha Maskvoiy pro Boy za Donestkee Aeraport" ("Echo of Moscow Forbidden Airtime about the battle of Donestk Airport"), Dax Ure YouTube channel, published on November 2, 2014, consulted on June 29, 2022, https://www.youtube.com/watch?v=DBNm-I56cAg.

67 "Sanksee? Ne Smaysheeteh Myee Iskandiereh", ("Sanctions? Don't make my Iskanders laugh"), RT YouTube channel, published on September 25, 2014, consulted on June 1, 2020, https://www.youtube.com/watch?v=JcMhih8E9l0.; "Ne Smaysheeteh Myee Iskandiereh", ("Don't make my Iskanders laugh"), Golos Islama website, published on September 26, 2014, consulted on June 30, 2022, https://golosislama.com/news.php?id=25004.

68 Varlam Shalamov, *Kolyma Stories*, (New York, New York Review Books, 2018), pages 414–417.

69 Simon Sebag Montefiore, *Titans of History: The Giants Who Made Our World*, (London, Weidenfeld & Nicolson, 2017), page number 534.
70 See, for example, the following videos published on the Om TV YouTube channel: "Tanke T-72B3, Katoreech 'Nyeh Bilya e Nyet'-I. Russian Tanks in Ukraine! Part 1" (The T-72B3 tanks which 'were not and are not there'-I), Om TV YouTube channel, published on September 5, 2015, consulted June 29, 2022, https://www.youtube.com/watch?v=gupUasybpuw; "Tanke T-64, Katoreech 'Nyeh Bilya e Nyet'-II. Russian Tanks in Ukraine! Part 2" (The T-64 tanks which 'were not and are not there'-2), Om TV YouTube channel, published on September 2015, consulted on June 29, 2022, https://www.youtube.com/watch?v=n0MzDo7HbyU, "Boleyeh sta Rassesskiech Tankov, Katoreech 'Nyeh Bilya e Nyet'-III" (More Than a Hundred Russian Tanks, that 'were not and are not there'-3), Om TV YouTube channel, published on January 16, 2015, consulted on June 29, 2022, https://www.youtube.com/watch?v=C4nZeG_Lzbs.
71 Vitaly Shevchenko, "Little green men" or "Russian invaders"?, BBC News website, published on March 11, 2014, consulted on February 17, 2021, https://www.bbc.co.uk/news/world-europe-26532154.
72 Kimberly Marten, "The Puzzle of Russian Behavior in Deir al-Zour", War on the Rocks website, published on July 5, 2018, consulted on February 17, 2021, https://warontherocks.com/2018/07/the-puzzle-of-russian-behavior-in-deir-al-zour/.
73 See, for example, "Bashir I Petrov Chastushki" (Bashirov and Petrov Chastushki"), Yuri Hovansky's YouTube channel, published on October 4, 2018, consulted on June 6, 2019, https://www.youtube.com/watch?v=LgFxMFfoB4g,; "Moi e Anyeggdoti Klasna Travim - Petrov I Bashirov za

Kadrom (Parodia), (We can Tell Jokes as Well – Petrov and Bashirov Behind the Scenes - Parody), Studia Kvartal 95 Online YouTube channel, published on November 3, 2018, consulted on June 6, 2019, https://www.youtube.com/watch?v=Vax3Y2Z9XE4,; Slepakov Semion Spili, published on the Serg Lus YouTube channel on October 10, 2018, consulted on June 6, 2019, https://www.youtube.com/watch?v=fMyFMyrvhh8.

74 David E. McNabb, *Vladimir Putin and Russia's Imperial Revival*, e-book, (London, New York, CRC Press, Taylor and Francis Group, 2016), page 55.

Chapter 10

Less Rape Jokes, More Rape

Political correctness began to be felt in the 1980s when, for example, *The Benny Hill Show* was cancelled despite it being a very popular TV programme. The problem? Sexism and misogyny according to many observers.[1]

As we will see, something else began in the 1980s, but it only became visible decades later. Gangs of men were given free rein to prey on young female children.[2] The political correctness was meant to protect the vulnerable.[3] What it actually achieved was the exact opposite, namely the wholesale abuse of the most vulnerable.

It was the abusers who were protected, as we will see in this chapter.

A Contradiction?

These days, the career of a politician may suffer because he allegedly touched the thigh of a woman decades ago.[4] Wolf whistling at a woman can be treated as a hate crime.[5] This suggests that British society has zero tolerance of sexual abuse.

Yet the same society tolerated the systemic and brutal abuse of thousands of underage girls for over a decade or, as the British prime minister at the time, David Cameron, put it, the rape of children on an "industrial scale".[6] As of 2019 the number is 19,000 for England alone but the overall number keeps being revised upwards.[7] The victims in Rotherham alone were 1400 to 1700.[8] There were thousands more in Rochdale, Oxford, Telford, Leeds, Birmingham, Norwich, Burnley, High Wycombe, Leicester, Dewsbury, Middlesbrough, Peterborough, Bristol, Halifax and Newcastle,[9] Huddersfield, Aylesbury.[10] The number of rapes runs into the millions, according to some estimates, because thousands of children were raped repeatedly for more than a decade.[11] The children were being raped (including many who were mentally ill), occasionally beaten up (sometimes to the point of hospitalisation), passed around, and in some cases enslaved.[12]

It seems that the picture is even grimmer than this because the British government refused to publish the report on these crimes in February of 2020.[13] It was still not published by the end of that year, despite the fact that a petition to the UK Parliament was signed by over 100,000 British citizens. In February 2022, an independent inquiry into child sexual abuse was published, which revealed that some police forces across England and Wales were still not recording the ethnicity of some suspects. Eighty-six per cent of offenders involved in child sex exploitation in Tower Hamlets (London) in 2019 did not have their ethnicity recorded.[14] The report also states that: "Police forces in Britain must start recording the ethnicities of suspects in cases of child sexual exploitation by criminal gangs."[15]

Zero tolerance of sexual abuse and tolerating sexual abuse on an industrial scale doesn't seem to tie up. It is like giving a pickpocket a 10-year jail sentence while letting serial killers get away with a slap on the wrist. As you will see, there's no contradiction here as both the strictness and the leniency stem from the same factor: political correctness.

In particular, political correctness dictates that rape jokes must not be allowed because they disparage the experience of the victims and make rape sound trivial and therefore acceptable. The writer Madeline Wahl argued the last by posing a question: "Moving forward, how can we stop rape? Sexual assault? Rape culture? Rape jokes?"

According to the same author, rape jokes are a part of rape culture.[16] Sargon of Akkad and Count Dankula, popular YouTubers and would-be politicians, joked about many things, but Channel 4 focused only on their rape jokes.[17] (This was the same Channel 4 that did not air a documentary about the Asian grooming gangs and raping of children back in 2004.[18]) The two were never given a chance to present their political ideas on TV and thus their political careers were over before they had begun. Two men who have not raped anybody were immediately associated with rape and punished for it. They lost the election. Bottom line: Channel 4 fought against rape jokes but not against rape.

The police too were quick to focus on the Sargon of Akkad for his rape joke,[19] but were reluctant to do something about the actual rapes that had taken place in Rotherham for many years.[20] Interestingly, the police were ignoring not only instances of rape, but also the drug dealing of the abusers, despite being given specific and accurate information, as long as the perpetrators were of "Asian" origin.[21] Therefore, the problem was not the type of crime (rape or drug dealing) but the skin colour of the suspects. Yet the same police quickly arrested the father of one of the girls who shouted racial abuse at her rapists, even though this happened at the place where the rape had taken place and the police could see evidence of this.[22] They also arrested children who were victims of rape to accuse them of procuring the rape of other children.[23] Eventually, police officers went as far as to threaten a victim that the perpetrators knew where she lived.[24] The police were not only ignoring crime, but were siding with the criminals against their victims.

The same factor, fear of being called racist, was working in the cases when the police were turning a blind eye and when they were arresting people.[25] The 14-year-old girl who was abused that night and arrested along with her father is just one example. When the police attended to two girls who had been hospitalised because they were assaulted, the officers did not arrest the assailants but focused on the racist language the victims were using when they talked about their assailants. Words mattered more than physical violence for the police.[26]

The police were not the only government institution to display this attitude. Council and social services officials did their best to silence the whistle-blowers as well. Files containing information about the rapists were taken away and censorship was imposed.[27] There was a cover up.[28]

Occasionally, it became absurd. The Pakistani abusers were referred to as "Asian", but that was still deemed too controversial so eventually the "Asian taxi drivers" became "men of certain ethnicity, engaged in a particular occupation".[29] The rapes were not the issue while the council was playing its little politically correct games; the council was considerate towards everybody except to the victims.

This would have been farcical if it were not so tragic. On one side of the barricade were the British TV, the British government, and the British criminals, while on the other side there were the children, lacking life experience and physically weak, mentally ill in some cases, often without parents, along with a handful of whistle-blowers who were being told not to talk of "Asian" men (one whistle-blower was even sent to a "diversity" training course[30]). The perpetrators were threatening the victims to remain silent.[31] Occasionally they were threatening their families as well.[32] Meanwhile, the police were helping the perpetrators by threatening the whistle-blowers to keep quiet. In other words, the police were committing crimes instead of investigating crimes. They were breaking the law rather than enforcing it. They were fighting the whistle-blowers instead of the rapists. To sum it up, the police were the problem rather than the solution.

This reminds us of some third world countries where the police are in cahoots with the criminals. However, corruption was not the problem in the UK,[33] political correctness was.[34] The British policemen did not know the criminals, but they did know their ethnicity. What that meant was that the police did not want to touch this hot potato for fear of being branded "racist", something that was eventually acknowledged in the official reports.[35] The bad guys were all of the same cultural background. They were not as diverse as in the politically correct adverts we see on TV which nowadays always pairs a white person with a brown person. This sameness of the skin colour of the abusers didn't tie up with the fight for political correctness. Crime is supposed to be colourless and a police force is supposed to be colour blind. There are white criminals, black criminals, and brown criminals. However, in this case, all criminals were of the same colour. That made them untouchable and this empowered them to continue raping.

Political correctness is meant to protect vulnerable people who may be unjustly stereotyped – tarred with the same brush, as the saying goes (such as associating Pakistani men with rape). On the other hand, the political correctness limits not only freedom of speech, but freedom of thought because whatever cannot be said cannot be thought. It is no accident that the expressions "freedom of speech" and "freedom of thought" are often used interchangeably. Not being able to say certain things in public means that these things may not be discussed and, subsequently, may not be considered, and will not be investigated. This is something Jayne Senior, the woman who fought to expose the Rotherham abuse scandal, was finding hard to grasp at first. She was puzzled as to why the police did nothing although there was so much information.[36] (The police had names, addresses, vehicle plate numbers, etc., for a full decade before it decided to investigate.)

Being politically correct, therefore, has a similar effect on our way of thinking as being racist: it is a prejudice. It leads to certain conclusions about an individual based on the colour of his or her skin before the facts are even examined. To illustrate, white people are presumed to be privileged while non-white people are presumed to be victims. The facts that support that politically correct assumption are taken into account while the facts that don't are never mentioned. The conclusion was that the "Asians" could not be blamed; this was reached from the beginning. From then on, the facts that pointed to the contrary were just a nuisance, and the people invoking them were considered to be time-wasters or trouble-makers. A later report on Rotherham Council defined this attitude as "a culture where bad news was not welcome".[37] From this point of view, political correctness was the new racism – it became what it was supposed to end. The officials became racist for fear of being called "racist".

In hindsight, it is ironic that the police behaviour was racist, precisely because they were trying so hard not to be racist. It was covering up the crimes and even threatening those who wanted to expose those crimes because of the skin colour of the criminals. Therefore, people were treated unequally based on the colour of their skin, which is the very definition of racist discrimination. Racism was re-born under the guise of fighting racism.

Brown Privilege

Was there "brown privilege" in the Rotherham abuse scandal?

Equating political correctness with racism sounds absurd at a first glance. Isn't rejecting racism part of political correctness? Not really, if we consider that it is politically correct to attack only one culture: that of the white West. There is "white guilt" but there is no "brown guilt". That is why Eastern Europeans living in the UK are confusing to the politically correct. On one hand, they are emigrants and therefore must be victims, but on the other hand they are white and therefore must be guilty. Incidentally, the whole of Eastern Europe is problematic to the left in the West. It is inhabited by white people who never enslaved anybody but were themselves enslaved by the Arabs and then the Ottomans who usually had a darker skin colour.

What is the summary here? That all cultures are equal, but some are more equal than others? Take the relatively new coining of the term "cultural appropriation". Pamela Anderson came under fire in 2019 because she was photographed wearing an American Indian headdress, but no American Indian will be criticised if he appears in a Western suit with a tie. Consistency dictates that being anti-white is as racist as being anti-black and yet this is not the case.

The child-slave-trade-grooming scandal does not sit well with the assumptions of the PC culture, which dictates that the privileged must be white and victims can't be white. That is why it should come as no surprise that a prominent UK politician re-tweeted and liked a social media message telling victims to shut up for "the good of diversity".[38]

This is not the only example. In Canada, a former Islamic State sex slave (Nadia Murad, now a Nobel Peace Prize winner), was to give a talk at a book club, but the head of the Toronto District School Board said the book would "incite Islamophobia" and refused to let her students attend the event.[39]

Censorship has been imposed for the best of reasons throughout history. From the Ancient Greeks who executed Socrates to Stalin, Hitler, and Mao who executed people for telling political jokes, no censor has stated that it curtails free speech to obtain power. It has always been done in the name of the nation, public order, good governance, morality, security, the protecting of core values, God, the bright future of humanity, and the good name of members of the public. Therefore, there is nothing new about the hate-speech laws being introduced in the West today, only the justification (protecting the vulnerable) is.

The decade of lawlessness in Rotherham cannot be blamed on this or that individual who was in charge in the police or in the council. Remarkably, what the authorities did in Rotherham resembles what was done in other cities.

Some sources suggest that the Home Office in London sent a letter to the local police forces instructing them not to deal with the child abuse caused by the Asian grooming gangs.[40] In November 2018, a request was raised under the Freedom of Information Act about said letter or circular. The Home Office replied: "We have not been able to identify any circular which includes the statement in your request."[41]

The police departments throughout the country ignored the law for a decade. This cannot be explained with a single document composed by a single individual. Different officials in different cities who did not know each other behaved remarkably alike as the circumstances were the same: brown men, white girls.[42] Since there's no hard evidence this letter ever existed, there's just one explanation left: the prevailing atmosphere of political correctness which was the same throughout the country.

Incidentally, even if such a letter existed, it will still not get political correctness off the hook. Britain is supposed to be a country with a rule of law, and laws are created by Parliament, not by the Home Office. As a solicitor would put it, letters are not a source of law. Twitter is also not a source of law. This applies to the politically correct opinion that brown people cannot be criminals and white people cannot be victims.

The law was another universal rule that applied to the whole country, the Sexual Offences Act 2003 being in force at the time. The police knew that some of the children involved were under 13. This would make any sexual activity with them a criminal offence under Articles 5, 6, and 7 even if no violence or threat of it has been used. The police were also informed that some of the girls were mentally ill (which would make any sexual activity with them a criminal offence under Articles 30 and 31 even if they were not under the legal age of consent). Then there were the threats and the violence which made such sexual acts a criminal offence whatever the age or the mental state.[43] Some policemen came up with the bogus excuse that the girls were prostitutes. There was no evidence that they were, but let's suppose, for the sake of argument, that there were some. What the "clients" of such "prostitutes" were doing would have still been a criminal offence because of the age and the mental state of the girls, not to mention the violence and the threat of it used to coerce them into this "prostitution".

It was not a prosecution that caused the pendulum to swing in the other direction but a publication in *The Times*. (The article was aptly called "Revealed: Conspiracy of Silence over UK Sex Gangs".[44]) In other words, it was public opinion and not some legal procedure that caused the shift. The law just followed the ensuing public uproar after the publication. All of a sudden there were official reports (law), investigations (law), and prosecutions (law). Public servants jumped ship. They began to enforce the law instead of enforcing the political correctness. Therefore, the law was irrelevant both before and after; it was not the reason the rapes were not investigated for a decade and it was not the reason they were eventually investigated. This suggests a troubling realisation that the law in the UK, just like the law in many developing countries, may be no more than a pretence of legality. Public officials may invoke it to give an appearance of legality to what they do, but what they really abide by is the mood of the day, the way the wind is blowing.

The Natives Are More Vulnerable

The Rotherham story demonstrates how easily all hard-won freedoms, freedoms that took many centuries to win, can be lost because they depend on public officials to enforce the law. It shows how vulnerable people are under certain circumstances in the Western world. They don't have large extended families to protect them; clan culture disappeared centuries ago, and people now rely on the police – that makes us easy prey if policing doesn't work. There's no Plan B, no second line of defence. This is not the case with emigrant communities coming from developing countries where cousins help cousins and gang culture is often a natural continuation of the traditional social organisation. I, being born in the East and emigrating to the West at the age of 42, had the opportunity to see the difference. A Westerner calls removal men when he has to move his furniture while an Easterner calls his friends or relatives. The Westerner goes on a cruise to be merry among random people while the Easterner typically celebrates within their own private community. The Westerner is alone when the bailiffs come to collect his debt while the Easterner often calls on extended family members to intimidate the bailiffs.[45] The Westerner, more often than not, calls the police when he is intimidated while the Easterner often calls, you guessed it, friends or relatives. Whereas a Westerner usually relies on the law, the Easterner will sometimes take the law into his own hands. Whereas a Westerner relies on the government, the Easterner usually relies on his own private circle. A well-known Bedouin proverb summarises the clan mentality: "Me against my brother, my brother and I against my cousin, and all of us against the stranger."[46]

These distinctions between modern and traditional societies have been recognised ever since Durkheim, who is known as the father of sociology, called them mechanical and organic solidarity. "Mechanical solidarity is the social integration of members of a society who have common values and beliefs. These common values and beliefs constitute a 'collective conscience' that works internally in individual members to cause them to cooperate."[47]

To make sense of this technical definition, think of a country where religion is not just about the church in which you hold your wedding, but determines in great detail how you dress, what you say, what your personal everyday life is and so on.

Naturally, nobody can afford to be different in such a society because they will be singled out and ostracised. This is how things used to be hundreds of years ago in the West (remember the Scarlet Letter[48]) and this is how they still are in most non-Western countries all over the world today.

Contrast this with the organic solidarity: "Society relies less on imposing uniform rules on everyone and more on regulating the relations between different groups and persons, often through the greater use of contracts and laws."[49]

Naturally, the members of such a society rely on paid professionals like policemen and judges when their rights are infringed, not on relatives and members of the community. They don't take the law into their own hands, they don't brawl, they expect the government to have the monopoly on violence, which any government by definition should have. That is something to keep in mind when the West opens its doors to mass immigration from countries with mechanical solidarity. The West, being a society with organic solidarity, cannot take in such immigrants indefinitely and keep its identity any more than a ship can take in water and keep afloat indefinitely.

The distinctions between traditional and modern societies are key to understanding why white British girls were considered to be "easy meat".[50] (That phrase caused a stir among the politically correct, but it was echoed by a judge who said, while sentencing some of the rapists, that the girls were treated "as though they were worthless".[51]) Jack Straw explained it well:

> These young men are in a Western society, in any event, they act like any other young men, they're fizzing and popping with testosterone, they want some outlet for that, but Pakistani-heritage girls are off-limits... So they then seek other avenues and they see these young women, white girls who are vulnerable...[52]

So, "easy meat" is a phrase that does not refer to girls being promiscuous but to the fact that they are not part of a self-help community. These girls, being Western, don't have extended families and neighbours who will stand behind them and their only recourse is the police when they are violated. Therefore, they have nobody to help them when the government refuses to enforce the law, as it did for a decade.

Was this taken into account by the British government? Did these girls get extra protection because they were vulnerable? No. On the contrary, they got less protection.

An example of this would be one young woman who was raped by her abusers hundreds of times and was let down repeatedly by the Police. On being interviewed for a BBC Radio 4 podcast, she said:

> So, I remember being raped, but they were just physically aggressive, so there's I think four, four or five – I can't remember – in the room. One of the men was raping me, and other men that'd be kicking me and beating me in the stomach, and I said to them that I'm pregnant.[53]

The abusers knew what they were doing: "they knew it would have been, like, potentially one of their children, or baby that I was carrying, and saying to me, like, well, I'm going to beat it out of you, it'll be the devil child."[54]

Yet the police did not identify her as a victim of modern slavery and did not refer her to the National Referral Mechanism. The NRM is a government system that could have given her access to a safe house, counselling, financial support, and legal aid, the things needed to escape her abusers. Isabel remembers:

> I asked my NRM worker about legal aid, because I had struggles with the police, I thought maybe like a solicitor

> or somebody could help me with this. And she started to be angry and she was like, you don't need that legal advice, because you're not an immigrant, so she was basically like, because you were born here, that you don't need support with anything legal.[55]

In a Home Office report on group-based child sexual exploitation, the Rt Hon Priti Patel MP said: "Victims and survivors of these abhorrent crimes have told me how they were let down by the state in the name of political correctness."[56]

Yet after all the right words were said, more of the same occurred. In June 2022 the Operation Linden Report about Rotherham was published by the Independent Office for Police Conduct. The perpetrators continued to be referred to as "Asians".[57] What made these crimes possible, the political correctness, continued to be practised.

In April 2023, the UK Home Secretary Suella Braverman said:

> We have seen institutions and state agencies, whether it's social workers, teachers, the police, turn a blind eye to these signs of abuse out of political correctness, out of fear of being called racist, out of fear of being called bigoted.[58]

The reaction? She was called racist.

After another decade of investigation, no police officers were sent to jail.

Little Bulgaria

Expressions like "Chinatown" or "Little Italy" do not just refer to neighbourhoods where one can eat fried rice or spaghetti, but to the fact that the rules of the game are as in China or as in Italy. I began to grasp this when I immigrated to the UK and found myself in a "Little Bulgaria" of sorts. It consisted of a single house in London. Although its "territory" was tiny, British laws and customs did not apply there. I had the unpleasant feeling that I was back in Bulgaria. There were no written contracts, receipts, bank transfers, or taxes when it came to renting. What happened in the house was a perfect example of a shadow (grey) economy. This is characterised by under-the-counter dealing and Bulgaria has the largest share of it among EU countries.[59] We, the tenants, did not know who our landlord was, we just knew the person who gathered the rent in cash. (The discrepancy between who is the owner on paper and who is the actual owner is typical of Bulgarian society where those who control an entity are often not mentioned in any documents or registers.) The tenants who did not pay or were disliked for some reason were thrown out without due legal process or bailiffs because they had no way of proving they were tenants. Throwing tenants out without going through the courts is a criminal offence both in Britain and Bulgaria, but it was practised in this house in Britain without any legal ramifications, just as it is practised all over Bulgaria.

The tenants were rude, edgy, noisy, and complained about each other. One could not sleep because another played loud music in the middle of the night. It was not clear who had to clean or take out the trash, and so it was dirty and smelly as a result. (Nobody wanted to be a sucker by doing more cleaning than the others.) Scores were settled by threats of physical violence and so "might was right". A guy who bragged that he was a former convict seemed to be the most authoritative figure.

There were bedbugs, and all attempts to exterminate them were unsuccessful because not all occupants of the house were co-operating. Bedbugs, it turns out, are like mosquitoes: they prefer certain humans if given a choice. Therefore, some of us were bitten during the night and others were not. Those who were not bitten did not care and did not want to wash their clothes at 90 degrees Celsius or have their belongings chemically treated. The Bulgarians in London could not get organised, just like their compatriots living in Bulgaria could not get organised. The better tenants left the house at the first opportunity as they could neither stand the worst ones nor put them in line. They "emigrated", so to say, to better houses in London, houses that were not occupied by Bulgarians (or bedbugs). Negative selection was at work in this house just as negative selection was at work in Bulgaria. I was stuck there for a while because I had given my address to several official institutions and I was waiting for letters to arrive which would confirm this was my current home address.

The same tenants who were inept against the bedbugs proved industrious when it came to giving bribes: all of us had CSCS (Construction Skills Certification Scheme) cards, but I was the only one who took the CSCS test. The rest had gained the cards "in the second way" as the Bulgarian expression for using unofficial means goes. (Something like "through the back door".) The rumour was that bribes were given to Romanians in positions of authority in the UK. This is to be expected given that Bulgaria and Romania are known for their corruption.

The tenants were all different individuals and yet they behaved like stereotypical Bulgarians when they were together.

While one cannot predict how an individual will behave by knowing their nationality, one can predict how a large number of individuals belonging to the same nation will behave if they live together. The larger the number, the more accurate the prediction. As a statistician would put it, "the larger the sample size, the smaller the margin of error".[60] In the case of the Bulgarians, most of them are gathered together in Bulgaria, in the case of the Chinese, most of them are gathered in China. There may be plenty of freedom-loving people in China (as the protests in Hong Kong in 2019 demonstrated), but China is known for its authoritarianism. There are plenty of honest people in Bulgaria, but as a whole the Bulgarians are known to bribe traffic policemen and Bulgarian traffic policemen are known for taking bribes. Studies suggest that Bulgaria is the most corrupt country in the EU.[61]

That is not stereotyping because it relates to communities, not to individuals, and it can be measured objectively. In fact, there's a science that does exactly that: it is called ethnography. Stereotyping by definition is judging somebody not according to his individual merits, but according to the assumptions we have about the group he belongs to (his ethnicity, race, culture, sexual orientation, profession, etc. – think of all those lawyer or blonde jokes). As Martin Luther King Jr. put it poetically in his "I Have a Dream" speech, it is judging someone by the colour of his skin, not the content of his character. (Note that he was talking about individuals, not about groups of people like nations or races: the exact quote in his speech was "my four little children".) Therefore, I will be stereotyping if I hear the name Abdul and suggest he is a misogynist simply because he is from Pakistan. The statistics about Pakistani men tell us nothing about Abdul in particular. He may well be from Pakistan and not be a misogynist, just as somebody may be a native of Africa and be white. However, it will not be stereotyping if I talk of a nation. Nations have individuality precisely because they are not just collections of individuals. Therefore, it can be said that Pakistani men (that is the men who live in Pakistan because obviously most Pakistani men live there) are more likely to be misogynist because we know how women are generally treated in Pakistan. (To illustrate, more than 1000 women are killed in Pakistan annually and most of these deaths happen within the family; Pakistan is the sixth most unsafe country for women in the world.[62]) Trevor Phillips, who led the Equality and Human Rights Commission for six years, seemed to be aware of this when he said that racial stereotypes are "largely true".[63] He should know given that he was the one in charge of the government institution whose job it was to prevent perpetuating those stereotypes.

This is something to remember when people casually talk of multiculturalism as though it is this colourful carnival taken out of a glossy holiday brochure. Ethnic identities are not just about cuisines and national costumes. Foreigners do not come with suitcases full of only clothes, they come with social baggage. They tend to recreate their own motherland way of life if they live, work, trade, and marry within their own ethnic communities in the countries they immigrate to. The stereotypical overtakes individual differences if the stereotypical is what individuals have in common. This is rather obvious when we think about it: what is stereotypical is also what they can agree on, what is self-evident to them all. Emigrants integrate in their new country only if they live, work, and interact with the natives and if integration is advantageous to them. This is why the US "melting pot" worked: the newcomers had to share the American values and the English language in order to prosper. This meant that their children were Americans and not Irish, Italians, or Poles. In a word, they integrated.

Far from integration being advantageous, the Rotherham story revealed that not integrating was actually advantageous in Britain. The "Asian" paedophiles were not prosecuted although the evidence was overwhelming (numerous victims, witnesses, medical and NGO reports) while natives accused of the same crime were prosecuted quickly even when the accusations were not credible or, more accurately, were simply incredible.[64] What was also incredible was that a Member of Parliament tried to rationalise the non-integration in a speech given at a conference dedicated to child abuse, in Rotherham of all places. He didn't do it explicitly but, in a roundabout, politically correct kind of way. He did not mention the word "paedophilia" but spoke of how we must learn to live together accepting each other's way of life.[65] With policies like these, it is not surprising that there's no such thing as a UK melting pot.

The Role of Religion

Speaking of "each other's" way of life, can the Rotherham story be explained in terms of religion? Maajid Nawaz made the connection with the Prophet of Islam who is venerated as the perfect Muslim (and therefore has to be emulated by Muslims) and who had sex with a girl as young as the youngest ones in Rotherham.[66]

However, even if religion were to explain why the abuse started, it cannot explain why the police refused to enforce the law for over a decade. There are criminals in every society and most of them find convenient excuses (often based on morality, ideology or common sense) for what they do. Robin Hood was a thief, but that was supposedly acceptable since he helped the poor. That was an idea which the likes of Al Capone and Pablo Escobar flirted with by setting up soup kitchens for the unemployed and erecting buildings for the homeless; Incidentally, the latter was nicknamed "Robin Hood".[67] The Cosa Nostra was originally posing as a protector of the locals, an idea echoed by the movie *The Godfather* where the mafia boss is expected to right the wrongs that the inefficient judiciary doesn't. The Communists were terrorists before they came to power and were raising funds by robbing banks, fraud, and racketeering,[68] but that was fine since it was for the good of the workers. Likewise, the Nazi stormtroopers were disrupting the meetings of political opponents because they pursued a supposedly just cause (given how unjustly Germany was treated after WWI, a subject covered in the "Making the World Unsafe for Democracy" chapter). In a similar fashion, the Antifa bullies its opponents today because the latter are presumed to be fascists or Nazis and in their mind that justifies intimidation.[69] This list can be continued as criminals in all times and places are good at convincing themselves that they are benign people.

Therefore, the important question regarding the child rape is not how the paedophiles justified it, but why the British police were in bed with them. The police are the real culprits here because crime exists in every country, however, there is still the rule of law as long as the government enforces it. Religion or not, the abuse would not have gone on for over a decade if the police had done its duty. Since the police were paralysed by political correctness, the crimes were tolerated because of this political correctness. This suggests that political correctness is incompatible not only with free speech, as has been acknowledged by many authors, but with the rule of law as well. Given that raping is breaking the law, it should come as no surprise that efforts to decrease rape jokes increases rape numbers.

Endnotes

1 See, for example, Justin Gray, "That's Not Funny, That's Sexist: The Controversial Legacy of Benny Hill", Vulture website, published on May 15, 2013, consulted on March 29, 2021, https://www.vulture.com/2013/05/thats-not-funny-thats-sexist-the-controversial-legacy-of-benny-hill.html.

2 Neal Baker, "TOWN OF SIN What was the Rotherham sex abuse scandal, who were the child grooming gang and are the law changes proposed?", published on November 28, 2018, consulted on December 22, 2020, https://www.thesun.co.uk/news/4302003/rotherham-sex-abuse-scandal-child-grooming-exploitation-sarah-champion-mp/.

3 That political correctness is there to protect the vulnerable is a recurring claim among its supporters. See, for example, "What's the deal with political correctness?", Reachout website, consulted on May 7, 2020, https://au.reachout.com/articles/whats-the-deal-with-political-correctness; Sandra Dzenis and Filipe Nobre Faria, "Political Correctness: the Twofold Protection of Liberalism", Springer Link website,

published on June 17, 2019, consulted on May 7, 2020, https://link.springer.com/article/10.1007/s11406-019-00094-4.

4 Kate Proctor and Heather Stewart, "No 10 denies claims Boris Johnson groped Sunday Times journalist", The Guardian website, published on September 30, 2019, consulted on October 29, 2019, https://www.theguardian.com/politics/2019/sep/29/no-10-denies-claims-boris-johnson-squeezed-thigh-journalist-charlotte-edwardes.

5 No author, "Wolf whistling can now be reported as a hate crime", BBC News website, published on July 20, 2016, consulted on March 1, 2020, http://www.bbc.co.uk/newsbeat/article/36835470/wolf-whistling-can-now-be-reported-as-a-hate-crime.

6 David Cameron said "UK children suffered sex abuse on 'industrial scale'", BBC News website, published on March 3, 2015, consulted on October 29, 2019, https://www.bbc.co.uk/news/uk-31691061.

7 Lizzie Dearden, "Grooming 'epidemic' as almost 19,000 children identified as sexual exploitation victims in England", published on December 28, 2019, consulted on July 6, 2023, https://www.independent.co.uk/news/uk/home-news/grooming-child-sex-abuse-exploitation-rotherham-rochdale-police-a9215261.html.

8 Jayne Senior, *Broken and Betrayed: The True Story of the Rotherham Abuse Scandal by the Woman Who Fought to Expose It*, (London, Pan Books an imprint of Pan Macmillan, 2016), page 291.

9 "Maajid Nawaz: It Is Not Racist To Talk About Muslims In Grooming Gangs", LBC website, published on December 10, 2017, consulted on October 31, 2019, https://www.lbc.co.uk/radio/presenters/maajid-nawaz/not-racist-talk-islam-grooming-gangs/.

10 Geraldine McKelvie, "Huddersfield grooming scandal is just the start – sick child rape gangs are littered across

our country", published on October 20, 2018, consulted on November 6, 2019, https://www.mirror.co.uk/news/uk-news/huddersfield-grooming-scandal-just-start-13450338.

11 "Lord Pearson Question in the House of Lords on Grooming Gangs 13 March 2018", Brian London YouTube channel, published on March 17, 2018, consulted on December 4, 2019, https://www.youtube.com/watch?v=BtRcdge3hTE.

12 Maggie Oliver, *Survivors: One Brave Detective's Battle to Expose the Rochdale Child Abuse Scandal*, (London, John Blake Publishing, 2019), page 270; Jayne Senior, *Broken and Betrayed: The True Story of the Rotherham Abuse Scandal by the Woman Who Fought to Expose It*, (London, Pan Books an imprint of Pan Macmillan, 2016), pages 77, 120, 136, 137, 215, 230.

13 Lizzie Dearden, "Grooming gang review kept secret as Home Office claims releasing findings 'not in public interest'", Independent website, published on February 21, 2020, consulted on February 22, 2020, https://www.independent.co.uk/news/uk/home-news/grooming-gang-rotherham-review-home-office-findings-a9344896.html.

14 "Child sexual exploitation by organised networks: investigation report February 2022", published on February 1, 2022, consulted on February 13 2022, https://www.iicsa.org.uk/reports-recommendations/publications/investigation/cs-organised-networks/part-h-profiling/h4-failures-record-victim-and-perpetrator-ethnicity.

15 Mark Duell, "Ethnicity of child abusers MUST be recorded to tackle grooming gangs, says landmark report – after police and councils 'failed, ignored and blamed' victims as young as 12 because authorities 'didn't want to become another Rotherham', published on February 1, 2022, consulted on February 12, 2022, https://www.dailymail.co.uk/news/article-10463833/Scathing-report-finds-extensive-failures-way-child-exploitation-tackled.html.

16 Madeline Wahl, "How Rape Jokes Contribute to Rape Culture", HuffPost website, published on April 30, 2014, consulted on December 19, 2019, https://www.huffpost.com/entry/how-rape-jokes-contribute_b_5240592?guccounter=1&guce_referrer=aHR0cHM6Ly93d3cuZ29vZ2xlLmNvbS8&guce_referrer_sig=AQAAAGnSHjIMcc7FvnUjD2ZUnECIsNp0VmyIFY1cjKRwzqGfma953Bt1zxncjckdrQZrgRMMhHM-nzRiQobscBVFh5vy_aid8botH5D1sJP-q-C8WKm44dRbCp-wQKdmnhPM-jhAb60I8QdVwXqlGU2emeMW_o0ngHkpE-fydsdIjqSc4Th.

17 "Ukip launch EU election campaign amid candidate controversy", Channel 4 News YouTube channel, published on April 18, 2018, consulted on October 30, 2019, https://www.youtube.com/watch?v=iRV8kwHyZJ0.

18 Matt Born, "Race fears halt film on Asian sex 'grooming'", The Telegraph website on May 21, 2004, consulted on October 30, 2019, https://www.telegraph.co.uk/news/uknews/1462413/Race-fears-halt-film-on-Asian-sex-grooming.html,; Owen Gibson, "BNP hits back over Channel 4 abuse film", published on May 26, 2004, consulted on December 15, 2020, https://www.theguardian.com/media/2004/may/26/broadcasting.elections2004.

19 Aidan Radnedge, "Police Probe Vile Ukipper Rape Threat", Metro newspaper, published on May 8 2019.

20 Jayne Senior, *Broken and Betrayed: The True Story of the Rotherham Abuse Scandal by the Woman Who Fought to Expose It*, (London, Pan Books an imprint of Pan Macmillan, 2016), pages 89, 90.; Maggie Oliver, *Survivors: One Brave Detective's Battle to Expose the Rochdale Child Abuse Scandal*, (London, John Blake Publishing, 2019), page 91.

21 Jayne Senior, *Broken and Betrayed: The True Story of the Rotherham Abuse Scandal by the Woman Who Fought to Expose It*, (London, Pan Books an imprint of Pan Macmillan, 2016), page 86.

22 Jayne Senior, *Broken and Betrayed: The True Story of the Rotherham Abuse Scandal by the Woman Who Fought to Expose It*, (London, Pan Books an imprint of Pan Macmillan, 2016), pages 92, 93.
23 Maggie Oliver, *Survivors: One Brave Detective's Battle to Expose the Rochdale Child Abuse Scandal*, (London, John Blake Publishing, 2019), page 149.
24 Jayne Senior, *Broken and Betrayed: The True Story of the Rotherham Abuse Scandal by the Woman Who Fought to Expose It*, (London, Pan Books an imprint of Pan Macmillan, 2016), page 117.
25 Maggie Oliver, *Survivors: One Brave Detective's Battle to Expose the Rochdale Child Abuse Scandal*, (London, John Blake Publishing, 2019), pages 97, 98.
26 Jayne Senior, *Broken and Betrayed: The True Story of the Rotherham Abuse Scandal by the Woman Who Fought to Expose It*, (London, Pan Books an imprint of Pan Macmillan, 2016), page 137.
27 Jayne Senior, *Broken and Betrayed: The True Story of the Rotherham Abuse Scandal by the Woman Who Fought to Expose It*, (London, Pan Books an imprint of Pan Macmillan, 2016), pages 109–119.
28 Jayne Senior, *Broken and Betrayed: The True Story of the Rotherham Abuse Scandal by the Woman Who Fought to Expose It*, (London, Pan Books an imprint of Pan Macmillan, 2016), page 338.
29 Jayne Senior, *Broken and Betrayed: The True Story of the Rotherham Abuse Scandal by the Woman Who Fought to Expose it*, (London, Pan Books an imprint of Pan Macmillan, 2016), page 337.
30 Jayne Senior, *Broken and Betrayed: The True Story of the Rotherham Abuse Scandal by the Woman Who Fought to Expose It*, (London, Pan Books an imprint of Pan Macmillan, 2016), page 114.

31 Jayne Senior, *Broken and Betrayed: The True Story of the Rotherham Abuse Scandal by the Woman Who Fought to Expose It*, (London, Pan Books an imprint of Pan Macmillan, 2016), pages 135, 182, 194, 217, 285, 286.; Maggie Oliver, *Survivors: One Brave Detective's Battle to Expose the Rochdale Child Abuse Scandal*, (London, John Blake Publishing, 2019), page 166.

32 Jayne Senior, *Broken and Betrayed: The True Story of the Rotherham Abuse Scandal by the Woman Who Fought to Expose It*, (London, Pan Books an imprint of Pan Macmillan, 2016), pages 162, 217.

33 Some of the police were corrupt as well, but that was rare and therefore not the main issue: Jayne Senior, *Broken and Betrayed: The True Story of the Rotherham Abuse Scandal by the Woman Who Fought to Expose It*, (London, Pan Books an imprint of Pan Macmillan, 2016), page 153; Maggie Oliver, *Survivors: One Brave Detective's Battle to Expose the Rochdale Child Abuse Scandal*, (London, John Blake Publishing, 2019), page 97.

34 See, for example, Maggie Oliver, *Survivors: One Brave Detective's Battle to Expose the Rochdale Child Abuse Scandal*, (London, John Blake Publishing, 2019), page 159.

35 Jayne Senior, *Broken and Betrayed: The True Story of the Rotherham Abuse Scandal by the Woman Who Fought to Expose It*, (London, Pan Books an imprint of Pan Macmillan, 2016), page 291.

36 Jayne Senior, *Broken and Betrayed*: The True Story of the Rotherham Abuse Scandal by the Woman Who Fought to Expose it, (London: Pan Books, 2016), pages 88, 89.

37 Jayne Senior, *Broken and Betrayed: The True Story of the Rotherham Abuse Scandal by the Woman Who Fought to Expose It*, (London, Pan Books an imprint of Pan Macmillan, 2016), page 339.

38 Ben Lazarus, ",SHUT YOUR MOUTH': Corbyn ally shares message telling Rotherham sex abuse victims to be quiet 'for

the good of diversity'", The Sun website, published on August 22, 2017, updated: August 24, 2017, consulted on December 28, 2019, https://www.thesun.co.uk/news/4299167/corbyn-ally-shares-message-telling-rotherham-sex-abuse-victims-to-be-quiet-for-the-good-of-diversity/.

39 Shannon Thaller, "Canadian school CANCELS event with ISIS survivor Nadia Murad because her harrowing description of torture and rape 'would be offensive to Muslims and foster Islamophobia'", published on November 26, 2021, consulted on November 28, 2021, https://www.dailymail.co.uk/news/article-10247301/School-CANCELS-event-ISIS-survivor-Nadia-Murad-saying-visit-offensive-Muslims.html.

40 Maggie Oliver, Survivors: One Brave Detective's Battle to Expose the Rochdale Child Abuse Scandal, (London, John Blake Publishing, 2019), page 118; also Nazir Afzal, "Three Girls: I prosecuted the Rochdale child grooming gang – it wasn't about race", International Business Times website, published on May 17, 2017, consulted on May 12, 2022, https://www.ibtimes.co.uk/i-prosecuted-rochdale-child-grooming-gang-it-wasnt-about-race-1621370.

41 "Child Grooming – circular to Police Forces in 2008", published on November 12, 2018, consulted on December 17, 2020, https://www.whatdotheyknow.com/request/child_grooming_circular_to_polic.

42 Not all victims were white but the vast majority were. Alexis Jay OBE, "Independent Inquiry into Child Sexual Exploitation in Rotherham 1997–2013", published on August 21, 2014, consulted on December 31, 2021, https://www.rotherham.gov.uk/downloads/file/279/independent-inquiry-into-child-sexual-exploitation-in-rotherham.

43 "Sexual Offences Act 2003", consulted on February 21, 2021, https://www.legislation.gov.uk/ukpga/2003/42/pdfs/ukpga_20030042_en.pdf.

44 A. Norfolk, "Revealed: Conspiracy of Silence over UK Sex Gangs", The Times Digital Archive, published on 5 January 2011, consulted on 10 January 2021, https://go.gale.com/ps/i.do?p=TTDA&u=wikipedia&v=2.1&it=r&id=GALE%7CIF0504169030&asid=1610341200000~904a260a.

45 You can see how this happens in "Can't Pay We'll Take It Away" Series 02 Episode 06 HD, HDSTUFF YouTube channel, published on September 7, 2020, consulted on May 12, 2022, https://www.youtube.com/watch?v=bf05qwrHoYA.

46 Alex Potter and Shaminder Dulai, "Me Against My Brother", published on September 29, 2014, consulted on May 10, 2021, https://www.newsweek.com/photos-me-against-my-brother-274000.

47 Mechanical and Organic Solidarity, Britannica website, consulted on February 16, 2020, https://www.britannica.com/topic/mechanical-and-organic-solidarity.

48 Ronan McDonald, "The Scarlet Letter", consulted on December 17, 2020, https://www.britannica.com/topic/The-Scarlet-Letter-novel-by-Hawthorne.

49 Mechanical and Organic Solidarity, Britannica website, consulted on February 16, 2020, https://www.britannica.com/topic/mechanical-and-organic-solidarity.

50 In the words of the former Home Secretary Jack Straw: David Batty and agencies, "White girls seen as 'easy meat' by Pakistani rapists", said Jack Straw, The Guardian website, published on January 8, 2011, consulted on May 12, 2022, https://www.theguardian.com/world/2011/jan/08/jack-straw-white-girls-easy-meat.

51 Maggie Oliver, *Survivors: One Brave Detective's Battle to Expose the Rochdale Child Abuse Scandal*, (London, John Blake Publishing, 2019), page 271.

52 "Jack Straw criticised for 'easy meat' comments on abuse", BBC News website, published on January 8, 2011, consulted on December 31, 2019, https://www.bbc.co.uk/news/uk-12142177.

53 “Isobel’s Story”, BBC Radio 4 “File on 4” podcast, page 11, published September 27, 2022, consulted on December 9, 2022, http://downloads.bbc.co.uk/rmhttp/fileon4/PAJ_4562_PG12_Isobel.pdf.

54 “Isobel’s Story”, BBC Radio 4 “File on 4” podcast, page 11, published September 27, 2022, consulted on December 9, 2022, http://downloads.bbc.co.uk/rmhttp/fileon4/PAJ_4562_PG12_Isobel.pdf.

55 Isobel’s Story”, BBC Radio 4 “File on 4” podcast, page 13, published September 27, 2022, consulted on December 9, 2022, http://downloads.bbc.co.uk/rmhttp/fileon4/PAJ_4562_PG12_Isobel.pdf.

56 “Group-based Child Sexual Exploitation Characteristics of Offending”, published on December 2020, Home Office website, consulted on March 22, 2022, https://assets.publishing.service.gov.uk/government/uploads/system/uploads/attachment_data/file/944206/Group-based_CSE_Paper.pdf.

57 The Operation Linden Report, IOPC website, published in June, 2022, consulted on June 22, 2022, https://policeconduct.gov.uk/operation-linden-report.

58 “UK Home Secretary Suella Braverman faces backlash over ‘racist’ comments about British-Pakistani men”, Middle East Eye YouTube channel, published on April 4, 2023, consulted on April 12, 2023, https://www.youtube.com/shorts/Pd0EkWURmFg.

59 Bulgaria has Europe’s largest grey economy, IMF says, IntelliNews website, published on February 8, 2018, consulted on June 1, 2020, https://www.intellinews.com/bulgaria-has-europe-s-largest-grey-economy-imf-says-136465/.

60 Jon Zamboni, “The Advantages of a Large Sample Size”, Sciencing website, published on May 15, 2018, consulted

on March 20, 2020, https://sciencing.com/advantages-large-sample-size-7210190.html.

61 Thomas Chenel and Qayyah Moynihan, "These are the 13 most corrupt countries in Europe", Business Insider website, published on February 13, 2019, consulted on May 13, 2022, https://www.businessinsider.com/these-are-the-13-most-corrupt-countries-in-europe-2019-2?r=US&IR=T.

62 M. Hanif, "Pakistan: where the daily slaughter of women barely makes the news", May 9, 2019, consulted on February 13, 2020, https://www.theguardian.com/commentisfree/2019/may/09/pakistan-murdered-women.

63 "Things we won't say about race that are true", a 2015 Channel 4 documentary, published on March 22, 2015, Mario YouTube Channel, consulted on April 30, 2021, https://www.youtube.com/watch?v=Tb2iFikOwYU.

64 Georgina Hayes, "Ex-MP Harvey Proctor wins Met payout for false child abuse claims", The Guardian website, published on November 29, 2019, consulted on November 30, 2019, https://www.theguardian.com/uk-news/2019/nov/29/ex-mp-harvey-proctor-wins-900k-from-met-over-false-child-abuse-allegations.

65 Jayne Senior, *Broken and Betrayed: The True Story of the Rotherham Abuse Scandal by the Woman Who Fought to Expose It*, (London, Pan Books an imprint of Pan Macmillan, 2016), pages 167, 168.

66 Maajid Nawaz On The Muslim Grooming Gangs In Telford Scandal, a debate on the BBC, published on the Patriotic Populist YouTube channel on March 24, 2018, consulted on October 31, 2019, https://www.youtube.com/watch?v=_KVtOzYn2Wg.

67 Amanda Macias, "10 Facts Reveal the Absurdity of Pablo Escobar's Wealth", Independent website, published on December 29, 2017, consulted on November 1, 2019, https://

www.independent.co.uk/news/people/pablo-escobar-worth-wealth-money-how-much-a8133141.html.

68 Edvard Radzinsky, *Stalin*, (Great Britain, Hodder & Stoughton, 1997), pages 56–61; Thomas de Waal, *The Caucasus: an introduction*, (United States of America, Oxford University Press, 2010), page 49.

69 Dinesh D'Souza, *The Big Lie: Exposing the Nazi Roots of the American Left*, (USA, Regnery Publishing, 2017), pages 209, 210.

Chapter 11

More Environmentalism, More CO_2

Environmentalism has been around for hundreds of years, but it turned into a mass movement in the 1960s. Global warming became one of its causes when it gained attention in the 1980s.[1] However, as we'll see in this chapter, the movement began to affect global warming long before that. In fact, environmentalists began to impact global warming without even realising it.

Environmentalists say global warming is real and many of them blame the free market for it.[2] People with conservative views, trying to keep the market free, usually dispute that global warming is real or that it is man-made. (For example, Trump expressed his scepticism because climate scientists "have a very big political agenda".[3]) As will be shown here, the facts suggest a third position and it is a surprising one: global warming is real and environmentalists are to blame for it.

Are Renewables the Answer?

We can judge environmentalists by what energy sources they promote.

Here's an example of what those pushing for renewable energy typically claim: that it is "the only real answer to tackling global warming" because it is "free, inexhaustible and clean"[4] ("inexhaustible" being just another word for "renewable"). This sounds plausible as long as the subject is treated in the cartoonish fashion we see in the infomercials of many environmental organisations: happy children running through green fields dotted with wind turbines.[5] Running through green fields is good, but running the numbers is better. As we'll see further, so-called free, clean, renewable energy is expensive, dirty, and not really renewable at all.

Free but not Free

The energy from renewable sources is called "free" because we don't pay for the sun to shine or the wind to blow. Under this logic, we may call fossil fuels free because we did not pay for the biological and geological processes that produced oil, coal, and natural gas. However, just like the extraction, transportation, and burning of these fuels costs money, so does the harnessing of wind and solar. If anything, wind and solar (not to mention biofuels and other exotic renewables) cost more since the energy produced using them is more expensive than that from coal due to larger capital and service costs. After all, this is why the "green" industries need $240 billion in subsidies worldwide every year.[6]

Yet according to a 2020 report, renewables are now cheaper than coal.[7] Such a bold claim must be taken with a pinch a salt. The global warming problem would already be solved if this was true because renewables would replace coal if they were cheaper. We would not need any subsidies or international treaties since energy producers would want to switch to renewables to save money.

Such reports are like comparing apples with oranges because the energy of renewables needs to be stored and the energy of coal doesn't. (You can store the actual coal instead of the energy it releases. Such comparisons would be meaningful if they factor either the cost of the energy storage or the adverse problems caused by the lack of it.)

The same goes for the infrastructure needed. The problem in this respect alone is three-fold. First, the location of wind turbines and solar panels is not about where the power is needed but where it is windy and sunny. That means erecting and maintaining tens of thousands of electric pylons criss-crossing the country in addition to the ones already in place. Second, there are sudden "jolts" in the supply whenever it is not sunny or windy. The solution here would be an absurdly massive and expensive battery, unless we kept the share of renewables low and expensive back-up generators ready (as it is now). For this reason, back-up plants are called "flexible". They might as well be called "inefficient" because the electricity generated by them is more expensive than it is for the plants that work continuously.[8] Thirdly, the electricity that comes out of wind turbines and solar panels does not have the necessary voltage, frequency or phase. This means that additional components like inverters are needed.[9] This alone translates into more expense, more complications, more things that can go wrong, and more maintenance. Here's the bottom line: actual generation accounts for only 44 per cent of the total cost of electricity production when it comes to renewables,[10] although promotional videos of the renewables industry leave the impression that it is all about wind turbines and solar panels. You don't see any "flexible" power plants in those videos, or inverters, or extra pylons. It is easy to prove that renewables are cheap if we take into account only 44 per cent of their expenses.

Here's another accounting trick: only the construction and maintenance costs are typically factored in the cost of the renewables. The cost must include the decommissioning, however, what it will really amount to be is anybody's guess, given that it hasn't been done on a large scale or with newer models yet.[11] But even maintenance costs are still not clear. For example, it turned out that wind turbines wear out sooner than expected.[12]

Then, on top of that, there are the complicated legalities and subsidies that distort the data because they transfer the true cost to the consumer or the taxpayer (thus hiding it), not to mention the confusing contractual terms of individual projects.[13] This poses a reasonable question: are they harnessing the sun or the public purse? Any energy source can be made the cheapest if it is subsidised enough. Actually, the cost can be made to be zero.

So, renewables can be free after all, but it would be a matter of clever accountancy, not clever engineering.

This is how the more expensive electricity produced by not so efficient diesel generators could outcompete the cheap energy generated by coal. Governments pay the solar farms so that the energy they produce is cheap and it can compete with the carbon-releasing businesses. This arrangement worked well in Spain until something odd was noticed: certain solar farms produced energy at night. It turned out that they used diesel generators, not solar panels. If the "solar" farmers hadn't been that greedy, if they had used the diesel generators during the day only, the scam may still be going on.[14]

This sounds like a joke, but what it suggests is far from amusing. Distorting the market with subsidies opens the door to waste and fraud. Bearing in mind that this happened in a Western European country, what can we expect to happen if subsidies are to be used in Africa, Asia, and Latin America where corruption is rampant and enforcement is weak?

Given all this, it is not surprising that although renewable technologies get cheaper, their implementation drives energy prices up.[15] There's no contradiction here: they get cheaper precisely because the energy gets more expensive.

There's one simple test that can settle the price dispute once and for all: competition. All it takes to perform it is to do nothing, to level the playing field, to introduce no subsidies or privileges. If fossil fuels win, we have a problem. If, however, renewables or any other source that does not emit CO_2 wins, all we need to do is get out of the way.

Yet this is the one test that environmentalists prevent by making sure some energy sources are favoured by the government. Given that, do they really believe that their pet source of energy is cheaper than coal?

If our energy becomes more expensive as a result of using more renewables, we'll have to pay more not only for it, but for everything else (food, transportation, accommodation, steel, etc.) because everything else requires energy to produce or move around. Therefore, even if solar and wind can be manufactured in sufficient quantities to replace all coal and nuclear, this will lead to a sharp lowering of standards of living since everyone will have less money for food, transport or a roof over their heads. Bearing in mind the pitiful results achieved by international climate treaties so far, it is unlikely that an agreement will be reached to fully switch to solar and wind. It is even less likely that it will be enforced if it is reached. Currently, 795 million people worldwide[16] don't have enough to eat. Expecting them to switch to solar and wind is expecting them to pay more for food. No government will be capable to enforce rules that increase food prices in poor countries. (At least, no democratic government. Maybe that is why some environmentalists began to support authoritarianism.[17] The North Korean government was not toppled although about 10 per cent of the population starved to death in the 1990s.) People tend not to vote for politicians who ask them to starve and even if such politicians come to power, the rules they enact will likely remain on paper.

Mentioning starvation brings us to another darling of many who speak in the name of the environment: biofuels, ethanol being the first among them. Although different plants have been considered,[18] it is usually extracted from corn that could otherwise be eaten. The frightening truth is that the world does not have enough land to produce enough biofuels in order to build a carbon-neutral economy, even if no land is left for food production.[19]

Then there's the problem that more energy is spent manufacturing ethanol than is gained by burning it and therefore it cannot be called an energy source at all, rather an energy drain.[20]

Still, none of this deterred the do-gooders and large subsidies were paid to make this impossible dream work. This did increase the price of food (which is critical for the aforementioned hundreds of million people all over the world who are malnourished) but did not decrease greenhouse gases. On the contrary, this "green" fuel has increased the emission of greenhouse gases, as well as increasing air and water pollution. This comes as a surprise because corn is a plant and plants use sunlight to grow. Isn't sunlight clean? It is, but farming corn is not since it increases nitrous oxide which is 296 times more of a potent greenhouse gas than CO_2 and this is on top of the CO_2 that is released in order to make and transport the ethanol.[21] Bottom line: the use of ethanol does not alleviate global warming, it exacerbates it.

Unlike biofuels, hydro energy works, but it cannot replace both coal and nuclear because most rivers suitable to generate electric power have already been dammed.[22]

Then there are a few really exotic renewables like geothermal (which works in rare and specific areas only, such as Iceland) or wave and tidal energy. Their share in the world's overall energy mix remains negligible despite the fact that research has been going on for decades.

Solar and wind can theoretically satisfy all of humanity's energy needs, but this will be too expensive[23] and that's assuming that the energy storage problem is solved (which it hasn't yet been).[24]

Remember the 240 billion dollars sunk into renewables annually? Given everything discussed so far, it is little wonder that the world is getting "virtually nil" impact from this colossal expense.[25] True, the efficiency of solar and wind is improving but so is any technology, including coal and nuclear.

Yet, there is something that can be said for solar and wind only. It is easy to use them, as long as their share in the overall energy consumption is small and, therefore, other energy sources can provide the slack needed when the sun is not shining and the wind is not blowing. This big disadvantage of wind and solar can still be compensated for because the steam turbines of coal and nuclear plants can provide electricity during the winter and in the evenings when it is dark and people come home to cook dinner and turn on the TV. Things would be different if solar and wind were to simultaneously replace nuclear and coal, the two sources that reliably provide us with electricity when we need it as opposed to when it is easy to produce it. (It's up to us when nuclear and coal work while it is up to the weather when solar and wind work.) That would still be a problem even if the efficiency of solar and wind were to become 100 per cent (which is impossible because of the laws of thermodynamics). Therefore, the improvements environmentalists talk about will become irrelevant after a certain point unless there is a way to store renewable energy.

The alternative is to supplement renewables by using local generators working on natural gas that take the aforementioned "slack" when the sun does not shine and the wind does not blow. A study found that a 0.88 per cent increase in renewables is associated with a 1 per cent increase in the use of such generators.[26] To put it crudely, for every watt of renewable generation capacity added we need to add an extra watt of fossil fuel generation capacity. The whole point of renewables was to get rid of fossil fuels. However, as it turns out, more renewables require more, not less, fossil fuel capacity.

This also makes energy production expensive as gas generators only work part time, in effect duplicating the capacity of the solar panels and the wind turbines. That is the opposite of two for the price of one: we pay twice the price to get one.

The bottom line: the more the renewable sources, the more expensive the lack of storage. There's no such thing as economy of scale here.

The Only Way to Win Is not to Play

Even if storage was available, the problems keep piling up. When we produce energy and use it at the same time, we only suffer the inefficiencies of production. Storing it also increases its loss. This part of the big picture is often missed when many are bogged down in the details of the latest storage craze. Sure, some storage technologies will work better than others and all will work better in the long run. However, whatever the technology, and no matter how mature it is, storage will result in energy losses. That is how it used to be a century ago, this is how it is now, and this is how it will be in the twenty-second century unless somebody finds a way to circumvent the laws of thermodynamics.

Let's illustrate this with a popular idea that the renewable energy enthusiasts push: thermal storage. It works like this: sunlight heats some material (say liquefied salt). Some heat energy is lost while the salt is being heated. Then the heated material "waits" until the moment when the sun is not shining. Naturally, more energy is lost during this waiting due to heat exchange within the environment no matter how good the thermal insulation is. Later, in a few hours or days, the heat has to be finally converted to electricity. This final stage means more energy losses because it works like a regular thermoelectric power plant with just one difference: instead of burning coal to produce heat, the stored heat in the salt is used. Thermoelectric plants waste 60 per cent of the heat released by coal or uranium, so there's no reason to expect that the thermal storage machinery will do any better during this final conversion. Given that most solar energy cannot be harnessed to begin with, just a fraction of it will be eventually used in our homes.

This applies to any energy storage. For example, electrical energy is converted into chemical energy in batteries when they are charged and then the chemical energy is converted back to electricity when they are discharged. Some energy is lost during the first conversion, some during the hours or the days while it is stored (as any mobile phone owner will attest), and then more is lost when the process is reversed and a chemical reaction produces electricity. Adding conversions increases waste and waste is neither free nor green.

The same goes for more fanciful ideas like using flywheels, compressed air,[27] liquefied air (which then boils into gas when exposed to the temperature of the surrounding environment and thus releases energy in the form of pressurised air that can rotate turbines or push pistons, much as steam does), synthetic fuels, or methods used presently like pumping water into reservoirs which is then released downhill through electricity generating turbines. There are physical, chemical, and biological processes that require energy to occur and there are processes that release energy when they do. They all can theoretically be used to store energy. In Greek mythology, Sisyphus rolled a boulder up a hill endlessly, thus converting the chemical energy in his muscles into the potential energy of the boulder being high on the top of the hill. Every time the boulder rolled back down, this potential energy was transformed into kinetic energy which was wasted in making heat and noise. If the kinetic energy was put to good use, Sisyphus's labour would have been a form of energy storage because a boulder on a hill has "stored" potential energy. We can toy with the idea of converting solar and wind energy into kinetic, potential, or chemical energy all we want, but each method boils down to adding more components, more steps, more complexities, more expenses, more maintenance, more inefficiency and therefore more energy loss.

Converting energy is like producing it several times over while putting it to good use only once. Any energy production is actually energy conversion. Navigating steamships by burning oil is converting the chemical energy of the oil into mechanical energy that rotates the ship's propellers. Sailing ships convert the kinetic energy of the wind into forward motion to navigate. Producing electricity using the same wind is converting the kinetic energy of the moving air into mechanical energy that rotates the generator, and so on.

Given all this, imagine that we store energy by converting CO_2 into C (carbon) and O_2 (oxygen). We can release the O_2 into the atmosphere and be left with something resembling a lump of coal. (If we are to split hairs, this lump will be cleaner than real coal since it will not contain sulphur, mercury, water, and many other substances, but this is irrelevant here.) The feasibility of using solar energy to do this has been studied.[28] The lump will be our "battery" and we will use the energy stored in it whenever we like by burning it. Burning such artificial "coal" will not cause a greenhouse effect since it cannot release more CO_2 than was extracted from the atmosphere in the first place to produce it. It will be, as the jargon goes, carbon neutral.

But burning it comes with all the inefficiencies associated with burning coal dug in a coal mine because we'll use the same boilers and steam turbines we use today. As has already been pointed out, around 40 per cent of the energy will be used and 60 per cent will be wasted in the form of heat. What's the difference with the actual coal, then? That the 60 per cent wasted burning it will be on top of the energy already lost in converting the CO_2 into C and O_2 in the first place. Therefore, the useful energy we will end up with after so many long-winded processes will be a fraction of the energy we started with.

Storing energy by producing artificial coal hasn't been proposed yet, but something similar has: storing energy in hydrogen. Hydrogen can be manufactured in several ways, one being by decomposing water into oxygen and hydrogen, which is then burned or used in some non-flammable chemical reaction (say in a battery) to release energy. (Presently it is mostly done by extracting the hydrogen from natural gas, but the idea is to make this carbon neutral, isn't it?) Provided we don't burn fossil fuels to produce the hydrogen, it amounts to the same thing in terms of carbon neutrality as hypothetical man-made coal.

Water is readily available while the share of CO_2 in the atmosphere is so low that it would have to be concentrated thus increasing the energy losses. However, this will not be necessary if CO_2 is collected when it is released from a chimney. Moreover, some bright minds propose combating global warming by burying the CO_2 in the ground but for that to happen it would have to be in a concentrated form. Why not decompose it instead of burying it? One convoluted hypothetical option would be to use actual coal, burn it, collect the CO_2 and then decompose it using wind or solar. This way we would make burning coal carbon neutral while removing the need for storage. Or we could continue the cycle as though we were using a rechargeable battery, repeatedly burning and decomposing. So, on the face of it, carbon does not have to be worse than hydrogen as an energy storage medium in terms of availability.

If anything, one could argue that carbon is better because storing hydrogen is harder since it is a gas. Hydrogen requires pressurised vessels or cryogenic installations which keep it so cold that it is a liquid (which wastes energy: first to liquefy it, then to keep it liquid). Moreover, hydrogen is not just any gas, it is the most volatile one and that means it can easily escape from a pressurised vessel. Incidentally, that makes it highly flammable as well, which means that storing and transporting it is dangerous. Hydrogen is also one of the hardest gases to liquefy cryogenically and therefore this option is even more expensive than pressurisation. The other way of storing hydrogen would be using hydrogen storage materials.[29] However, this too adds to the cost and complexity of its use. Coal, in contrast, can be simply piled up in the open: risk-free and free of charge.

Moreover, using coal for heat releases less CO_2 than hydrogen.[30] The study is about the hydrogen derived from natural gas, but there's no reason to think that the other types would do any better given the inefficiencies involved. And that's assuming that the CO_2 released during the production of hydrogen could be stored safely and indefinitely, which is over-optimistic.

Wouldn't manufacturing this artificial coal be stupid? Sure, it would. But how come manufacturing hydrogen is any better?

"Stupid" is the exact word Elon Musk used to describe the push for using hydrogen, only he prefixed it with the phrase "mind-bogglingly". His opponents objected that he had a vested interest because he is in the lithium battery business (therefore competing with other forms of storage),[31] but they did not refute his argument (which is basically the argument about hydrogen given here).

The problems with storage don't end there. Adding conversions not only wastes energy, it also leads to less reliability because there are more things that can go wrong. This is something engineering students learn during their first year at university.

The best solution to storing energy is not to store it. This means that it must be made when needed, not just when the sun shines and the wind blows. Therefore, we are left with the options we have right now: fossil fuels and nuclear energy. Given that fossil fuels cause global warming, that narrows the choice down, doesn't it?

It is this stark choice that environmentalists don't want to face when they oppose both coal and nuclear. Since they are better at preventing the construction of new nuclear power plants instead of coal power plants, it turns out that they actually promote coal, even though they are supposedly against it. The results are evident in Germany where environmentalists began to close nuclear power plants. The promotion of the renewables was enough to increase the electricity price but was not enough to decrease the burning of fossil fuels and so the net result was more CO_2 emissions.[32] While 61 per cent of Germany's electricity supply comes from CO_2-emitting sources, only 14 per cent does in France, where nuclear is widespread. This is despite the fact that German electricity is 1.7 times more expensive than French.[33] So the bottom line is: more "green" policies, more greenhouse gases.

The German approach gives us the worst of both worlds: one of free market and one of environmental sustainability. We sacrifice our freedom to choose the energy we want, but this sacrifice does not stop global warming in return. Environmentalists want us to give up our freedom in exchange for environmental sustainability, but the result is that we have neither.

Clean but not Clean

Ironically, the widespread use of wind turbines may even increase the CO_2 emissions. Remember the so called "flexible" power plants that provide back-up using fossil fuels when the wind is not blowing and the sun is not shining? These plants are less efficient than those working full time since they are designed to be switched on and off at short notice.[34]

While we may argue whether the turbines increase or decrease CO_2, one thing is certain: they increase another greenhouse gas. SF6 is used in the electrical industry (including wind turbines). SF6 leaks in the EU in 2017 "were the equivalent of putting an extra 1.3 million cars on the road. Levels are rising as an unintended consequence of the green energy boom".[35] We can imagine how many more cars its effect will be equal to if wind power expands as much as environmentalists would like. It's good for the environment that wind energy is not more developed yet.

Greenhouse gases are just part of the problem. Arsenic, selenium, indium, gallium, and siloxanes are used in the manufacture of solar panels and will be released into the environment when the panels are scrapped in a decade or so. A million tonnes of these dangerous chemicals will be used if the USA's electricity needs alone are to be satisfied with solar. Nuclear energy is far greener by comparison, emitting only 3000 tonnes of waste per year to produce the same amount of energy.[36]

Renewable but not Renewable

The very term "renewable" is a misnomer. It is based on emotions rather than on sound scientific logic. The idea is that certain resources (like coal, oil, gas, and uranium or thorium ore) are limited and will therefore be depleted while others (like solar, biofuels, wind, hydro, and geothermal) will run on forever. However, the energy of renewables either comes from the sun (solar, wind, hydro, biofuels) or from the earth (geothermal). The energy of the sun and the earth are both generated by nuclear reactions (fusion within the sun and fission within the earth). Both will not last forever since the hydrogen in the sun's core is being depleted and the same goes for the radioactive elements that decay within the earth's core. Both fusion and fission are irreversible and therefore these forms of energy should not be called renewable.

One may argue that they will last forever since the sun will shine and the earth will have its molten core for billions of years, but the same argument can be made for some nuclear fuels, for example, thorium. It, too, will last for billions of years, and its energy also comes from nuclear fission. Yet thorium, along with uranium and other nuclear fuels, is classed as non-renewable. Environmentalists have double standards here because an objective classification does not fit into their propaganda.

After all, they want subsidies for their pet forms of energy, and nuclear is not among them, whatever the facts.

"Renewables" divert not just public funds but public attention. All this talk of solar and wind leaves the impression that something is being done about global warming. It is not. The problem is getting worse. Humanity wastes time because it takes decades until the futility of the renewables become apparent to every voter.

Nuclear Cars

People associate nuclear energy with production of electricity. Some are aware that there are ships running on it as well (a number of submarines, icebreakers, and aircraft carriers).

But this does not have to be the limit since heat and electric energy can be used for production of synthetic fuels from air and water. These in turn can be used in cars, trucks, ships, aeroplanes, rockets, bulldozers, diggers, tractors, and locomotives.[37] Synthetic fuels are not only carbon neutral but are lighter than electric batteries (which is important for all forms of transport and crucial for aeroplanes and rockets).[38]

Synthetic fuels can also be used for the production of cement, bricks, for distillation, for smelting of metals, and all the other processes that require heat. Therefore, the argument that nuclear reactors are too expensive, heavy, complicated, dangerous, and cumbersome to be used in all types of vehicles or industries is groundless. Reactors need not be used directly so that their energy is used. This way even a chainsaw or a home stove burning synthetic fuels could be nuclear powered, just like our electrical appliances at home could be nuclear powered if the electricity came from a nuclear plant many miles away. What is more, this can be done by using much of the existing infrastructure for the transportation of gas and petroleum while renewables require new infrastructure.

Theoretically, renewables can also be a source of both electricity and heat to manufacture synthetic fuels. In practice, they have no chance of satisfying our need of electricity, let alone producing so much of it that the surplus can be used for fuel production and heating

The Safest Energy Isn't What You Think

Environmentalists object that nuclear energy is not safe.[39]

Three incidents are named whenever its safety is mentioned: Three Mile Island, Chernobyl, and Fukushima. Nobody died during the first.[40] Less than a hundred deaths were confirmed as a direct result of the Chernobyl disaster.[41] There are no confirmed deaths due to radiation in Fukushima according to some sources and there's one death according to other sources.[42] Contrast that with the hundreds of thousands of people who die each year as a result of coal being used for energy production. Even the use of renewables, whose share in the energy mix continues to be small, results in more deaths per single year than the number of fatalities due to use of nuclear energy during its entire history. The data is unequivocal: nuclear is by far the safest and no other form of energy production comes close.[43]

Chernobyl was not only the worst nuclear accident in history, it was the worst that could possibly happen because the reactor melted, blew up, and much of its fuel became airborne (half of it, according to some sources).[44] The worst-case scenario was no longer some hypothetical doomsday, it became reality. That said, fewer than one hundred people died as a result.[45] The land around it was supposed to be uninhabitable for thousands of years, we were told, yet most of it is already safe with the radiation levels comparable to the natural levels in many countries.[46] The only thing that is still not safe is growing crops in certain parts – that will have to wait a few more decades. This is something to remember when we are fed apocalyptic fables about radioactive wastelands and thousands of lives at risk from a nuclear accident. There is hard evidence and it refutes these fears. Chernobyl is considered a PR disaster for the nuclear industry, but it can be argued that it is just the opposite because it demonstrated that even the worst-case scenario was not as bad as it was thought to be.

The safest form of energy is popularly considered the most dangerous. *The China Syndrome*, a successful Hollywood movie about Three Mile Island, suggests why this is so. Nobody was in danger of dying during the actual incident, however, the movie script writers invented a story where a major disaster was averted. But they are in the money-making and not in the educating-the-public business.

What is perceived as dangerous by the public does not necessarily relate to what is really dangerous. That is why *Jaws* instilled a fear of sharks into audiences although sharks have killed fewer than 500 people since 1958[47] and mosquitoes kill a million (by spreading malaria) each year.[48] That makes mosquitoes 100,000 times deadlier than sharks, but it would be tricky to make a blockbuster about a mosquito chasing people. Attempts have been made, but the creators of *Mosquito* (1994) had to come up with a far-fetched plot with mosquitoes biting aliens so that they could mutate and become larger than eagles.

Environmentalists have tapped into this popular misconception that nuclear energy is not safe and therefore have a vested interest that it is not refuted.[49] That nuclear was proven to be the safest form of energy, including the renewables,[50] doesn't sit well with what they have asserted for decades. That explains why environmentalists dispute the numbers. Greenpeace put the Chernobyl death toll at about 90,000. As may also be expected, experts in the field called this conclusion "bad science".[51] Nobody has seen these tens of thousands of corpses, nobody has noticed so many people missing – there's no record of them.

But let's suppose, for the sake of argument, that the 90,000 figure is correct. That would still mean that **all** deaths for **all** the years nuclear energy has existed is still several times smaller than the number of those dying because we use coal in a **single** year.

Environmentalists not only invent data, they cherry-pick from the existing data. For example, they won't tell you that "the fly ash emitted by a power plant – a by-product from burning coal for electricity – carries into the surrounding environment 100 times more radiation than a nuclear power plant producing the same amount of energy".[52]

Like good con artists, environmentalists use the oldest trick in the book: the assumptions of the public. People assume that nuclear is associated with radioactivity because it is called "nuclear". They cannot imagine that the radiation it releases is so low that it is less than that of coal.

The word "nuclear" is used when one talks of bombs and when one talks of electric power production. This gives rise to another fallacy: that a nuclear reactor can explode in the same way a nuclear bomb does. In fact this is impossible, even if the engineers servicing it deliberately want to sabotage it.[53] It is incredibly complicated and hard to cause a nuclear explosion, even if one has all the uranium and plutonium in the world.[54] First, the fuel has to be enriched as what is used in a civilian power plant reactor is not the same as what is in a bomb.[55] Then it must be shaped in a particular and precise way, then surrounded by explosives that are also shaped in a particular and precise way, then the last must detonate in a very specific manner using specialised and hard to come by electronics. Tired of this list? It goes on. Each of these operations in itself is a technical feat of engineering that requires unique machines, highly qualified experts, and months of work – and that is just what is declassified, in other words just the problems we know of. None of this can be achieved in a nuclear power plant unless somebody equips it with large machine workshops full of centrifuges, chemical separation plants, tools, and much else. However, in this case the power plant will eventually be a small part of a vast industrial park and what will explode will still not be its reactor but a purposefully manufactured nuclear bomb. To expect that it can occur accidentally would be the same as putting some of the cogs of a disassembled watch in a hat, throwing away the rest, then shaking what's left in the hat and miraculously find a ticking watch inside. That is why we haven't had a terrorist with a nuclear vest and why Iran has been so slow to manufacture a nuclear bomb.

Unlike chemical explosives, nuclear materials do not blow up if they are set alight, heated, hit, squashed, dropped, spilled, mixed with other materials, etc. While piling up a large quantity of them in one spot can cause an uncontrollable chain reaction, this may lead to releasing enough heat to melt them but not to cause a nuclear blast.[56] You will have something resembling lava that will slowly flow for a few metres until it cools down enough to freeze in a glass-like mass. This is what a reactor meltdown looks like, and you can actually see it in Chernobyl.[57]

People are surprised to hear that the explosions in Chernobyl and Fukushima were chemical and not nuclear. The assumption that nuclear reactors can blow up like nuclear bombs is widespread.

Another misconception spread by environmentalists is that nuclear power plants create a lot of dangerous, radioactive waste which cannot be stored safely. In fact, nuclear is the only "green" industry as it releases no waste into the environment, unlike coal burning plants that pollute the atmosphere, and solar panels that leave large quantities of highly toxic chemicals behind. Moreover, nuclear waste is far less dangerous than many chemicals routinely used in other industries.[58]

In fact, there is no actual waste from nuclear power plants at all, only by-products. Far from being "waste", these are valuable and some are useful even today.[59] There are several technologies being developed that allow energy production from the so called "waste".[60] One is the TerraPower, a reactor that can not only burn its own waste, but utilise the "waste" that has been accumulated in the previous decades.[61] Another technology uses the depleted uranium to convert ethylene into ethane, which could be used to create valuable commodity chemicals or new energy sources.[62] In 2020, a US company unveiled a battery that uses nuclear waste and lasts up to 28,000 years.[63] So, it is not a stretch of the imagination to say that all of the by-products will be used eventually.

The present-day situation reminds us of the infancy of the oil industry more than a century ago when certain valuable oil fractions had to be disposed of because they were not useful yet. It sounds ridiculous now, but gasoline was among those. The same went for natural gas. So, money was spent getting rid of them instead of money being made by selling them. They were considered to be waste instead of being a resource.[64] The difference between the oil industry then and the nuclear industry now is that the first wasted this pseudo waste, harming the environment in the process, while the second stores the by-products that are not used today for future use.

But even if the technology never improves, nuclear storage would not be an issue. The waste is solid (so it cannot leak as it does in B-movies) and can be kept in geological formations that have been stable for millions of years. In the unlikely event that these are flooded, and the canisters containing the waste rusts through (impossible since they are made of thick stainless steel), the danger to the groundwater is still remote. After all, radioactivity is not invented by man. These same materials have existed in nature and most still do. Releasing the waste would be, as a physicist puts it, *'like adding a few grains of sand to the Sahara Desert'*.[65] That is not an exaggeration given that the waste volume per year per person who uses electricity from a nuclear power plant amounts to the size of one aspirin tablet.[66]

Although there is no issue with the current storage, the US government wanted to improve on the situation by putting nuclear by-products into one central storage place. That was delayed because of anti-nuclear "politicking".[67] So, the only real problem is the one artificially created by the opponents of the nuclear energy.

The same may be said of the transportation. It should present no problem since the quantities involved are tiny compared to coal or oil. Spent nuclear fuel is moved in collision-proof casks which have been extensively crash-tested and stay intact in the event of a head-on collision between a cask-carrying truck and a full-speed train. The casks are designed to tolerate external bomb blasts. Even if a spent fuel element were exposed to air, the solid form of the radioactive products prevents them from becoming radioactive aerosols. The risk is 50,000 times less than the estimated death caused by coal transports.[68]

So, in absence of a real issue, the environmentalists did what any good campaigner would do: they created one. To illustrate, in 1997 a shipment of radioactive waste was moved a few hundred miles in Germany for storage:

> Over the course of four days, 10,000 protesters clashed with 30,000 police at a cost of about $100 million. Some of the tactics used by protesters were: chaining 80 tractors together to blockade the road, cementing themselves to the railroad tracks, use of children to block railroad tracks, tunnelling under the roads along the route to undermine their integrity, and erecting barriers in the road and setting them on fire.[69]

The environmentalists did their best to make nuclear energy expensive and then they complained it was expensive.[70]

Moreover, epic stunts like this not only cost money, they spread the idea that nuclear energy is something to be feared.

Some object that it is not just about scare tactics because the nuclear energy must be closely controlled by the government since it can be used to make materials for weapons of mass distruction. That may be true of the uranium based designs still being used in the 2020s, but thorium is by and large impractical for making nuclear bombs. As for "dirty" bombs, it turns out that no reactor would be useful at all, thorium-powered or otherwise.[71] Thorium's radioactivity is so low that it is used in some welding rods handled by humans[72] and can be found in every home (in the magnetron lamp of your microwave, the part that heats up your food). Yet thorium is often subjected to similar mining regulations as uranium. That red tape is one more consequence of the fearmongering surrounding all things nuclear.

Nuclear Cheaper Than Coal

Although nuclear energy is safe as it is, it is getting safer with the introduction of thorium as a nuclear fuel in the near future. This was tested in Oak Ridge National Laboratory in the 1960s and 1970s.[73] The programme was cancelled for reasons that had nothing to do with its feasibility, one being that, as was already mentioned, thorium is not suitable for the production of nuclear weapons. (That was a disadvantage during the Cold War; it is an advantage now.) So, the thorium energy is not something that must be invented, it must merely be commercialised. China, a country which specialises in replicating and refining foreign technologies, has begun to do precisely that. India is not far behind.[74]

The reactors based on thorium (and molten salt thorium reactors in particular) are better on every count: they do not operate under high pressure, they don't need large containment buildings, they don't need electrical power in order to be shut down, they are regulated by physical laws rather than by a device, and cannot experience a meltdown since the fuel is already liquid. Each of these characteristics is ground-breaking.

Take the liquid part. All you need to grasp its significance is to compare boiling potatoes to boiling couscous. The first don't need stirring as the water can circulate freely in the pot and thus transfer the heat evenly. The second can't flow and therefore will burn if it is not stirred. Likewise, the fuel in a liquid fluoride thorium reactor moves freely about while the uranium rods in the present-day reactors need to be "stirred" as they are solid and neither the reaction nor the temperature in the reactor is uniform as a result. This "stirring" is not only expensive, but it also requires the reactor to be stopped and, on top of that, does not help much as most of the fuel remains unused despite all the complicated procedures.

No high pressure means that you don't need all the expensive plumbing which keeps current reactors cool and makes them prone to accidents. It also means that a thorium reactor does not need a big building to keep the steam from escaping in case of a leak. (The reactors of today use water as a coolant and liquid water expands hundreds of times when vaporised; hence, they need a big building to contain all that steam in case of an accident.) In fact, there could be no building at all to house a thorium reactor as the whole assembly could conceivably be no bigger than a shipping container. (That was one of their selling points originally as the Americans considered to use them in bombers which could stay airborne indefinitely during the Cold War.) This, in turn, not only lowers the price, it means that we can install these everywhere and thus get away with the expensive and vulnerable electrical infrastructure that covers the landscape with all those steel high-voltage pylons and which wastes around seven percent of the energy manufactured.

A thorium reactor is self-regulating: "If the fuel overheats, it expands considerably, which, due to the liquid nature of the fuel, will push fuel out of the active core region. In a small or well-moderated core this reduces the reactivity."[75]

An operator could be asleep at the controls because he doesn't need to do anything. American physicists used to leave the thorium reactor in Oak Ridge unattended when they went home at the weekends.[76] This is something you can never do with a present-day water-cooled reactor as it requires constant monitoring.

This alone makes the thorium reactor safe, but there are additional security features. If there is loss of electrical power, the reactor shuts down by itself. It needs power in order to stay hot as without it a fan stops blowing air and a frozen blockage melts. (The blockage is just frozen fuel in a pipe. No valve is needed and that matters because any valve could break, but melting frozen fuel is a physical process which always occurs in the same way.) Melting it drains the fuel into another tank, the geometry of the latter stopping the nuclear reaction. No electricity is needed for the liquid to flow down as anybody who has seen a river or a kitchen sink knows: gravity does the job. Contrast this with current reactors which need electrical power in order to be shut down.

Therefore, thorium reactors are what the engineers call fail-safe. They revert to a safe condition in the event of a breakdown. They rely on the laws of thermodynamics and gravity for safety, not on moving parts and computers that can fail or on human operators who can make mistakes. Gravity doesn't need supervision.

On top of it, thorium reactors are way more efficient, and the material used to power them is practically unlimited.[77] Environmentalists never mention this technology as it doesn't fit into their narrative. They need nuclear energy to be expensive, dangerous, and complicated.

Thorium reactors are not only safer, but cheaper as well. That is not too good to be true because thorium reactors have fewer components, and every engineer will tell you that a machine that has fewer components is simultaneously cheaper, more efficient, and less likely to fail. All three characteristics stem from a single one: simplicity. Fewer components means that fewer of them need to be manufactured, which reduces the price of production. It also means that there are fewer components that can fail which improves reliability. Finally, fewer components have to be moved and that reduces not only the wear and tear, but the energy loss. Present-day reactors have high-pressure valves, water pumps, complicated plumbing, controlling rods, electric motors, back-up generators, and much more that is absent in the thorium ones.

In fact, the energy that can be produced by thorium reactors is so cheap that it is cheaper than coal.[78] That should come as no surprise given that nuclear reactions are at least a million times more energetic than the chemical ones.[79] This contrast is so incredible that it is hard to visualise. Imagine a million freight cars in a train that is over 10,000 kilometres long. That's more than the length of Russia, the largest country on Earth, comprising 11 time zones. If all of these cars are full of coal, their energy content would still not exceed that of a single freight car full of thorium, a car which is a little over 10 metres long.

Less Pain, More Gain

It turns out that the greenest energy of them all, the one which releases least pollutants, can also be the cheapest.

This simple fact refutes all the arguments of the environmentalists. They tell us that we must pay more for energy in order to prevent global warming. The opposite turns out to be true: we must enjoy cheaper energy in order to prevent global warming. Thorium has no carbon footprint yet the more expensive coal has. Environmentalists tell us that global warming can be prevented by regulating CO_2 emissions. However, less environmental regulation turns out to be the answer because everybody prefers what is cheaper if given a choice (a choice the regulations deny). We don't have to force people to pay less. Therefore, the free market can eliminate CO_2 for free (because we wouldn't have to pay bureaucracies to enforce the regulations). After all, we did not need international treaties or enforcing bureaucracies in order to switch from inefficient vacuum tubes to energy-saving transistors. We also didn't need treaties or bureaucracies to increase the efficiency of the steam engine and yet it was increased 92 times over the last three centuries. Modern steam engines are up to 46 per cent energy efficient[80] (Some go as high as 63 per cent) while the original one (invented in 1712) was only 0.5 per cent efficient.[81] (That means that the ones today release 92 times less CO_2 to produce the same amount of energy. Note: this is *times*, not per cent!) It was the free market that did this, not the environmentalists, and it was done because it happened to be cheaper.

The staggering advantage nuclear energy has over coal has not translated into economic gains so far because the development of the technology has been held back since its inception. What we use in nuclear plants in the 2020s are just refined 1950s designs. Apart from being complicated (and therefore expensive to manufacture and maintain), these use less than 1 percent of the energy value of the nuclear fuel.[82] The fact that they are still able to compete with other forms of energy production, given this staggering inefficiency, is testimony to how great the potential of nuclear fuel is.

So, current nuclear reactors are inefficient just like early steam engines were. Similar comparisons can be made with cars, aeroplanes, and computers. Any technology is inefficient at first. Compare the current nuclear design stagnation to the incredible development computers underwent since the 1950s. A 2020s nuclear plant would be recognisable to a 1950s nuclear engineer, while a modern computer would be baffling to a 1950s computer engineer, who would expect to see vacuum tubes, punch cards, and electro-mechanical relays. Part of the explanation is that the computers were left to the market while nuclear energy was heavily regulated by governments. Regulation stifles innovation. To illustrate, current nuclear plants use water pumps to cool their cores and it is crucial that these pumps work continuously to prevent overheating. That is why the regulating government agencies want to make sure that many redundant water pumps are used in a nuclear reactor. However, a liquid fluoride thorium reactor doesn't use water as a coolant. Naturally, there are no water pumps. It will be hard to apply for a licence for such a reactor, given that its creators will have to fill in forms about the water pumps they are going to use.

This brings us to the environmentalists again, since it is they who are to answer for this overregulation, scaring a public that is not educated in nuclear physics. In modern society, too many causes compete for our attention and our attention spans get shorter. We are a culture that learns physics from the *Chernobyl* TV series, although it has as much to do with actual science as *'Allo, 'Allo!* has to do with the real history of WWII.[83] A lecture on physics has little chance of getting through given the noise the likes of Greta Thunberg and the Kardashians make. Just look at the numbers of views below a celebrity video and the number below a physics lecture on YouTube. The first will be in the millions while the second will be in the hundreds. The environmentalists have an advantage over scientists here: they can generate news by blocking roads, riding motorboats, dressing colourfully, posing as seals and whales, staging shows, and other stunts. They can influence the popular mood and government agencies take these moods into account, whether they are grounded in reality or not. Politicians are not physicists and, even if they are, they are not voted into office by the scientific community. The public may not know what an atom is but, in a democracy, it ultimately decides what atomic technologies are to be developed. While wind turbines and solar panels are popularly associated with green fields and running children, nuclear is associated with children growing tails or having two heads. This is how we come to a weird situation. We depend on competent engineers to provide us with energy and yet we let PR artists tell us how energy must be provided.

Greenpeace, Extinction Rebellion, Insulate Britain – these are not solutions to environmental problems, they are memorable catchphrases expertly chosen to be repeatable and thus to create maximum noise. The environment is about molecules and degrees, not about PR brilliance. One may argue that PR is needed to get a message across, but it can equally be used for self-serving promotion. Sure, real chemistry will never make it onto the nine o'clock news if for no other reason than because it will take eight hours to explain. But replacing it with one-liners is not a good substitute, as the history of social engineering has demonstrated. The more simplified a message becomes, the greater its chance to find a following, but the further away this following gets from reality. The PR surrounding environmentalism is, therefore, self-defeating: the more influential it is, the less useful it is. If you hear somebody's message, it must be a lie as it must be a one-liner. If it is true, you won't be given a chance to hear it as it will be long-winded and therefore obscure.

Given that the first functioning thorium reactor was successfully run in the 1960s, we could have used thorium energy for decades now, thus emitting no CO_2 and enjoying a higher standard of living into the bargain. Alas, the development of nuclear technology was artificially hindered and we ended up with global warming. We have the environmentalists to thank for that.

Endnotes

1 Environmental Movement, published on Encyclopedia website, updated on May 18, 2018, consulted on March 29, 2021, https://www.encyclopedia.com/earth-and-environment/ecology-and-environmentalism/environmental-studies/environmental-movement.

2 Phil McDuff, "Ending climate change requires the end of capitalism. Have we got the stomach for it?", The Guardian website, published on March 18, 2019, consulted on 28 March 2021, https://www.theguardian.com/commentisfree/2019/mar/18/ending-climate-change-end-capitalism.

3 Andrew Glover, "If You Want to Save the Planet, Drop the Campaign Against Capitalism", Quillette website, on October 29, 2018, consulted on March 28, 2021, https://quillette.com/2018/10/29/if-you-want-to-save-the-planet-drop-the-campaign-against-capitalism/.

4 Ian Sample, "Clean, abundant and free", The Guardian website, published on April 30, 2008, consulted on April 2, 2021, https://www.theguardian.com/technology/2008/apr/30/greentech.scienceofclimatechange.

5 See, for example, the boy flying a kite among the windmills on "25 Best Climate and Renewable Pages" by Amanda Gaser-Bligh, Eon website, consulted on May 25, 2019, https://www.eon.com/en/new-energy/new-energy-world/25-best-climate-and-renewable-pages.html.

6 Copenhagen Consensus Centre Director Bjorn Lomborg according to "World spending $240b on green subsidies for 'virtually nil impact'", Sky News Australia website, published on August 11, 2019, consulted on April 21, 2020, https://www.skynews.com.au/details/_6071657727001.

7 Jonathan Chadwick, "Producing energy from wind or solar is now CHEAPER than coal as campaigners demand power stations are shut down", Daily Mail website, published on March 24, 2020, consulted on June 1, 2020, https://

www.dailymail.co.uk/sciencetech/article-8104801/Energy-renewables-cheaper-coal-says-report.html.

8 Brian Murray, "The Paradox of Declining Renewable Costs and Rising Electricity Prices", Forbes website, published on June 17, 2019, consulted on June 2, 2020, https://www.forbes.com/sites/brianmurray1/2019/06/17/the-paradox-of-declining-renewable-costs-and-rising-electricity-prices/#668aae7661d5.

9 A.S. Creviston, Tony Soverns, and Gary Gengenbach, "DISTRIBUTED POWER, RENEWABLES, STORED ENERGY AND THE GRID BLINKLESS® SYNCHRONOUS INVERTERSYSTEMCAPABILITIESANDAPPLICATIONS", page 2, Go Electric Inc website, consulted on June 2, 2020, https://goelectricinc.com/wp-content/uploads/2017/08/Distributed-Power-Renewables-Stored-Energy-and-the-Grid.pdf.

10 Brian Murray, "The Paradox of Declining Renewable Costs and Rising Electricity Prices", Forbes website, published on June 17, 2019, consulted on June 2, 2020, https://www.forbes.com/sites/brianmurray1/2019/06/17/the-paradox-of-declining-renewable-costs-and-rising-electricity-prices/#668aae7661d5.

11 Rick Kelley, "Retiring worn-out wind turbines could cost billions that nobody has", Energy Central website, published on February 21, 2017, consulted on June 2, 2020, https://energycentral.com/news/retiring-worn-out-wind-turbines-could-cost-billions-nobody-has.

12 Charles Rotter, "Wind farm turbines wear sooner than expected, says study", Watts Up With That website, published on December 29, 2018, consulted on June 2, 2020, https://wattsupwiththat.com/2018/12/29/wind-farm-turbines-wear-sooner-than-expected-says-study/.

13 Details see in the lecture "The True Cost of Wind-Ryan M. Yonk", Independent Institute YouTube channel, published on

December 8, 2015, consulted on June 29, 2022, https://www.youtube.com/watch?v=WC8z9GTQOYA&list=WL&index=6.

14 "Spanish nighttime solar energy fraud 'unlikely in UK'", The Ecologist website, published on April 16, 2010, consulted on January 10, 2021, https://theecologist.org/2010/apr/16/spanish-nighttime-solar-energy-fraud-unlikely-uk.

15 Brian Murray, "The Paradox of Declining Renewable Costs and Rising Electricity Prices", Forbes website, published on June 17, 2019, consulted on June 2, 2020, https://www.forbes.com/sites/brianmurray1/2019/06/17/the-paradox-of-declining-renewable-costs-and-rising-electricity-prices/#668aae7661d5.

16 Marc Porubcansky, "795 million people don't have enough to eat – why that's actually good news", Minnpost website, published on June 8, 2015, consulted on June 27, 2019, https://www.minnpost.com/foreign-concept/2015/06/795-million-people-don-t-have-enough-eat-why-s-actually-good-news/.

17 Ross Mittiga, "Political Legitimacy, Authoritarianism, and Climate Change", Cambridge website, published December 6, 2021, consulted on February 4, 2022, https://www.cambridge.org/core/journals/american-political-science-review/article/abs/political-legitimacy-authoritarianism-and-climate-change/E7391723A7E02FA6D536AC168377D2DE.

18 John Abraham, "Biofuels can help solve climate change, especially with a carbon tax", The Guardian website, published on March 14, 2018, consulted on April 2, 2021. https://www.theguardian.com/environment/climate-consensus-97-per-cent/2018/mar/14/biofuels-can-help-solve-climate-change-especially-with-a-carbon-tax.

19 Eerkens, *The Nuclear Imperative: A Critical Look at the Approaching Energy Crisis (More Physics for Presidents)*, (Dordrecht Heidelberg London New York, Springer, 2010), pages 24, 66–68.

20 William A. Sherden, *Best Laid Plans: The Tyranny of Unintended Consequences and How to Avoid Them*, (California, Colorado, England, Praeger, 2011), Chapter 2, section "The Ethanol Enterprise".
21 William A. Sherden, *Best Laid Plans: The Tyranny of Unintended Consequences and How to Avoid Them*, (California, Colorado, England, Praeger, 2011), Chapter 2, section "The Ethanol Enterprise".
22 Eerkens, *The Nuclear Imperative: A Critical Look at the Approaching Energy Crisis (More Physics for Presidents)*, (Dordrecht Heidelberg London New York, Springer, 2010), page 74.
23 Eerkens, *The Nuclear Imperative: A Critical Look at the Approaching Energy Crisis (More Physics for Presidents)*, (Dordrecht Heidelberg London New York, Springer, 2010), pages 69–73.
24 Eerkens, *The Nuclear Imperative: A Critical Look at the Approaching Energy Crisis (More Physics for Presidents)*, (Dordrecht Heidelberg London New York, Springer, 2010), page 75.
25 Copenhagen Consensus Centre Director Bjorn Lomborg according to "World spending $240b on green subsidies for 'virtually nil impact'", Sky News Australia website, published on August 11, 2019, consulted on April 21, 2020. https://www.skynews.com.au/details/_6071657727001.
26 Chris Mooney, "Turns out wind and solar have a secret friend: Natural gas", The Washington Post website, published on August 11, 2016, consulted on April 3, 2021, https://www.washingtonpost.com/news/energy-environment/wp/2016/08/11/turns-out-wind-and-solar-have-a-secret-friend-natural-gas/.
27 "Compressed Air Energy Storage", Science Direct website, consulted on June 29, 2022, https://www.sciencedirect.com/topics/engineering/compressed-air-energy-storage.

28 James E. Miller, "Why not split harmful carbon dioxide into harmless carbon and oxygen?", Scientific American website, published on July 9, 2009, consulted on April 3, 2021, https://www.scientificamerican.com/article/splitting-carbon-dioxide/.
29 Materials-Based Hydrogen Storage, Office of Energy Efficiency and Renewable Energy, Energy Gov website, consulted on February 13, 2021, https://www.energy.gov/eere/fuelcells/materials-based-hydrogen-storage.
30 David Kindy, "'Blue' Hydrogen May Not Be a Very 'Green' Energy Source After All", Smithsonian Magazine website, published on August 17, 2021, consulted on September 21, 2021,https://www.smithsonianmag.com/smart-news/blue-hydrogen-20-worse-burning-coal-study-states-180978451/.
31 Alex Ivanenko, "It's Time For Elon Musk To Admit The Significance Of Hydrogen Fuel Cells", Forbes website, published on November 2, 2020, consulted on March 29, 2021, https://www.forbes.com/sites/forbestechcouncil/2020/11/02/its-time-for-elon-musk-to-admit-the-significance-of-hydrogen-fuel-cells/.
32 Daniel Oberhaus, "Germany Rejected Nuclear Power – and Deadly Emissions Spiked", Wired website, published on January 23, 2020, consulted on February 14, 2021, https://www.wired.com/story/germany-rejected-nuclear-power-and-deadly-emissions-spiked/.
33 "The Complete Case for Nuclear", Environmental Progress website, consulted on April 4, 2021, https://environmentalprogress.org/the-complete-case-for-nuclear.
34 Robert Hargraves, "Thorium energy cheaper than coal – ThEC12" lecture, gordonmcdowell YouTube website, December 9, 2012, consulted on May 13, 2019, https://www.youtube.com/watch?v=ayIyiVua8cY.
35 Matt McGrath, "Climate change: Electrical industry's 'dirty secret' boosts warming", September 13, 2019, BBC News

website, consulted on 14 September 2019, https://www.bbc.co.uk/news/science-environment-49567197.

36 Eerkens, *The Nuclear Imperative: A Critical Look at the Approaching Energy Crisis (More Physics for Presidents)*, (Dordrecht Heidelberg London New York, Springer, 2010), page 23.

37 Eerkens, *The Nuclear Imperative: A Critical Look at the Approaching Energy Crisis (More Physics for Presidents)*, (Dordrecht Heidelberg London New York, Springer, 2010), page xix.

38 Eerkens, *The Nuclear Imperative: A Critical Look at the Approaching Energy Crisis (More Physics for Presidents)*, (Dordrecht Heidelberg London New York, Springer, 2010), page 79.

39 Michael Shellenberger, "The Real Reason They Hate Nuclear Is Because It Means We Don't Need Renewables", Forbes website, published on February 14, 2019, consulted on April 4, 2021, https://www.forbes.com/sites/michaelshellenberger/2019/02/14/the-real-reason-they-hate-nuclear-is-because-it-means-we-dont-need-renewables/?sh=67ca4f1c128f.

40 Eerkens, *The Nuclear Imperative: A Critical Look at the Approaching Energy Crisis (More Physics for Presidents)*, (Dordrecht Heidelberg London New York, Springer, 2010), page ix.

41 "Chernobyl, the true scale of the accident", World Health Organization website, published on September 5, 2005, consulted on May 23, 2019, https://www.who.int/mediacentre/news/releases/2005/pr38/en/.

42 "Fukushima Daiichi Accident", World Nuclear Organisation website, updated on April 2021, consulted on March 18, 2022, https://world-nuclear.org/information-library/safety-and-security/safety-of-plants/fukushima-daiichi-accident.aspx,; Sharon Marris, "Fukushima worker dies of cancer

caused by radiation seven years after disaster", Sky News website, published on September 6, 2018, consulted on March 18, 2022, https://news.sky.com/story/fukushima-worker-dies-of-cancer-caused-by-radiation-seven-years-after-disaster-11491282.

43 James Conca, "How Deadly Is Your Kilowatt? We Rank the Killer Energy Sources", Forbes website, published on June 10, 2012, consulted on May 23, 2019.
https://www.forbes.com/sites/jamesconca/2012/06/10/energys-deathprint-a-price-always-paid/#3b7cf014709b,; "Mortality rate worldwide in 2012, by energy source", Statista website, published on January 29, 2021, consulted on 26 April 2022, https://www.statista.com/statistics/494425/death-rate-worldwide-by-energy-source/.

44 Von Charles Hawley and Stefan Schmitt, "The Chernobyl Body Count Controversy", Spiegel website, published on April 18, 2006, consulted on June 22, 2021, https://www.spiegel.de/international/greenpeace-vs-the-united-nations-the-chernobyl-body-count-controversy-a-411864.html.

45 Eerkens, *The Nuclear Imperative: A Critical Look at the Approaching Energy Crisis (More Physics for Presidents)*, (Dordrecht Heidelberg London New York, Springer, 2010), page x.

46 "Chernobyl: The end of a three-decade experiment", BBC website, published on February 14, 2019, consulted on May 25, 2019, https://www.bbc.co.uk/news/science-environment-47227767.

47 "Shark Attack", article from Wikipedia website, consulted on May 23, 2019, https://en.wikipedia.org/wiki/Shark_attack#cite_note-5.

48 "Who is the biggest killer on the planet?", Hardy Diagnostics website, consulted on May 23, 2019, http://www.hardydiagnostics.com/wp-content/uploads/2016/05/The-Most-Deadly-Animals.pdf.

49 Michael Shellenberger, "The Real Reason They Hate Nuclear Is Because It Means We Don't Need Renewables", Forbes website, published on February 14, 2019, consulted on April 4, 2021, https://www.forbes.com/sites/michaelshellenberger/2019/02/14/the-real-reason-they-hate-nuclear-is-because-it-means-we-dont-need-renewables/?sh=67ca4f1c128f.

50 "The Complete Case for Nuclear", Environmental Progress website, consulted on April 4, 2021, https://environmentalprogress.org/the-complete-case-for-nuclear.

51 Von Charles Hawley and Stefan Schmitt, "The Chernobyl Body Count Controversy", Spiegel website, published on April 18, 2006, consulted on May 24, 2019, https://www.spiegel.de/international/greenpeace-vs-the-united-nations-the-chernobyl-body-count-controversy-a-411864.html.

52 Mara Hvistendahl, "Coal Ash Is More Radioactive Than Nuclear Waste", Scientific American website, published on December 13, 2007, consulted on April 24, 2020, https://www.scientificamerican.com/article/coal-ash-is-more-radioactive-than-nuclear-waste/.

53 Eerkens, *The Nuclear Imperative: A Critical Look at the Approaching Energy Crisis (More Physics for Presidents)*, (Dordrecht Heidelberg London New York, Springer, 2010), pages 33, 34.

54 On some of the problems involved see Rhodes, *The Making of the Atomic Bomb*, (New York, Simon and Schuster, 1988).

55 Eerkens, *The Nuclear Imperative: A Critical Look at the Approaching Energy Crisis (More Physics for Presidents)*, (Dordrecht Heidelberg London New York, Springer, 2010), page 125.

56 "Matt Bunn-How Nuclear Bombs Work", Ronald Veisenberger YouTube channel, published on YouTube November 21, 2017, consulted on June 29, 2022, https://www.youtube.com/watch?v=jqLbcNpeBaw.

57 You can see photos of it if you google the phrase "Elephant's Foot".

58 Eerkens, *The Nuclear Imperative: A Critical Look at the Approaching Energy Crisis (More Physics for Presidents),* (Dordrecht Heidelberg London New York, Springer, 2010), page 129.

59 Eerkens, *The Nuclear Imperative: A Critical Look at the Approaching Energy Crisis (More Physics for Presidents),* (Dordrecht Heidelberg London New York, Springer, 2010), page 36.

60 David Szondy, "Feature: Small modular nuclear reactors – the future of energy?", New Atlas website, published February 16, 2012, consulted on November 6, 2019, https://newatlas.com/small-modular-nuclear-reactors/20860/.

61 Kevan Weaver, Ph. D, "A Solution to the Nuclear Waste Problem", TerraPower website, published October 29, 2015, consulted on November 6, 2019, https://terrapower.com/updates/a-solution-to-the-nuclear-waste-problem/.

62 University of Sussex, "Chemists Have Found a Productive Use for Stockpiles of Nuclear Waste", SciTechDaily website, published on January 10, 2020, consulted on January 12, 2020, https://scitechdaily.com/chemists-have-found-a-productive-use-for-stockpiles-of-nuclear-waste/.

63 Dimitris Mavrokefalidis, "US startup unveils battery made from nuclear waste that could last up to 28,000 years", Energy Live News website, published on September 2, 2020, consulted on September 4, 2020, https://www.energylivenews.com/2020/09/02/us-startup-unveils-battery-made-from-nuclear-waste-that-could-last-up-to-28000-years/.

64 'Petroleum Technology History Part 1 - Background', consulted on May 11, 2019, http://www.greatachievements.org/?id=3677.

65 Eerkens, *The Nuclear Imperative: A Critical Look at the Approaching Energy Crisis (More Physics for Presidents),*

(Dordrecht Heidelberg London New York, Springer, 2010), page 129.

66 Eerkens, *The Nuclear Imperative: A Critical Look at the Approaching Energy Crisis (More Physics for Presidents)*, (Dordrecht Heidelberg London New York, Springer, 2010), page 35.

67 Eerkens, *The Nuclear Imperative: A Critical Look at the Approaching Energy Crisis (More Physics for Presidents)*, (Dordrecht Heidelberg London New York, Springer, 2010), page 35.

68 Eerkens, *The Nuclear Imperative: A Critical Look at the Approaching Energy Crisis (More Physics for Presidents)*, (Dordrecht Heidelberg London New York, Springer, 2010), pages 35, 36, 120.

69 Ellen L. Watson, Roy F. Weston, Inc., "TRANSPORTATION OF RADIOACTIVE WASTE - PLANNING FOR CONFLICT", consulted on May 24, 2019, http://www.wmsym.org/archives/1998/html/sess24/24-05/24-05.htm. Some details vary in other sources: Alan Cowell, "Nuclear Waste Convoy Stirs Angry Protests in Germany", New York Times website, published on March 4, 1997, https://www.nytimes.com/1997/03/04/world/nuclear-waste-convoy-stirs-angry-protests-in-germany.html.

70 "Nuclear Power", consulted on April 24, 2020, https://www.greenpeace.org.uk/challenges/nuclear-power/.

71 Eerkens, *The Nuclear Imperative: A Critical Look at the Approaching Energy Crisis (More Physics for Presidents)*, (Dordrecht Heidelberg London New York, Springer, 2010), page 131; A.K. Nayak, Bal Raj Sehgal, *Thorium-Energy for the Future*, (Singapore, Springer Nature Singapore Pte Ltd, 2019), pages 17, 112.

72 "Thorium Containing Welding Rod" (1990s), Museum of Radiation and Radioactivity website, consulted on May 18, 2019, https://www.orau.org/health-physics-museum/

collection/consumer/products-containing-thorium/welding-rod.html.

73 A.K. Nayak, Bal Raj Sehgal, *Thorium-Energy for the Future,* (Singapore, Springer Nature Singapore Pte Ltd, 2019), page 97.

74 Smriti Mallapaty, "China prepares to test thorium-fuelled nuclear reactor", Nature website, published on 9 September 2021, consulted on September 21, 2021, https://www.nature.com/articles/d41586-021-02459-w.

75 Badawy M. Elsheikh, Journal of Radiation Research and Applied Sciences, "Safety assessment of molten salt reactors in comparison with light water reactors", Science Direct website, published on October 26, 2013, consulted on January 16, 2020, https://www.sciencedirect.com/science/article/pii/S1687850713000101.

76 ORNL Thorium Molten Salt Reactor Experiment Researchers – Dick Engel and Syd Ball – Dinner & Interview, the gordonmcdowell YouTube Channel, published on September 28, 2012, consulted on December 14, 2020, https://www.youtube.com/watch?v=ENH-jd6NhRc.

77 A.K. Nayak, Bal Raj Sehgal, *Thorium-Energy for the Future,* (Singapore, Springer Nature Singapore Pte Ltd, 2019), pages 98–113.

78 The case for this was made by Robert Hargraves in a "Thorium energy cheaper than coal – ThEC12" lecture, gordonmcdowell YouTube channel, published on December 9, 2012, consulted on May 13, 2019, https://www.youtube.com/watch?v=ayIyiVua8cY.

79 "Matt Bunn-How Nuclear Bombs Work", Ronald Veisenberger YouTube channel, published on YouTube November 21, 2017, consulted on June 29, 2022, https://www.youtube.com/watch?v=jqLbcNpeBaw.; A.K. Nayak, Bal Raj Sehgal, *Thorium-Energy for the Future,* (Singapore, Springer Nature Singapore Pte Ltd, 2019), page 99.

80 John Voelcker, "Steam Under The Hood", May 13, 2008, consulted on February 18, 2021, https://www.popsci.com/scitech/article/2008-05/steam-under-hood/.
81 Gerald Muller, "The atmospheric steam engine as energy converter for low and medium temperature thermal energy", Faculty of Engineering and the Environment, University of Southampton website, consulted on February 18, 2021. https://eprints.soton.ac.uk/348565/1/Muller%2520RENE%25202013.pdf.
82 "Kirk Sorensen @ MRU on LFTR-Liquid Fluoride Thorium Reactors", on gordonmcdowell YouTube channel, published on May 24, 2011, consulted on May 13, 2019, https://www.youtube.com/watch?v=D3rL08J7fDA.
83 "HBOs Chernobyl: BUSTED!", Thunderf00t YouTube Channel, published on June 12, 2019, consulted on October 6, 2019, https://www.youtube.com/watch?v=SsdLDFtbdrA.

Chapter 12

Feminism to End Female Rights

Feminism demographically undermines the only society in the world where women have rights: Western society. This chapter explores how feminist policies could serve to Islamise the West, which would be the end of the rights Western women presently enjoy.

Birth Control

Feminism is associated with voting rights, not birth rates. But the Suffragettes are only one part of the story. The very phrase "birth control" was coined in 1914 by a prominent, perhaps the most prominent, feminist, Margaret Sanger, who said: "Woman must have her freedom, the fundamental freedom of choosing whether or not she will be a mother."[1]

Incidentally, Sanger was among those who provided inspiration for the Nazi eugenics[2]: the doctrine that humans must be artificially selected like cattle or cabbages in order to breed only the best. Birth control was essential, Sanger insisted: "In animal industry, the poor stock is not allowed to breed. In gardens, the weeds are kept down."

America had to get rid of the "human weeds"[3] This seemed logical because "the most urgent problem today is how to limit and discourage the over-fertility of the mentally and physically defective".[4]

She must have been aware that these ideas were shocking even at the time because she wrote in a private letter: "We do not want word to go out that we want to exterminate the Negro population."[5]

Sanger is not some obscure feminist; she, along with Sylvia Pankhurst, is the embodiment of feminism. Every book on the history of feminism starts with her. Fittingly, Hillary Clinton acknowledged her:

> Now, I have to tell you that it was a great privilege when I was told that I would receive this award. I admire Margaret Sanger enormously, her courage, her tenacity, her vision... And when I think about what she did all those years ago in Brooklyn, taking on archetypes, taking on attitudes and accusations flowing from all directions, I am really in awe of her.[6]

Naturally, fighting for the right to have an abortion was the next step feminism made,[7] given that abortion was viewed as another form of birth control.

Once gender began to be about rights and not about making babies, why have sex with men at all? In the 1960s, some feminists claimed that heterosexuality was a way for men to control women. That's why, for some, lesbianism became a form of liberation. Penetration began to be viewed as an act of violation by men through which women were "invaded". Employing military terminology did not end there: men were identified as the "enemy".[8]

Biology was further taken over by politics in the 1980s. Heterosexuality was proclaimed to be imposed on women by society and was called a "political institution".[9] In other words, men and women were not together because they need each other or because humanity needed to procreate to survive, they were together because society expected them to be. Thus, family began to be viewed as a problem and not as a solution.

As we can see, the feminist arguments from the end of the twentieth century differ from those at the beginning of the movement, but the basic idea is the same: motherhood is not a fact of life when one is female, it is a choice.

However, choosing to be a mother was deemed as choosing to be controlled by society, while choosing not to become a mother was equated with being free. So, it followed, motherhood was a choice only as long as a woman chose not to have children. Women were free to choose as long as they chose not to have children.

We can see how the roots of feminism have made transgenderism possible. If sex is not grounded in biology, if it is not about having babies and breastfeeding, then why shouldn't a man identify as a woman?

Who Needs a Family?

Feminism affected birth rates not only directly, but also by reducing marriage rates. In order to grasp this, we need to take a step back and understand why the family unit was needed in the first place.

The female usually takes care of offspring in the animal kingdom. This could not work with humans because walking on two legs rather than four means that the human pelvis must be strong enough to bear the full weight of the mother's body. This means the birth canal must be narrow. Therefore, the head of the baby has to be small, which is not possible if the brain is big. However, one needs a big brain to be intelligent. What is the solution to this biological predicament? The solution natural selection came up with was that a woman must give birth before the baby's brain is fully developed. This way, fitting through the pelvis would be possible and the mother would still be able to walk on two legs.

However, this solution came at a price. A brain that is not fully developed translates into a baby that is helpless. Unlike the babies of animals that walk on all fours, human babies need somebody to care for them for months and even years. The mother alone could not do that while foraging for food and fending off predators. A second parent was needed.[10]

But this opened another can of worms because males prefer babes to babies. In this respect, human males resemble stags. They feel the urge to compete with other males (in other words to assert themselves) and to copulate with as many females as possible, but not to stay around after they have done what it takes to impregnate them. A bull can mate with as many as 100 cows within a 30-hour observation.[11] That makes perfect sense in terms of gene spreading: a cow cannot be impregnated twice and therefore it is better to copulate with two cows once rather than with one cow twice. Bulls don't invite cows over to their grassy field to bond over Netflix and share their innermost secrets. A bull that wastes time bonding will not spread his genes as much as the one that moves on to the next cow and therefore the next generation consists only of bulls that don't feel the urge to bond. This is how natural selection works. It favours those males who "pump and dump" as the expression goes, and thus it is no wonder that males are born with the urge to be pumper-dumpers.

Studies show that things are not so different with apes, from whose ancestors we are also descended. The chimpanzee is our closest relative. A male of that species has no further part in the child's development after mating. He is only interested in females when they are in heat. We think that single-mother families are a modern development, but chimpanzees only have single-mother families. Single motherhood is the norm in the animal world. As a scholar summarised it: "Before there were humans, there were no fathers."[12]

Social pressures played a role with making human males into fathers, because they would behave like bulls or chimpanzees if left to their instincts. Men were incentivised by sex (which conservative societies do not allow outside marriage – in other words unless the man commits, invests his time, and resources). The burden of being a father also came with the perk of being respected both within the family and in the wider world. Unmarried men in a traditional society are "not only sexually frustrated but also socially marginalised. In many traditional societies, a man is not considered an adult until he has found a wife and sired children".[13]

Therefore, the two things that a male of any species aspires to (sex and respect) were channelled in a productive direction by making him a father. There are different ways to look at this. The one favoured by feminists is that this was the subjugation of women by the patriarchy. Another is to see marriage as exploiting the males by tricking them to do something which goes against their biological nature.

The "biological nature" phrase requires some explanation. Copulation does not involve much investment for a male since his body can produce sperm in their millions and he would have wasted just a few hours if he had sex with a wrong female (say, one that did not have good genes). Females, however, get pregnant (and the gestation period takes months, not hours) and are then stuck with an infant who needs care for years. Therefore, she can ill afford to sleep around because this would mean to waste her precious few opportunities to have offspring if she is with a male whose genes are not good or who will dump her, thus reducing her and her child's chances of survival. Therefore, the invention of marriage was in the woman's best interest because it was she who needed security and monogamy.

No matter how we look at marriage, one thing is certain: it was a way for humanity (men and women) to survive walking on two legs and having large brains. Since walking on two legs and having large brains is what distinguishes us from other creatures, a case can be made that finding a way to get males involved was key to becoming human. Marriage, therefore, allowed humans to become intelligent and build something no other animal could: civilisation.

Reluctant to Marry? I Don't Blame Ya!

When a man and woman kiss at the end of a romantic movie, she thinks of their wedding whereas he thinks of all the sex they will have.

Marriage worked until the twentieth century when the feminists began to boldly tinker with it.

The free love movement was the first blow to the family. The name says it all: it came with no price tag attached to it. But there was a hidden cost – free love for women meant free love for men, and men would not commit if they could have sex without commitment. Feminism may not have been the reason for the sexual revolution, but it "ratified it", as Mona Charen eloquently observed:

> Without women's seal of approval, the sexual revolution would have been nothing more than another attempt in a long history of men urging women to let down their guard. Thousands of years of civilizational evolution had been necessary to get men to subordinate their natural desire for lots of sex with many partners to women's preference for monogamy and faithfulness.[14]

Why this matters is evident from a study where men cited three reasons for not getting married: they can have sex without marrying, they can enjoy cohabiting without marrying, and they can avoid the financial risks of divorce.[15]

The last reason brings us to the enactment of laws that made divorce easy for women and costly for men. Men are less likely to keep their children or property in the event of a divorce and are more likely to pay alimony as well. In 2011 there were an estimated 50,000 people imprisoned for non-payment of child support in the USA alone, and the majority of them were men. Many could not pay alimony because they were simply poor or unemployed.[16]

Marriage is meant to be a contract and therefore a compromise between men and women. That is the essence of striking any deal: it has to be acceptable to both parties. It won't be concluded if all rights are for one party and all obligations are for the other. Feminism may fight for women's rights when it comes to marriage, but what's the use of these rights if the contract of marriage becomes so one-sided that men no longer wish to marry? Men must consider the legal risks of marriage and that makes them reluctant.[17] They don't want to be financially used and dumped just like women don't want to be sexually used and dumped.

This situation can be compared with minimum wage laws. Employers and employees are better off together because otherwise the employers will have no business and the employees will have no wage. However, the minimum wage law made the agreement disadvantageous to employers when the minimum wage prescribed exceeded the productivity of an employee. (This is covered in the "Raising the Minimum Wage Lowers the Income" chapter.) Just like employers did not want to hire in such a case, men did not want to marry if it meant pain with no gain for them. Employees lost out because of politicians enacting laws that supposedly favoured employees; women lost out because of feminists lobbying for laws that supposedly favoured women. As a worker has no use for such laws if he is unemployed, so a woman has no use for such laws if she is unmarried.

Some authors add another factor brought about by feminism: single-mother benefits. According to their explanation, many women are not that eager to marry because the government has replaced their potential husbands as a provider.[18] However, this cannot explain the falling birth rates because they are falling in much the same way in Eastern Europe and Russia too, but the welfare benefits there are hardly enough to support single mothers.

The Empowerment

Feminism found a new buzz word in the last few decades: empowerment. It aims at giving women confidence to stand their ground against men, and this is reflected in the number of films released showing that women can be action heroes too, from *Charlie's Angels* to *Captain Marvel.*

However, beauty to a woman is what strength is to a man. This follows from the biological roles the two sexes have. While a man has to be confident and prevail over other males, a woman must have sex appeal and prevail over other females by being more attractive. As long as this is the case, men compete with men and women compete with women. Therefore, the two sexes don't compete with each other, instead they co-operate and ensure the propagation of our species. You can see this idea depicted in porn movies that reduce the interaction between the sexes to basic biology: while the male stars are cast for being able to hold an erection (in other words, to be confident), female stars are selected for their attractive shapes. This point of view may be called old fashioned or primitive (and it is), but so is breathing and eating. Biology does not care about our views.

Feminists call these biological facts of life "objectifying" because women are seen as bodies and not as individuals. They are correct. However, men are also objectified because women value them in terms of material resources, social status, and ambition.[19] This explains the popularity of wrinkly rock stars such as Mick Jagger who never fail to win over the charms of young models over the decades. The only difference is the criterion by which each sex objectifies the other. If women are sex objects, men are marriage objects. Objectifying has negative connotations these days because people forget its biological function. Each of us may be spiritually unique, but we all are biologically similar. Most people share most of each other's genes (99.9 per cent of each other's genes to be precise).[20] This is what makes all humans belong to the same species. It also means that whenever a baby is born, 99.9 per cent of our genes are being passed on although we are neither its mother nor its father. Each of us objectively needs certain typical traits in a representative of the other sex in order to procreate. Because they are certain and typical, they don't relate to each individual subject. (Hence the term "objective", the opposite of "subjective".) The importance of these traits can be easily explained by the natural sciences. Beauty is biology: "In both sexes, an attractive body may be an indicator of underlying genotypic quality, hormonal and health status (including freedom from parasites), competitive ability, reproductive potential, or some combination of these factors."[21]

Therefore, the chances are that the children of healthy women will be healthy as well. This, in turn, increases the chances of a male to pass on his own genes if he impregnates a beautiful woman. The same applies to women too. They too have a better chance to pass on their genes if they have children with men who are industrious. Also, such men will have higher social status and therefore can help their children socially as well as genetically. (A child of a rich dad will have better chances of having children with a healthy and rich representative of the opposite sex.) Thus, this objectifying allowed humans to be healthy and to survive for tens of thousands of years, as those humans with better genes left more children. (This reminds us of eugenics, but there's a key difference: this is natural selection whereas eugenics is artificial.) We should appreciate this aspect of objectifying because we are all happy to exist rather than to be extinct, whether we like to be objectified or not.

In this respect, humans are not that dissimilar from other animals. Two rams will clash until one of them wins. The female waits to mate with the winner, therefore making sure that her offspring will have a better chance of survival since her genes will be paired with the genes of the winner (which have been proven to be better by winning the fight).

One may object that we are not mere animals and that genes are not everything. That is so, but our individuality is a by-product of our biology, not vice versa. To illustrate, we can live without being spiritually unique, provided our kidneys work well. We die if our kidneys don't work well no matter how spiritually unique we are.

Feminism does not consider any of this when it pedals empowerment, when it encourages women to compete like men: by fighting instead of by being pretty. That inevitably means they will compete with men. What if they win (as they do in the movies)? Being defeated to a man is as humiliating as being ugly is to a woman. Empowerment, therefore, dismantles the illusions of grandeur, the heroism, which men were historically fed in order to be involved in the rearing of the children.

Sure, women can be heroes too, any person can be. But a culture that celebrates female heroes clashes with biology and therefore the society that procreates such culture doesn't procreate biologically. This is easy to explain. Heroism is about winning. A boy wins and gets the girl. What does a winning girl get – a boy? But biologically she does not need to win to get a boy, she can have any boy since males are programmed to copulate with as many females as possible while the females are picky. Sleeping with somebody is not her problem, sleeping with the right somebody is. That is why in the animal kingdom males fight for females and not vice versa. What is more, human females have an additional problem: having this somebody stay around after copulation.

Encouraging women to make careers has a similar effect. Careerism from a biological point of view is a way for males to compete among themselves. When women become careerists too, the sexes again find themselves competing with each other rather than with the representatives of their own sex. Males competing with males and females competing with females is a situation beneficial to a species because it ensures that the individuals with the best genes of each sex will be paired with the individuals with the best genes of the opposite sex. Those with the best genes will have healthy and numerous offspring as a result, which translates into good genes being passed down through the generations and improves the chances of survival of the species as a whole.

To take it a step further, the education of women and their participation in the workforce directly lowers birth rates.[22] Girls spend their 20s – the period when they are most attractive, healthy, and fertile – making careers instead of children. Lower rates of childbirth among twenty-somethings are "likely to continue".[23]

Meanwhile, happiness has decreased during the last few decades among Western women, although their standard of living has risen during the same time.[24] Likewise, marriage rates are plummeting in the West. In the USA, for example, they have reached their lowest point ever.[25]

Any country needs 2.1 children to be born on average to every 2 adults in order to sustain its population. Across Europe, the birth rate has fallen below these levels.[26] Europe as a whole has a rate of 1.38.[27]

The Achilles Heel of Feminism

Birth rates among emigrants from traditional societies where sex goes with marriage and women are not "empowered" do not have the same record. They are not falling.

People who identified as "white British" in the 2011 census will cease to be a majority in the United Kingdom by the 2060s.[28] The most popular baby boy's name in England and Wales in 2021 was Muhammad.[29] Muhammad also topped the list of baby names in Glasgow in 2020.[30] The rising population of the United Kingdom is now almost entirely due to immigration and higher birth rates among immigrants. In 2014, women who were born overseas accounted for 27 per cent of all live births in England

and Wales, and 33 per cent of newborn babies had at least one immigrant parent, a figure that has doubled since the 1990s.[31] Since 2010, the number of those in the United Kingdom who were born outside it has grown by 1.4 million. During the same period, 940,000 children were born in Britain to foreign-born mothers.[32]

In 1990, non-European immigrants counted for just 3 per cent of Sweden's population. By 2016 that figure had increased to around 13–14 per cent and is now growing at between one and two percentage points a year. In Malmo (Sweden's third largest city) non-ethnic Swedes already constitute almost half of the population. Within a generation, other cities will follow and ethnic Swedes will be a minority in all major cities: partly as a result of immigration, partly as a result of higher birth rates among immigrants, and partly as a result of ethnic Swedes abandoning areas where immigrants dominate.[33] Demographic studies show ethnic Swedes becoming a minority in Sweden within the lifetime of most people alive today.[34]

The majority of Austrians under the age of 15 will be Muslims by the middle of this century.[35] Are Muslims trying to outbreed Europeans from within Europe? In 1974, the former Algerian president told the General Assembly of the United Nations:

> One day millions of men will leave the southern hemisphere of this planet to burst into the northern one. But not as friends. Because they will burst in to conquer, and they will conquer by populating it with their children. Victory will come to us from the wombs of our women.[36]

Ultimately, it is immaterial whether the immigrants desire this or not, because it will happen either way.

What will be the result of this demographic replacement of native populations? To address this question, we need to bear in mind that in the majority of cases the immigrants keep their own culture, that they do not integrate with the natives. One consequence of this was the failure of the rule of law in some spheres of British life because the British police refused to investigate certain crimes committed by immigrants for over a decade. (The details are given in the "Less Rape Jokes, More Rape" chapter.) Here is an example of these crimes:

> The January before the release of the 2011 census results a gang of nine Muslim men – seven of Pakistani origin, two from North Africa – were convicted and sentenced at the Old Bailey in London for the sex trafficking of children between the ages of 11 and 15. On that occasion one of the victims sold into a form of modern-day slavery was a girl of 11 who was branded with the initial of her "owner" abuser: "M" for Mohammed. The court heard that Mohammed "branded her to make her his property and to ensure others knew about it"... This happened in Oxfordshire between 2004 and 2012.[37]

Britain is not an exception when it comes to the effect immigration has on law and order. A clear statistical connection was observed between rapes and migrants who came from cultures where "women have no value of their own".[38]

> In September 2015 officials in Bavaria began to warn local parents to ensure their daughters did not wear any revealing clothing in public. "Revealing tops or blouses, short shorts or miniskirts could lead to misunderstandings", one letter to locals warned. In some Bavarian towns ... police warned parents not to allow their children to go outside alone. Local women were advised not to walk to the railway station unaccompanied.[39]

There are even some European courts of law that show leniency towards immigrant rapists because their cultural background is one where the maltreatment of women is not punished.[40] While immigrants keep their culture, children will typically inherit the culture of their parents. Genital mutilation has been illegal in Britain for over three decades now, however, more than 130,000 women have suffered this treatment and there have still been no successful prosecutions for this crime.[41] Genital mutilation involves both immigrants and their offspring who have been born in the West.

By 2015 more British Muslim citizens were fighting for the Islamic State than for the British Armed Forces.[42]

> In 2014 a leaked report from Britain's Ministry of Defence revealed that military planners believed that "an increasingly multicultural Britain" and "increasingly diverse nation" meant that British military intervention in foreign countries was becoming impossible. The government would gain less and less public support for British troops being deployed in countries "from which UK citizens, or their families, come".[43]

Douglas Murray observed:

> The Muslim father does not want his daughter to become like Western women, because he sees some Western women and knows what they do. He does not want his daughter to become obsessed with consumerist culture when he sees all that it produces. That which he would refute is in the society all around him. Perhaps in time, rather than become more like the society into which they have moved, such people will become more entrenched in their own ways precisely because of the society into which they have moved. At the same time the evidence to date suggests that it is unlikely Europeans will much defend their own values before such people.[44]

These developments should not come as a surprise to those who have studied history. Any culture tends to spread as much as the people who share it. We can think of many examples. The spread of the British settlers throughout North America, Africa, and Australia also meant the spread of the English language and Common Law. Conversely, the demographic decline of a population often means the decline of its culture. To illustrate, the Shakers were a Christian sect of people who lived in celibacy. Because they did not marry and had no children, they could increase their numbers only "by gaining converts and through adoption".[45] There were only two Shakers left in the world by 2017, both very old.[46]

Western Europe is on its way to becoming Islamic. What the implications for female rights will be is suggested by what these are throughout the Muslim world today. To begin with, Islam decrees that women's rights are not the same as men's: "Allah commands you as regards your children's (inheritance): to the male, a portion equal to that of two females ... (the distribution in all cases is) after the payment of legacies he may have bequeathed or debts (al-Nisa' 4:11).[47]

In Saudi Arabia, a man can have several wives, but a woman cannot have several husbands. Marriages are often arranged by the family. In 2005, forced marriages were banned in Saudi Arabia, but marriage contracts are still between the husband-to-be and the father of the bride, not the bride herself.[48] A Saudi religious authority has ruled that women are allowed to ride bikes and buggies, on condition that they dress modestly and a male guardian accompanies them.[49] In United Arab Emirates one reads job adverts saying that only female candidates on spouse visas are required to apply.[50] Others look for a female to be on husband/father sponsorship.[51]

Apart from the official rules, there's the reality of what happens on the ground in Islamic societies. Around 5000 honour killings take place per year all over the world, of which about 1000 occur in Pakistan and 12 in the UK[52]:

> UK police forces recorded 11,744 honour-based crimes between 2010 and 2014, including forced marriage, FGM (female genital mutilation), sexual and physical assault, and murder. Between 2014 and 2017, the number of incidents reported to the police increased by 53 per cent. And given that honour crimes are often unreported, these figures are likely to underestimate the true scale of abuse. Shockingly, in 2016/17 just 5 per cent of incidents were referred by the police to the Crown Prosecution Service, the lowest in five years.[53]

But wait, some may object, you are mixing two separate subjects here: feminism is about the rights of women, not about immigration. However, the two don't exist on different planets. They cannot be separated just as the minimum wage cannot be separated from protectionism (something covered in the "Raising the Minimum Wage Lowers the Income" chapter) or the British war guarantee to Poland could not be separated from the Soviet plans to invade Europe (covered in the "Attempts to Prevent WWII Made It Happen" chapter). The fact that we've put them in different books, articles, or chapters is only because they are separated in our minds, not in the real world. As investigators of aeroplane crashes and industrial accidents will tell you, these are usually caused by a combination of factors. Yet students are trained to focus on one single subject when they write essays and publishers reject manuscripts if their concept cannot be put down in a sentence; One-liners pay off in both talk-shows and T-shirts as people have neither the time nor the patience to listen to lectures or read thick books. Considering all the angles doesn't pay emotionally either as it teaches humility, makes us feel small and confused, doesn't allow us to vent off steam/unwind by chanting slogans.

Endnotes

1 *The Feminism Book,* (London, Dorling Kingsley Limited, A Penguin Random House Company, 2019), pages 100–102.

2 Dinesh D'Souza, *The Big Lie: Exposing the Nazi Roots of the American Left,* (USA, Regnery Publishing, 2017), pages 27, 154, 155.

3 Dinesh D'Souza, *The Big Lie: Exposing the Nazi Roots of the American Left,* (USA, Regnery Publishing, 2017), page 156.

4 Jennifer Latson, "What Margaret Sanger Really Said About Eugenics and Race", Time website, published October 14, 2016, consulted March 1, 2020, https://time.com/4081760/margaret-sanger-history-eugenics/.

5 Rebecca Hagelin, "Margaret Sanger Founded Planned Parenthood on Racism", Washington Times website, published on April 23, 2017, consulted on May 4, 2021, https://www.washingtontimes.com/news/2017/apr/23/margaret-sanger-founded-planned-parenthood-on-raci/.

6 Kevin Vance, "Sec. Clinton Stands By Her Praise of Eugenicist Margaret Sanger", Washington Examiner website, published on April 15, 2009, consulted on May 3, 2021, https://www.washingtonexaminer.com/weekly-standard/sec-clinton-stands-by-her-praise-of-eugenicist-margaret-sanger.

7 *The Feminism Book,* (London, Dorling Kingsley Limited, A Penguin Random House Company, 2019), page 157.

8 *The Feminism Book,* (London, Dorling Kingsley Limited, A Penguin Random House Company, 2019), pages 180, 181.

9 Adrienne Rich quoted in *The Feminism Book,* (London, Dorling Kingsley Limited, A Penguin Random House Company, 2019), page 194.

10 Bill Bryson, *A Short History of Nearly Everything,* (Black Swan), page 536.

11 P. J. Chenoweth, Sexual Behaviour of the Bull: A Review, Journal of Dairy Science, Volume 66, Issue 1, January 1983,

page 174, consulted on January 14, 2020, https://www.sciencedirect.com/science/article/pii/S0022030283817706.

12 Sebastian Kraemer, The Origins of Fatherhood: An Ancient Family Process, Sebastian Kraemer website, consulted on January 11, 2020, http://sebastiankraemer.com/docs/Kraemer%20origins%20of%20fatherhood.pdf.

13 Tom Standage, *Seriously Curious: The Economist Explains the facts and figures that turn your world upside down,* (London, Profile Books Ltd, 2018).

14 Mona Charen, *Sex Matters: How Modern Feminism Lost Touch with Science, Love, and Common Sense,* (United States of America, Crown Forum, a division of Penguin Random House LLC, 2018), Page 45.

15 Helen Smith, *Men On Strike: Why Men Are Boycotting Marriage, Fatherhood, and the American Dream – and Why It Matters,* (New York, London, Encounter Books, 2013), page 14.

16 Helen Smith, *Men On Strike: Why Men Are Boycotting Marriage, Fatherhood, and the American Dream – and Why It Matters,* (New York, London, Encounter Books, 2013), page 61; Douglas A Galbi, "incarcerating child-support debtors without the benefit of counsel", Purple motes website, published on March 22, 2011, consulted on May 8, 2021, https://www.purplemotes.net/2011/03/22/persons-in-jail-for-child-support-debt/, Douglas A Galbi has a Ph.D. in Economics, Massachusetts Institute of Technology, M.Phil. in Economics, Oxford University, B.S.E. in Electrical Engineering and Computer Science, Princeton University.

17 Helen Smith, *Men On Strike: Why Men Are Boycotting Marriage, Fatherhood, and the American Dream – and Why It Matters,* (New York, London, Encounter Books, 2013), pages 28–40.

18 Lynn D. Wardle, "Relationships between family and government", Core website, published in the Fall 2000, page 16, https://core.ac.uk/download/pdf/232621187.pdf.
19 The relevant study is quoted by Mona Charen, *Sex Matters: How Modern Feminism Lost Touch with Science, Love, and Common Sense,* (United States of America, Crown Forum, a division of Penguin Random House LLC, 2018), page 79.
20 Genome Variations, Genome News Network website, updated on January 15, 2003, consulted on February 29, 2020, http://www.genomenewsnetwork.org/resources/whats_a_genome/Chp4_1.shtml.
21 "Fluctuating asymmetry and preferences for sex-typical bodily characteristics", William M. Brown, Michael E. Price, Jinsheng Kang, Nicholas Pound, Yue Zhao and Hui Yu, National Center for Biotechnology Information website, published September 2, 2008, consulted on February 19, 2021, https://www.ncbi.nlm.nih.gov/pmc/articles/PMC2529114/.
22 Max Roser, "Fertility Rate", OurWorldInData website, published on December 2, 2017, consulted on January 15, 2020, https://ourworldindata.org/fertility-rate.
23 Valentina Romei, Half of women in England and Wales do not have children by age 30, https://www.ft.com/content/2928092e-1d57-4dff-9062-f66d8f64fb48, published on January 27, 2022, consulted on January 28, 2022.
24 Mona Charen, *Sex Matters: How Modern Feminism Lost Touch with Science, Love, and Common Sense,* (United States of America, Crown Forum, a division of Penguin Random House LLC, 2018), page 8.
25 Helen Smith, *Men On Strike: Why Men Are Boycotting Marriage, Fatherhood, and the American Dream – and Why It Matters,* (New York • London: Encounter Books, 2013), pages 2, 3.

26 Douglas Murray, *The Strange Death of Europe,* (London, Bloomsbury Continuum, 2017), page 44.

27 Mark Steyn, *America Alone: the end of the world as we know it,* (United States of America, Regnery Publishing, Inc. 2006), Chapter 1, page 2; Douglas Murray, *The Strange Death of Europe,* (London, Bloomsbury Continuum, 2017), page 45.

28 Douglas Murray, *The Strange Death of Europe,* ((London, Bloomsbury Continuum, 2017), page 34.

29 "UK's most popular baby names of 2021 so far", Independent website, published on June 15, 2021, consulted on April 12, 2023, https://www.independent.co.uk/life-style/health-and-families/baby-names-popular-uk-2021-b1866059.html.

30 "Babies' First Names 2020", National Records of Scotland website, published on March 23, 2021, consulted on February 3, 2022, https://www.nrscotland.gov.uk/files//statistics/babies-names/20/babies-first-names-20-report.pdf.

31 Douglas Murray, *The Strange Death of Europe,* (London, Bloomsbury Continuum, 2017), page 34.

32 Douglas Murray, *The Strange Death of Europe,* (London, Bloomsbury Continuum, 2017), page 317.

33 Douglas Murray, *The Strange Death of Europe,* (London, Bloomsbury Continuum, 2017), page 254.

34 Douglas Murray, *The Strange Death of Europe,* (London, Bloomsbury Continuum, 2017), page 263.

35 "The Vienna Institute of Demography" reported by Douglas Murray, *The Strange Death of Europe,* (London, Bloomsbury Continuum, 2017), page 312.

36 Douglas Murray, *The Strange Death of Europe,* (London, Bloomsbury Continuum, 2017), page 147.

37 Douglas Murray, *The Strange Death of Europe,* (London, Bloomsbury Continuum, 2017), page 28.

38 Douglas Murray, *The Strange Death of Europe,* (London, Bloomsbury Continuum, 2017), page 56.

39 Douglas Murray, *The Strange Death of Europe*, (London, Bloomsbury Continuum, 2017), pages 195, 196.
40 Elan Journo, "Ayaan Hirsi Ali on Migration, Islam and Women as Prey", Ayn Rand Institute New Ideal website, published on August 28, 2021, consulted on July 11, 2021, https://newideal.aynrand.org/ayaan-hirsi-ali-on-migration-islam-and-women-as-prey/.
41 Douglas Murray, *The Strange Death of Europe*, (London, Bloomsbury Continuum, 2017), page 226.
42 Douglas Murray, *The Strange Death of Europe*, (London, Bloomsbury Continuum, 2017), page 313.
43 Douglas Murray, *The Strange Death of Europe*, (London, Bloomsbury Continuum, 2017), 314.
44 Douglas Murray, *The Strange Death of Europe*, (London, Bloomsbury Continuum, 2017), page 226.
45 Jaimie Franchi, "Shakers", New Georgia Encyclopaedia website, last edited on September 10, 2013, consulted December 10, 2020, https://www.georgiaencyclopedia.org/articles/arts-culture/shakers.
46 Erin Blakemore, "There Are Only Two Shakers Left in the World", published January 6, 2017, consulted December 10, 2020, https://www.smithsonianmag.com/smart-news/there-are-only-two-shakers-left-world-180961701/.
47 "Division of parents' estate between sons and daughters", February 1, 2004, consulted on February 12, 2020, https://islamqa.info/en/categories/very-important/60/answers/47057/division-of-parents-estate-between-sons-and-daughters.
48 Carla Bleiker, "Women's rights in the Islamic world", Deutsche Welle website, September 27, 2017, consulted on February 13, 2020, https://www.dw.com/en/womens-rights-in-the-islamic-world/a-40714427.
49 "On your bike! Saudi women allowed to ride bicycles, buggies in public", Al Aribiya News website, April 1, 2013,

consulted on February 13, 2020, http://english.alarabiya.net/en/News/middle-east/2013/04/01/On-your-bike-Saudi-women-allowed-to-ride-bikes-in-public.html#.

50 Indeed.ae website, https://www.indeed.ae/Female-jobs-in-Dubai-Free-Zone?vjk=db7ccd607cc0108e, consulted on March 24, 2020.

51 MNC Jobs Gulf website, consulted July 3, 2022, https://www.mncjobsgulf.com/jobs/female-accountant-on-husbands-or-fathers-sponsorship-abu-dhabi-1292663.

52 "Statistics and Data", Honour Based Violence Awareness Network website, 'http://hbv-awareness.com/statistics-data/', consulted on February 13, 2020.

53 Julie Bindel, "Britain's honour crime shame", published January 14, 2019, consulted on February 11, 2020, https://unherd.com/2019/01/britains-honour-crime-shame.

Chapter 13

Afterword

Will the West become like Muslim countries today? This is not certain given what this book demonstrates: humans are not good at predicting the future. There may be some factors yet unnoticed that will prevent this development.

On the other hand, if feminism results in the daughters of today's feminists having fewer rights than their mothers, that will not be the first time that social engineering has backfired. It hurts mostly those who are meant to benefit from it, given the history of socialism, minimum wage laws, foreign aid, political correctness, and all the other half-baked attempts to improve the lives of the disadvantaged. Feminists think that they are winning. But so did the workers when the Communists were coming to power and yet they ended up enslaved in the 1930s. So did the Germans when they voted for Hitler, but by 1945 most of them ended up homeless, raped or dead. Given all that, perhaps the future of women in the West may be summarised in three words, Kinder, Kuche, Kirche, (German for Children, Kitchen, Church), the difference being that there will be a Mosque instead of a Church.

More stories could be added to this book. The Prohibition Era was supposed to reduce crime, but it created the likes of Al Capone. The New Deal was meant to end the Great Depression, yet it made it worse.[1] Legislative measures to lower rent all over the world increased it.[2] The raising of taxes in the USA decreased the amount collected by the taxman.[3] The excessive zeal to uproot what's left of racism in the Western world may rekindle it. (This is covered in the "Less Rape Jokes, More Rape" chapter.) The data suggests that the measures to stop the spread of the Covid-19 virus in order to save lives achieved the opposite.[4] Putin wanted to eradicate the Ukrainian nationhood when he invaded in 2022, instead his invasion strengthened it by making the Ukrainian speaking population brothers in arms with the Russian speaking population of Ukraine. The Crusaders were supposed to counteract the spread of Islam, but they achieved the opposite because they weakened the Eastern Roman Empire, which was holding back the Islamic invaders and the Ottoman Empire managed to advance deep into Europe as a result.

Whatever the examples, the conclusion is always the same: we cannot foresee the consequences of our actions. Our world is not planned, it emerges as a result of trial and, mostly, error.

Endnotes

1 Thomas Sowell, *Intellectuals and Society*, (Basic Books – a member of the Perseus Books Group, New York, 2011), pages 84–88.

2 Thomas Sowell, *Basic Economics: A Citizen's Guide to the Economy*, Chapter 3, Price Controls, The Politics of Rent Control, (United States of America, Basic Books, 2004).

3 Thomas Sowell, *Intellectuals and Society*, (Basic Books – a member of the Perseus Books Group, New York, 2011), pages 148–157.

4 Scott W. Atlas, John R. Birge, Ralph L. Keeney and Alexander Lipton, "The COVID-19 shutdown will cost Americans millions of years of life", The Hill website, published on May 25, 2020, consulted on July 5, 2020, https://thehill.com/opinion/healthcare/499394-the-covid-19-shutdown-will-cost-americans-millions-of-years-of-life.

About the Authors

Vladislav Bogorov is a published author with a background in journalism. He was conscripted into the Bulgarian Army as a tankman. He is probably the only certified welder who has won four cases before the European Court of Human Rights (as a lawyer). Having been born in Bulgaria, Vladislav now resides in the United Kingdom. He has a Law Degree and an MSc in Russian, East European, and Eurasian Studies.

Allison McKenzie is no stranger to writing, having written many shopping lists and lottery tickets over the years. With only high school education, she learned about the Nazis from *'Allo, 'Allo!* and *Indiana Jones* and was surprised when Vladislav invited her to join in this book project. It was her ignorance of history that enabled her to edit the book so that it may be enjoyed by everyday people.

Note to Reader

The book is a collaboration between Vladislav Bogorov and Allison McKenzie. They contributed equally to it although the first-person singular pronoun is used in the passages that reflect Vladislav's experience only.

Please feel free to add your review of our book at your favourite online website.

If you would like to get in touch with the authors, they can be contacted at whenhistoryhadotherplans@hotmail.com

Appendix 1

WWII is called a tank war, so let's focus on the tanks. Going into the details is necessary here because many people assume the Germans were well equipped and yet few bother to familiarise themselves with the actual characteristics of the actual tank models.

The Germans didn't have Tigers or Panthers in 1941. On the other hand, the Soviets already had the magnificent T-34. It is usually the first Soviet tank that comes to mind as it was far superior to any tank in the world in 1941, but it was not the only one. The KV-1 had anti-shell armour (while Germany or any other nation had no such machines). T-37, T-37A, T-38, and T-40 were amphibious (Germany had no amphibious tanks). The models of the BT series were ultra-fast (way faster than the German ones; they would be considered fast today).[1] Even the oldest Soviet models like the Vickers-based T-26 still had a 45 mm cannon capable of penetrating all German tanks from long distances at that time while the German tanks were not capable of doing this.[2] Soviet tanks were superior to German tanks in every respect: reliability, fire-resistance (as most had diesel engines while all German tanks had petrol engines), cross-country passability (as they had wider tracks and more powerful engines), manoeuvrability, speed (even the heavier Soviet models like T-34 were way faster than the lightest and fastest German models[3]). Suffice it to say that modern tanks all over the world resemble the Soviet ones and not the German. Modern tanks have sloped welded armour, low silhouette, diesel engines, high-velocity/high-calibre guns, simple designs that are both reliable and easy to service. Not surprisingly, the German generals who had to face the Soviet tanks thought them better than their own.[4]

The German models were hopelessly outdated. There were four of them and they are easy to remember as their designations were PZ-1, PZ-2, PZ-3, and PZ-4. Apart from these, there was a negligible quantity of Czechoslovakian tanks.

PZ-1 did not have a cannon, just two 7.92 mm machine guns. That's the same calibre as a handgun. Therefore, it had no chance against even the oldest Soviet tank, T-26, as the war in Spain demonstrated. Four hundred and ten PZ-1s were sent to the USSR in 1941. General Halder, the Chief of the German Army General Staff, thought that PZ-1s were not suitable for action and should be sent to the rear. Soviet tankmen did not have to waste shells to fight them, they could just use their 12.7 mm machine guns as the armour of the German tanks was so pathetic.[5]

To put the last fact in perspective, the USSR had aeroplanes which were impervious to the same 12.7 mm machine guns. These were the legendary IL-2s. (The IL-2s were also better armed than the PZ-1s having 20 or 23 mm cannons, 37 mm in some modifications, not to mention rockets, but let's focus only on the armour here.) Just pause for a second to grasp how incredible this was: a tank, a crawling tracked vehicle, was less armoured than a machine that could fly. Maybe it could not fly very fast, but it was still many times faster than any tank at the time (or even today). The problem with armour is weight – whether we talk of tanks or of aeroplanes – but it is a way bigger problem for aeroplanes than for tanks. While adding an extra tonne was tolerable for most WWII tanks, adding a mere hundred kilograms was a big deal for any fighter plane or ground attack aircraft (which the IL-2 was). Yet the Soviet designers succeeded in protecting an aeroplane better than their German counterparts succeeded in protecting a tank.

A calibre of 7.92 mm may seem 2.5 times less than 20 mm, but this is misleading because we are talking about the diameter of a circle here, not the length of a rope. To appreciate the difference between 7.92 mm and 20 mm, we need to remember that the area of a circle (which is what a bullet or a shell is if we slice across its width) quadruples if the calibre is doubled. Double 7.92 mm and you get 15.82 mm, but the surface area actually grows from 49.265 mm^2 to 197.060 mm^2. Raise the calibre to 20 mm and you get an area of 314.195 mm^2. The mass of the projectile rises even faster given that its length increases on top of the increased width. So does its kinetic energy when it leaves the muzzle. This, in turn, translates into a flatter trajectory (which makes the weapon more accurate) and into more damage caused when it reaches the target (in particular, it can penetrate thicker armour). Bottom line: 20 mm is not 2.5 times larger compared to 7.92 mm, it is as different as a tennis ball is to a ping pong ball or a boulder to a pebble. But the Soviet tanks did not have 20 mm cannons; the smallest one was 45 mm and the biggest was 76 mm. A more apt comparison, therefore, would be that of a ping pong ball to a football or a pebble to a rock.

The German PZ-2 was somewhat better than PZ-1 as it had a 21 mm cannon. But this was still useless against most Soviet tanks except the amphibious models. The Germans had 746 of them when they invaded the USSR.[6]

Apart from PZ-1 and PZ-2, the Germans had a small quantity of Czechoslovakian tanks that had roughly the same characteristics and were notoriously unreliable on top of this.[7] All these were similar to the Soviet amphibious models except that the German and the Czech ones could not swim.

The PZ-3 had a 37 mm cannon (a small number was fitted with 50 mm). Therefore, this tank could at least be used against the oldest Soviet model (the already mentioned T-26) and against the Soviet BTs. But it had no chance against T-34 let alone against KV-1. Apart from these limitations, it couldn't handle rough terrain. Germany had 965 of these against the USSR at the outbreak of the war.[8]

The PZ-4 was supposedly an improved version of PZ-3. It had a 75 mm cannon, a calibre comparable to the 76 mm gun of the Soviet T-34 and KV-1. However, the German gun was short, and this made the velocity of the projectile low; the accuracy and the armour penetration suffered as a result. To put it in layman's terms, although the calibres were similar, the German cannon was like a pistol while the Soviet one was like a rifle. Consequently, the PZ-4 needed to get close to have any chance of harming a Soviet tank while the Soviet one could destroy the PZ-4 from a long distance. The off-road performance of the PZ-4 was equally dismal. The Germans had 439 of those against the USSR.[9]

Given the superiority of the Soviet tanks, just a few hundred of them would have been enough to stop the 3000 the Germans had. This is illustrated by a case where a single Soviet KV-1 tank held an entire German tank group destroying many vehicles and guns in the process. The KV could not manoeuvre because it was out of fuel. The Germans eventually succeeded to disable it by sending engineers to place explosives on it during the night.[10]

What if the lonely KV was not out of fuel? A German general gives the answer. He witnessed how one of his light tanks was bogged down in the mud while the heavy KV was easily driving through this same mud. (The German tank was so poorly designed that it sank although it was light.) The KV simply drove over the German machine. Then the Germans hit it from point blank range with a 150 mm howitzer, but the KV turned towards the howitzer and drove over it too.[11] Perhaps this one was out of ammunition instead of out of fuel and had to fight with its tracks instead of its gun.

The invasion would have been stopped at the border if all 636 KV-1s were used in the war, if they were supplied with fuel and ammunition, and if they were supported by infantry. (For one thing, the Germans would not have been able to attach explosives to them during the night.) Besides, those 636 tanks were just those already in the armed forces; additional vehicles were being mass produced while Germany did not even have a drawing of a comparable model at this point. (Fortunately for the Germans, their advance disrupted the Soviet production although the USSR still managed to out-produce its adversary many times over during the war.)

Taking into account the staggering technological superiority of the Soviet tanks, a number smaller than that of the German ones should have been enough for the USSR to win the war in 1941. But the USSR did not have less tanks than Germany. It did not even have an equal number. It had about 10 times more tanks on 22 June 1941.

The problem with giving the exact ratio is not that modern scholars disagree on the number of the Soviet tanks (let alone of the German ones), it is that they disagree on which machines should be counted as tanks. For example, the USSR had towing vehicles which are usually described as "tractors" in Soviet literature, the model's name was T-20 "Komsomolets". These tractors, however, were armoured and armed; their armour and armament were equal to that of the German PZ-1 which is counted in the literature as a tank. But the Soviet "tractors" until recently were not. The number of such "tractors" built until June 1941 was 7700.[12] The USSR also had 3258 armoured trucks that were armed with a tank turret and a 45 mm gun. This is clearly not a tank the way we understand this word now, but such a vehicle was still better armed than any German tank in 1941. Even if the armoured tractors and trucks are not counted, the USSR still had 25,886 tanks,[13] which is over seven times more than all the tanks with which Hitler invaded the USSR.

Endnotes

1 You can actually see how they moved in this footage: "Soviet Tank BT-7 (Red Army)", "yolkhere" YouTube channel, published on February 3, 2012, consulted on June 30, 2021, https://www.youtube.com/watch?v=Jzpom1gZcag.

2 On the number and the quality of the Soviet tanks see Vladimir Beshanov, *Tankaviy Pagrom: Kuda Ischesley 28 Teysciatch Soviestskyekh Tankov (The 1941 Tank Rout: How 28 Thousand Soviet Tanks Disappeared)*, (Minsk, Harvest, 2004), and Mark Solonin, 22 *Yunya: Anatomya Catastrophyee, (June 22: Anatomy of the Catastrophe)*, (Moscow, Yauza-Press, Eksmo, 2009), pages 189–207. On the inefficient German tank 'canons' and their poor reliability compared to the Soviet ones see. Details see in Viktor Suvorov, *Vzemum Si Dumitay Nazad , (I Take it Back)*, (Sofia, Fakel Express publishing, 2004) pages 516, 521.

3 Mark Solonin, 22 *Yunya: Anatomya Catastrophyee, (June 22: Anatomy of the Catastrophe)*, (Moscow, Yauza-Press, Eksmo, 2009), page 202.

4 Vladimir Beshanov, *Tankaviy Pagrom: Kuda Ischesley 28 Teysciatch Soviestskyekh Tankov (The 1941 Tank Rout: How 28 Thousand Soviet Tanks Disappeared)*, (Minsk, Harvest, 2004), page 102.

5 Vladimir Beshanov, *Tankaviy Pagrom: Kuda Ischesley 28 Teysciatch Soviestskyekh Tankov (The 1941 Tank Rout: How 28 Thousand Soviet Tanks Disappeared)*, (Minsk, Harvest, 2004), page 83.

6 Vladimir Beshanov, *Tankaviy Pagrom: Kuda Ischesley 28 Teysciatch Soviestskyekh Tankov (The 1941 Tank Rout: How 28 Thousand Soviet Tanks Disappeared)*, (Minsk, Harvest, 2004), page 84.

7 Vladimir Beshanov, *Tankaviy Pagrom: Kuda Ischesley 28 Teysciatch Soviestskyekh Tankov (The 1941 Tank Rout: How 28 Thousand Soviet Tanks Disappeared)*, (Minsk, Harvest, 2004), page 86.

8 Vladimir Beshanov, *Tankaviy Pagrom: Kuda Ischesley 28 Teysciatch Soviestskyekh Tankov (The 1941 Tank Rout: How 28 Thousand Soviet Tanks Disappeared)*, (Minsk, Harvest, 2004), pages 87, 88.

9 Vladimir Beshanov, *Tankaviy Pagrom: Kuda Ischesley 28 Teysciatch Soviestskyekh Tankov (The 1941 Tank Rout: How 28 Thousand Soviet Tanks Disappeared),* (Minsk, Harvest, 2004), page 88.

10 For more details see Prit Buttar, *Between Giants: The Battle for the Baltics in World War II,* (Oxford, Osprey Publishing), page 85.

11 Mark Solonin, *22 Yunya: Anatomya Catastrophee, (June 22: Anatomy of the Catastrophe),* (Moscow, Yauza-Press, Eksmo, 2009), page 207.

12 Vladislav Savin, *Razgadka 1941: Preecheeney Catastrophee. (Solving the Mystery of 1941: The Reasons for the Catastrophe),* (Moscow, Yauza-Press, 2010), page 137.

13 Vladimir Beshanov, *Tankaviy Pagrom: Kuda Ischesley 28 Teysciatch Soviestskyekh Tankov (The 1941 Tank Rout: How 28 Thousand Soviet Tanks Disappeared),* (Minsk, Harvest, 2004), page 119.

Appendix 2

One needs to understand what the Dutch Disease is in order to understand how aid stifles the economic development of Africa. To understand this, however, we need to know how currency exchange rates affect the trade balance of an economy and to get this, in turn, requires knowing what inflation and money truly are.

Money appeared to overcome the problems associated with bartering. A peasant needs meat and a shepherd needs bread. They can trade without money: meat for bread. But what if the peasant needs a tool, the shepherd needs bread, and the blacksmith needs meat? The transaction becomes harder and harder to arrange the more players and products there are.[1]

The way out of it is to designate a good (be it bread, meat, tools, or something else) which is used by all. Theoretically it can be anything, but in practice there are limits. Bricks are too heavy to carry around, cows can move on their own but are complicated to keep, sand is too common and therefore worthless. (Water can conceivably be used in a desert, but not where there are springs or lakes.)

Precious metals seem to fit the bill, however, not everything that glitters is gold. Not everybody can evaluate the weight and content of an ingot. A way out of this is to standardise the ingots, to form them into bars of equal volume and weight and to stamp them so that it is certain they are made of a certain metal – say gold. By doing this, we now have something reminding us of coins. The next step would be to associate the value with the stamp and not the material. We would already have money the way we understand that word now: a commodity that is used as a medium of exchange, and which may not have a value on its own (like paper money).

All these goods that could potentially be used as money (gold, cigarettes, rice, salt, seashells have actually been used[2]) have their own price and the same goes for any other money, including the paper kind. We think of money as something used to buy things and therefore of something used to place a value on things: a loaf of bread costs £2. However, we can turn this around and say that £1 costs half a loaf or that we can buy £1 with half a loaf of bread. In much the same way, we can buy £1 by paying, say, $1.50.

Like the price of any goods, the price of money is determined by supply and demand. The price of the British pound will fall if the supply of pounds is increased by, say, the British government printing too many pounds. From this point of view, inflation is just lowering the price of a given currency because too much of it has been put in circulation, that too much of it has been supplied. In reality it is a bit more complicated than that because of something called the "velocity of money". (Still, these details are immaterial when it comes to a really large increase of the money supply as the history of hyperinflation demonstrates: from Weimar Germany and post-WWII Hungary to Zimbabwe and Venezuela at the beginning of the twenty-first century.) In the same way, the price of socks will fall if too many of them are manufactured all of a sudden, the only difference being that we don't use socks to buy everything else. This cheapening of the money manifests itself as raising the prices of everything else because everything else is bought with money. Remember the £2 loaf of bread? It costs £3 now because the pound has inflated. We usually say that the price of the bread has risen, but it would be more accurate to say that the price of the currency has fallen provided that all goods (bread, oil, property, electronics, etc.) have risen by the same percentage.

The price of sterling will increase if the demand is increased by, say, too many foreign investors buying property in London.

They need sterling to buy in the UK and so will have to buy sterling in order to buy property. (Selling properties to foreign investors is an export from an economic point of view although the properties are not physically moved abroad.)

As the last example suggests, exporting and importing affects the value of a currency. The value of sterling will increase with the increase of the British exports (because more foreign importers will need sterling to pay for the British goods they obtain in order to sell them outside Britain). The value of sterling will decrease the more Britain imports foreign goods (because British importers will have to exchange sterling for foreign currency in order to pay for these goods). Example: a Japanese importer of Scottish whisky will need British sterling to buy the whisky which he will then sell in Japan just like a Scottish importer of Japanese Toyotas will need Japanese yen to obtain the Toyotas which he will then sell in Scotland. So, exporting whisky strengthens the pound and importing Toyotas weakens it. (To use the financial jargon, sterling that has become less valuable is "weaker" and the more expensive sterling is "stronger".)

Stronger sterling means less competitive British exports because British goods cost more to the foreign buyers. Weaker sterling will mean it is cheaper for foreign buyers to obtain British goods because they cost less to those foreign buyers. Thus, in an ideal world (providing that monetary policies do not distort the market by, say, artificially setting a foreign currency exchange rate by law), the exchange rate of a currency regulates an economy. That is to say, it doesn't allow it to go too far either exporting or importing and this way keeps the two in a relative equilibrium. Each national economy is part of the world economy. It has to export in order to import. From the point of view of production, it has to produce in order to consume foreign produce. Just like a person needs to earn money in order to spend, a national economy needs to give something to the international market in order to take from it.

This brings us to Dutch Disease because the last disturbs this equilibrium between exporting and importing. The Dutch Disease is the reduced competitiveness of all local exporters because particular exports (say gas exports) have increased the value of the national currency.[3] It goes like this: The foreign buyers buy the currency of the gas manufacturer in order to buy the gas. (In practice it is not that simple because the dollar is usually used as international currency in oil and gas trading, but let's simplify the picture for the sake of argument.) The increased demand for the local currency strengthens it and this makes all the goods that are exported more expensive to foreign buyers. The Dutch currency that was in circulation when this phenomenon was observed was the guilder. Let's create an example in order to illustrate the problem. A guilder costs, say, 80 US cents before the extraction of gas starts. It increases to 1 US dollar after the gas begins to be exported. A Dutch motorcycle costs, say, 1000 guilders. Before the gas was found, the motorcycle was sought after by American buyers as it was relatively cheap to them: they had to pay 800 dollars for it. After the gas was exported, the motorcycle still cost 1000 guilders, but the actual price of the motorcycle has been increased for the American buyer by 20 per cent now as the price of the guilder has increased by 20 US cents in the dollar. The American buyer will have to pay 1000 dollars instead of 800 dollars for the motorcycle now. That makes the Dutch motorcycle exporters less competitive on the American market (and on any other market outside the Netherlands). Therefore, Dutch industrial exports suffer because of the success of the Dutch gas exports.

So, the strengthening of the local currency stifles exports. But that's just half of it since it also encourages imports. The foreign goods are cheaper to local consumers now since their guilders buy more of these goods; 1000 guilders used to buy 800 dollars of foreign-made goods. The same 1000 guilders buy 1000 dollars of foreign-made goods now. That means that more foreign made, say, alcohol will be sold in the Netherlands and this, in turn, means that less of the domestically manufactured alcohol will be sold. The Dutch producers, therefore, will lose market share not only internationally but within the Netherlands as well.

The reduced sales, in turn, result in less production which means less employment. In the long run, it results in less development of the local industries. The country falls behind economically.[4]

What does all this have to do with foreign aid? It turns out that aid can have the same effect as gas exports.[5] The aid comes in the form of foreign currency (say, US dollars). These are exchanged for the national currency of the recipient country. The national currency of the African country increases in value as a result. (Its value increases because it is being bought, in other words, because the demand for it increases.) This means that importing becomes easier for the African consumer because the same sum of domestic money now buys more denims, TV sets, and bottles of whisky that are manufactured all over the world. At the same time, exporting becomes harder for the African producers as, with the Dutch motorcycle manufacturer, the locally produced sugar, clothing, and rum now cost more abroad. The result is increased consumption and decreased production. The population may live better for a while (while this shopping spree is fuelled by foreign aid), but the country's economy becomes unproductive and falls behind. Just like an individual on welfare benefits consumes and doesn't contribute anything to his national economy, the African country that gets the aid consumes and doesn't contribute anything to the international economy. This way, the country becomes more dependent on aid (because, with the ruining of the exporting industries, aid become its only source of foreign currency).

The economy of the African country will have no source of foreign currency if the aid is stopped. The local currency will crash. (It will crash as nobody will care to buy it.) Foreign goods will become prohibitively expensive while the local labour will become attractive to foreign investors as it will be cheap. The last may attract investors to move their manufacturing base to the African country. (The word "may" is key here because there are more factors at play in the real world. For example, a foreign investor will not move his factory to a country if there's no law and order there. Nobody builds a factory if it will be burned down, no matter how cheap the labour is. Civil wars, terrorism, organised crime, corruption and lack of law enforcement all play a role too.)

China used to be as poor as Africa, but it did not rely on foreign aid. Moreover, it kept its currency cheap. Correspondingly, the effect was the opposite of the effect of Dutch Disease. Foreign goods were expensive to the Chinese consumer and Chinese exports were cheap to the rest of the world. China, therefore, manufactured goods instead of importing them. The result was that it developed while Africa stagnated.

These examples suggest that being successful is more about good old-fashioned hard work and not so much about the sophisticated mumbo-jumbo of modern finance with its exchange-trade derivatives, hedge funds, and credit default swaps. It all boils down to producing more and consuming less, while foreign aid boils down to producing less and consuming more. If this is true, giving aid to a country is the perfect tool to keep it poor.

Just like a generous welfare system erodes incentives to work and erodes the work ethics of the individuals within a nation, foreign aid erodes the efficiency of an entire nation within the world economy. Just like the Western welfare system did not end the poverty within Western countries, Western foreign aid did not end poverty in foreign countries.

Endnotes

1 This simplistic account of the origin of money is given in economics textbooks ever since it was introduced by Adam Smith. It is disputed by David Graeber in "The Myth of Barter" chapter in his book *Debt: The First Five Thousand Years* (New York, London, Melville House Publishing, 2014).

2 Timothy Ho, "5 Types Of Alternative Money That Have Been More Useful Than Legal Currencies We Use Today", Dollars and Sense website, published on July 2, 2015, consulted on March 28, 2020, https://dollarsandsense.sg/5-types-of-alternative-money-that-have-been-more-useful-than-legal-currencies-we-use-today/.

3 The original Dutch Disease story involves natural gas, but this industry is just an example. The process has been observed throughout the world since then and it could involve oil or any other export industry. That is why the Investopedia website defines the Dutch Disease as decreasing the price competitiveness of exports of the affected country's manufactured goods and increasing the imports, both coming as a result of increasing the value of the local currency. James Chen, "Investopedia website", updated October 31, 2021, consulted June 29, 2022, https://www.investopedia.com/terms/d/dutchdisease.asp.

4 Dutch Disease, Corporate Finance Institute, updated February 12, 2021, consulted on February 25, 2021, https://corporatefinanceinstitute.com/resources/knowledge/economics/dutch-disease/.

5 Dambisa Moyo, *Dead Aid: Why Aid Is not Working and How There Is a Better Way for Africa,* (New York, Farrar, Straus and Giroux, 2009), pages 67–69.

Appendix 3

The Cold War Was Not Won

Robert Gates, a former director of the Central Intelligence Agency, served under five presidents in the USA, as he did not fail to remind us.[1] He assumes, by the very title of his book, that the Cold War was won; what remains for him is just to describe the details of how it was done. (The self-serving implication of this view is: certain American officials deserve the credit for it.)

Scholars have been less presumptuous, but many still share similar views. To illustrate, according to one notion, Ronald Reagan said everything like it was and this damaged Soviet propaganda, he supported the dissidents and other anti-Communists, and his Star Wars program dragged the USSR into a new technological arms race, which it could not afford.[2] The Helsinki Final Act contained a set of human rights provisions and compliance review procedures that, according to this notion, gave "a new, and ultimately irresistible, impetus to the political dynamics that eventually created the Revolution of 1989 in Central and Eastern Europe". Helsinki monitoring groups sprung up throughout the socialist world.[3]

The winning notion is related to the idea that the USSR collapsed because its economy was weak and that it was weak because of the escalation of Cold War military spending.

Let's start by examining the idea of "winning", point by point, in the next subchapters.

Afghanistan and Poland

According to this notion, the myth of the Red Army being invincible collapsed with its defeat in Afghanistan. Its enemies within the Soviet empire rose as a result; the USSR was overstretched, and this eventually toppled it. Poland also played a substantial role according to one of the variants of this notion: "How did the Lenin Shipyards in Gdansk become the twentieth-century's version of the Bastille? How could a non-violent resistance movement topple an empire that had been built on violence, cruelty and repression?"[4]

To begin with, this was not the first defeat of the "invincible" Red Army. It had lost another war with Poland in 1920.

The Red Army broke the Mannerheim Line in 1940 but did not decisively win the war with Finland and the latter did not become a Soviet "Democratic Republic". (That this had been the original plan is evident from the fact that a "Finnish" puppet government was prepared in advance headed by Otto Kuusinen.)

Then, during 1941, the Red Army suffered a defeat so complete that it can hardly be compared to any other in history. (This is covered in the "Stalin Lost Because He Prepared Too Well" chapter.)

None of this led to the fall of socialism (at least not in all Soviet territory, if we speak of 1941) and yet we are expected to believe that the 1979–89 war in Afghanistan caused it.

Even if the Afghan War shattered the belief in an invisible army within the Soviet Block, it is still not evident that this mattered to Eastern Europe. The crushing of the independence movements there, from 1953 to 1968, was not about whether the Soviet Army was considered powerful enough to do it, it was about whether it would be sent over there to do it. The Germans in 1953, the Hungarians in 1956, and the Czechs in 1968 did not need an Afghan War to rise. The problem for socialism in the late 1980s in Eastern Europe was that Gorbachev refused to send in the army when Poland and Hungary were breaking apart. Hence, the fall of socialism in Eastern Europe was an effect, rather than the cause, of the decline of the Soviet empire.

Besides, the Polish Communists proved capable in taking care of the "Solidarity" Trades Union in the early 1980s even without Soviet assistance. It was Gorbachev's perestroika that re-activated the anti-Communist movement there and therefore caused the aforementioned breaking-apart problem.

That would be the picture assuming that the Soviet Army was really defeated in Afghanistan. However, it was not. The Soviets more or less expected the problems they later encountered prior to the invasion.[5] The USSR did not win the war but was not militarily defeated any more than the Americans in Vietnam were. The Soviets left only because they chose to leave. They decided to pull out instead of escalating the conflict any further. This was not necessarily the result of Soviet casualties but rather of perestroika. The USSR had priorities other than military expansion in the late 1980s.

As for the casualties, the West is inclined to consider them high and subsequently to evaluate the whole affair as a catastrophe but that is only because it measures the USSR with its own yardstick. Thousands of soldiers killed was not a significant number for the Soviet Union; just think of the millions it lost in WWII. Besides, the Soviets were doing better in Afghanistan than the Americans in Vietnam. The number of their soldiers killed did not exceed 25,000 (some sources even speak of 15,000[6]) as opposed to 58,000 of Americans killed in Vietnam.

The number of servicemen sent to Afghanistan was also far lower than that of the Americans in Vietnam: 120,000 as opposed to more than 500,000.[7] Although some reservists were mobilised in the Soviet 40th Army, there was no need for mass drafts the way the USA needed them during its war.[8] The Soviet Army was not noticeably expanded compared to its peace-time numbers. It would be an overstatement to say that the USSR was totally committed in this war.

There was no draft-dodging and there were none of the other problems that plagued the USA during the Vietnam War. In particular, there was no anti-war movement. George Crile points out that the mothers of the dead soldiers started to form social circles and so did the Afghan veterans.[9] But all this was possible only because the perestroika was already underway by this time. Nothing of the kind happened under either Brezhnev, or Andropov, or Chiernenco although there were killed soldiers under their rule too and they also had mothers.

The Soviets could have escalated. No amount of Stinger missiles would have saved the "holy warriors" if the Communists used, say, half a million men and a corresponding quantity of hardware. That was the opinion of both the CIA and the military dictator of Pakistan at the time, General Zia-ul-Hag. That is why in the pre-perestroika era, the CIA supplied the Afghan resistance not with modern weapons but mostly with WWI rifles and occasionally with AK-47s which the mujahideen supposedly captured from Soviet soldiers. The Americans were afraid that if they supplied them openly, the Soviets would escalate the war and that would be the end of the resistance, if not the end of Pakistan.[10]

As for Afghanistan, the totalitarian state was still not established there at the time the mujahideen fought the Soviet Army. The population was not included in mass government organisations like Komsomol and professional unions; every village was not infiltrated by the secret police, did not have a party secretary, the border was not closed, the concentration camp system was not yet functioning. Likewise, it was still possible to have pockets of open resistance here and there in the USSR itself before the totalitarian state was fully established in the early 1920s. If we consider the Afghan resistance to be the cause for the Soviet collapse in 1991 then, by the same token, we should ask why armed resistance did not bring it down during the Russian Civil War of 1918–1922. Once the security apparatus of the totalitarian state infiltrated the population of the USSR, the borders closed, and the initial terror was carried out, such resistance was no longer possible. The Soviets never reached this point in Afghanistan. There's no reason to doubt that if the same methods – and in particular the same scale of mass murder – were used in Afghanistan (as in, say, Ukraine in the early 1930s), socialism would have worked in Afghanistan too. After all, it worked in other Muslim communities within the USSR which were not that dissimilar to the Afghans. In particular, it worked on the Tajik population, a people that comprised part of the Afghan nation as well. But the events in Afghanistan coincided with the downfall of socialism in the Soviet Union itself and so the process of establishing socialism in Afghanistan remained incomplete. The Afghans were lucky. Therefore, it was the Soviet downfall that caused the Afghans not to be sovietised rather than the Afghan resistance that caused the Soviet downfall.

Crucially, the Communists did not isolate the Afghan population from neighbouring Pakistan and Iran. Therefore, the Afghans enjoyed not only free Stingers and free food but other necessities the White Army or the Ukrainians could not even dream of during 1919–1922.[11] The porous borders gave the Afghans the opportunity to flee to safe heavens and to use a neighbouring country as a guerrilla base. Correspondingly, no one from abroad supported the Ukrainians and, as for the Whites, the support they received from the West was insignificant.

So, Afghanistan could have been subdued if its population had been incorporated into the Soviet empire. Making analogies with the British, who did not succeed in conquering it in their time would be misleading. The British Empire did not have a system equal to totalitarianism in its potential to control the population.

Apart from all this, the world was different in the 1980s compared to the 1920s and 1930s. It was by and large indifferent to the plight of the Ukrainians during the Soviet famine of 1932–33 that was planned and enforced by the Communists. Killing millions more in the same manner in the 1980s would have made it into the news.

Of course, the war was not irrelevant; it was indeed an economic drain and this may have helped the election of Gorbachev. After all, some of the Politburo members had been tricked into voting for him with a promise of economic improvement.[12] However, the greatest losses occurred after the Americans supplied the Stingers, the Milan Anti-Tank Light Infantry Missile, and the rest of the modern weapons. This happened well after the perestroika was underway.[13] So we cannot explain the launching of perestroika with the Afghan losses.

Reagan did not do it

According to one hypothesis, Reagan's policies brought the USSR down. He always spoke frankly and this supposedly damaged Soviet propaganda. He supported the dissidents living under socialism, and his Star Wars program – a missile defence system intended to protect the United States from attack by nuclear weapons – was the final nail in the coffin for the Soviet economy.[14]

These are strange assertions. To begin with, Reagan's speeches were not aired within the Soviet Bloc. What we (in the People's Republic of Bulgaria) learned of them, assuming we were interested (and most of the people I knew were not), was so distorted that it constituted Communist propaganda in itself.

Still, even if these speeches were aired (and translated, as very few spoke English in those days), it could not have damaged Soviet propaganda because it was not taken seriously within the Soviet empire at the time. The propaganda may have fooled some socialists in the West, but it had little effect on us who were living under socialism. It was no more than background noise to us, which we were used to disregarding.

Moreover, even if Reagan's eloquence had a profound effect on our mentalities, this would still not have affected the system because it was based primarily on fear and not on illusions.[15] We knew that we lived worse off than people in the West, that the Party functionaries were privileged, that there was no "bright future" (as the slogans proclaimed) and so on. Reagan's speeches could not have shattered our belief in socialism as it had already been shattered before he came to power. Still, we could not do anything about it. Moreover, we accepted the existence of the system as natural and did not seriously think it could be otherwise.

The dissidents may have been elated by Reagan's speeches, but the dissidents themselves were largely irrelevant. While the rare public actions of dissidents like Andrei Sakharov may have looked impressive in the Western media, these were easily counteracted by the authorities domestically and the majority of the population have either not heard of them or were hostile towards them.[16] The reason ordinary people were indifferent to dissidents was not just lack of information, but lack of interest.[17]

The Helsinki Final Act did not do it

The Helsinki Final Act of 1975 contained a set of human rights provisions and compliance review procedures that, according to this notion, gave "a new, and ultimately irresistible, impetus to the political dynamics that eventually created the Revolution of 1989 in Central and Eastern Europe". Helsinki monitoring groups sprung up throughout the socialist world.[18]

To begin with, none of these groups would have sprung up if the people comprising them were shot as people were under Lenin or Stalin. Therefore, it was the easing of terror that made this possible.

Furthermore, these groups came into being after signing the Helsinki Act. Why, then, did this not destabilise socialism in the 1970s? There is no correlation.

Above all, it is not clear how such agreements could have mattered given that they were legalities and legalities were by and large irrelevant under socialism. That, by the way, is why Brezhnev had no problem signing them. Likewise, Stalin agreed upon free elections with his allies after WWII and this meant little. As George Weigel justifiably asks, why did the Helsinki Act "not go the way of the 1948 Universal Declaration of Human Rights and the U N Covenant on Civil and Political Rights, both of which were promptly signed, and just as promptly ignored, by the regimes within Stalin's empire?"[19]

The same goes for North Korea today: "By imprisoning its citizens inside the country, North Korea defies an international agreement it has pledged to uphold."[20]

So what? There is no state of states which will come and arrest the government of North Korea. Needless to say, no groups ever spring up to monitor the implementation of this agreement within the DPRK because, if they do, they will disappear so fast that we will never hear of them.

The appearance of the Helsinki groups may have damaged the image of socialism in the West, but socialism did not depend on its popularity abroad, it depended on the fear it could instil domestically. The Western public did not vote in the socialist elections and furthermore there were no real elections. So why did the image matter? After all, the image North Korea has today cannot be worse and yet the government there does not crumble because of this.

No Economic Collapse

That the USSR collapsed because it was economically inefficient has become the conventional wisdom in many circles. President

Trump added his voice to the choir by saying: "Russia used to be the Soviet Union. Afghanistan made it Russia because they went bankrupt fighting in Afghanistan."[21]

The economic collapse thesis looks plausible on the surface. The Soviet economy, like any non-market economy, was inefficient. The fall in the price of oil in 1986[22] made things worse. At the same time, Cold War military expenses were enormous. On top of it, the Soviets were eventually losing something like a helicopter or a jet fighter daily (which meant 10 to 20 million dollars lost per day not counting the other expenses) in Afghanistan.[23] Chernobyl and the Armenian earthquake were two additional blows. According to this notion, perestroika was launched to address the economic issues.[24] It will be demonstrated here that while all these facts are true, they still don't explain the fall.

To begin with, any hypothesis that claims to explain the fall of socialism in economic terms has also to explain why this system still survives in North Korea. After all, we can list the same problems about the latter and then some: it is a socialist state, its economy is inefficient, the fall of the USSR hit it hard on top of it leaving it with no oil, and so on. In fact, the situation in North Korea was far worse in the early 1990s than both before and after Gorbachev came to power:

> By 1995, North Korea's economy was as stone-cold dead as the Great Leader's body. Per capita income was plummeting, from 2460 dollars in 1991 to 719 dollars in 1995. North Korea's merchandise exports dropped from 2 billion dollars to about 800 million dollars.[25]

By contrast, there was no famine in the USSR during the 1980s, while a certain percentage of the North Korean population died from it a decade later; transport was working in the USSR, while the roads were deserted in North Korea; there were no power outages in the USSR while the industry stayed idle in the North because of these.[26] All the comparisons are in the Soviet Union's favour. North Korea exports little except rockets and nuclear weapons technology,[27] recreational drugs[28] and counterfeit currency,[29] some labourers, and, correspondingly, it has almost no source of foreign currency. Its international trade volume is 224 times smaller than that of the South and its economy is 38 times smaller than the South's.[30] North Korea, survived despite the fact that about 10 per cent of its citizens died of malnutrition in the 1990s.[31] It is not comparable to the USSR industrially, technologically, or militarily. The North Korean regime should have collapsed long ago if the economic factors are the explanation.

There are other facts this hypothesis also does not correspond well with. The Soviet economy, although falling further behind the West, was continuing to grow in the mid-1980s and could at least satisfy basic needs.[32] The annual growth of 3 per cent[33] seems modest only when compared to South-East Asia and India because it is comparable to that of most Western countries today. The budget deficit in the USSR was still measured in single digits at the worst time in the late 1980s, while the same cannot be said of many leading economies these days. The budget deficit was a little bit above 4 per cent in 1985.[34] Falling oil prices to a large extent were compensated for by the opening of a new pipeline.[35]

The Afghan losses were significant and yet not significant enough to bankrupt the country.[36] Moreover, even if these have been enough to bankrupt it, the Soviets could have simply left the war like they eventually did. It was an economic drain only because the USSR allowed it to be. Therefore, Afghanistan was a self-imposed problem. Above all, the already mentioned per day losses began in 1987[37] and therefore they could not explain why perestroika was launched before that.

The economic hypothesis for the demise of socialism has much to do with Western preconceptions and little with the realities of socialism. A government is expected to fall in the West if the population faces hardship. Nothing of the kind can be observed throughout Soviet history. If anything, some of the hardships strengthened the Communist Party and were designed by the Kremlin to do so. Take the Ukrainian famine in the 1930s.[38] About seven million people were purposefully starved to death, more than the number of the Jews killed by the National Socialists.[39] The aim was not only to export the bread of the Ukrainians but to break their spirit of resistance, and it worked.

One has to remember that economic problems are not that dangerous for a totalitarian government as they are for a democratic one. If there is a sharp hike in prices in, say, the USA, politicians will be wary, the press will be outraged, the opposition will exploit the opportunity, the opinion polls will reflect all this; there will be protests, perhaps riots, and, of course, there will be consequences come election time. None of these things are applicable to socialist countries.

The economic situation was far worse under Lenin than either before Gorbachev's rule or at any point during it. Not only around five million people died of starvation,[40] but industry was ruined, and infrastructure destroyed.[41] During the Civil War the workers often stole and sold what they could from the factories in order to buy food. The hungry workers made axes and other primitive implements to sell privately on the black market in exchange for bread. This was done in factory workshops once tooled for the production of automobiles, tanks, aeroplanes, and howitzers. The former Russian Empire during the 1920s is reminiscent of the former Roman Empire during the Dark Ages, when the Roman bathhouses were used as living spaces and those who lived in them could not manage to maintain what the Romans had constructed let alone match it. Ninety-three factories were closed down just in 1921, among these some of the biggest in the country.[42]

"The decline of large-scale industry was truly catastrophic: industrial output was only one fifth of what it had been during the last year of peace."[43]

"As the market economy ceased to function, the cities were inadequately supplied with food, and the collapse of the transportation system made matters worse."[44]

The popular opinion is that the Russian economy was agrarian until the Communists came and industrialised the country. In fact, the opposite was true. The country was deindustrialised under Lenin.

Incidentally, something similar happened after socialism collapsed. I remember how the factories for the manufacturing of machines in my home city of Pernik were left idle and the turners were not paid for months. These highly qualified workers were making a living by taking small-time errands using the factory lathes behind the back of their superiors. Therefore, the machine shops equipped for mass production of sophisticated tools were used for the repairing of cheap implements brought in by local people. This under the counter business made no economic sense from the point of view of the economy as a whole because the said implements could have been cheaply mass produced instead of repaired using expensive equipment. Needless to say, the period was one of poverty.

Stalin succeeded to reverse the process in the USSR during so-called industrialisation, but in WWII the infrastructure of half the USSR (and the most developed half at that) was devastated along with most of its industry. Only part of the latter was salvaged by transferring it to the eastern parts of the Soviet Union. For example, the Soviet Union capacities for aluminium production rivalled that of the USA, however, it lost 60 per cent of these in the first months of the war.[45] Factories, bridges, railways, power stations, dams, houses, and even roads were blown up. This was done by both the retreating Soviets in 1941 and the retreating Germans in 1943, not to mention the damage done by the partisans in-between.

Starvation was a part of life in the USSR for most of its history and in that respect, the period before Gorbachev came to power was one of plenty. People had difficulty buying oranges and meat, but no one suffered malnutrition. On the other hand, millions died for lack of bread in the 1920s. The cannibalism was such that when a woman and her children were caught eating their husband and father, they did not want to give what was left of the corpse claiming that "he" was theirs. It was dangerous to travel on foot in some regions for fear of being killed and eaten.[46] Then even more died in 1930,[47] not to mention what happened in Ukraine and in some regions of Russia and Kazakhstan in 1932–1933, when Soviet authorities purposefully killed about seven million people through an artificially organised famine. Naturally, there were severe food shortages during WWII.

The conditions went from bad to worse again when the American food aid was stopped after WWII. Khrushchev said: "There was terrible famine in Ukraine in 1947. There were cases of cannibalism."[48]

He got reports that "people went mad of hunger and ate their own children. Corpses were discovered showing evidence that meat had been gnawed from the bones".[49]

That is not the cannibalism of 1922 or 1933.[50] That is yet another one and that is not counting the Leningrad famine during WWII, a cannibalism which, as a new study shows, was also of Soviet making.[51]

Is Khrushchev to be believed? After all, he lied on other occasions in order to discredit Stalin. For example, he repeated stories that Stalin has "decapitated" the army because of a German provocation.[52] He, being one of those closest to Stalin, must have known that this was a lie.

The first quotation, however, was not intended for publication. Moreover, Khrushchev is not the only source. Said Kosigin, the Deputy-Chairman of the Council of Ministers of the USSR and the one who managed the food relief in the worst hit areas in 1946–1947[53] claimed "many people were dying of starvation in many regions".[54]

Besides, these statements are in agreement with other facts. In 1956 there were still fewer cows in the Soviet Union than there had been before WWI in the Russian Empire.[55]

Peasants were so weak with hunger in the late 1940s that they often could not work.[56]

All this was in sharp contrast with the early 1980s. The infrastructure was working as was industry. The USSR was an economic giant, albeit not enjoying efficiency and the latest technologies. Soviet society was not affluent but certainly no one died for the lack of bread prior to Gorbachev. On the contrary, for the first time in Soviet history, bread was easy to buy and its cost was negligible. Bread, in fact, was so cheap and accessible, that it was used to feed pigs.[57] (The same, by the way, was going on in the People's Republic of Bulgaria, I still remember how many people used to buy up to ten loaves daily for that purpose.) Watch contemporary talk shows on Russian TV channels today and you will see that many people still remember the pre-perestroika days as a golden era. Consumer living standards were rising, doubling between the end of WWII and 1970.[58]

Reagan's Military Spending

According to one variant of the economic collapse hypothesis, Reagan's Star Wars program was the straw that broke the Soviet economic back.

However, Reagan's Star Wars program was a non-issue as the technology was nowhere near being operational and the Soviets knew it. The fact that even today this programme is considered not feasible is testimony to this. This was the conclusion of the Soviet physicists who advised the Kremlin.[59] Correspondingly, this is the opinion of the insiders:

> The notion that Gorbachev's perestroika was started as a result of Reagan's Star Wars program was concocted in the West and is completely absurd. In reality, nobody cared and nobody considered a practical response to the Star Wars program.[60]

Nothing came out of this programme except its non-cosmic component: anti-rocket missiles. Even these can, at best, only fight outdated Iskanders, if that, and had no chance against the Soviet ICBMs plunging to Earth at up to 7 km per second. Today, in the twenty-first century, after a lot of modernisations, these anti-rocket missiles still cannot destroy a few primitive North Korean rockets let alone hundreds of sophisticated Soviet ones.

But even if the Star Wars program was feasible, it was still a non-issue. Let us suppose that it was possible to destroy most of the Soviet ICBMs in mid-flight and only a very small percentage reached the USA. That begs the question: how small is small? America would have been devastated even if just one per cent of the warheads had reached US soil.

Let us suppose, for the sake of argument, something completely unrealistic: that no nuclear weapons could ever reach America and not only that, but that it was impossible to reach the American allies as well. That still meant that the USSR was a deadly adversary. First, it could have "bombed" the US by smuggling such weapons onto American soil not to mention the Soviet submarine fleet patrolling along the American shores.

That is not all because even if the USSR could not deliver a single nuclear weapon, that still did not mean that it could be invaded. North Korea today is not capable of showering the

USA with nuclear weapons, not to mention that its conventional military capabilities are not comparable to that of the former USSR. Still, it cannot be engaged militarily because the cost of the damage it could inflict using conventional weapons would still be too high.

Moreover, it was not possible for the USSR to be attacked for political reasons. Short of an accidental nuclear launch, WWIII could be started only by the USSR. While the USA was arming to make war impossible, the USSR was arming to make it possible. No democratically elected government could hope to start a war that would devastate the country and stay out of jail, let alone in power. However, this was possible for a totalitarian government. Examples: Stalin staying in power when the Germans were at the gates of Moscow, and Hitler staying in power when the Soviets were in Berlin. Therefore, the USA was in danger of being attacked if it lagged behind in the Cold War military build-up, but the USSR was not in danger of being attacked if it could not keep up in this race. The Soviet Union was not compelled to participate in an economic war of attrition provided it gave up any hopes of achieving military superiority.

The West puts too much emphasis on self-serving notions that give it a central role in what happened in 1991. (This, ironically, is characteristic of die-hard Communists in Russia who do not want to admit the fundamental problems with socialism and instead blame everything on Gorbachev and the West. Like post WWI Germany embraced the "stab in the back" myth, so the die-hard Communists are convinced that the USSR may have survived.) While the West played an indispensable role in containing socialism and supplying real information to the nations under it (with both having detrimental consequences for socialism in the long run), it is a stretch to think that Afghanistan or Reagan's Star Wars were the reason for the fall and that what happened was actually a defeat. No amount of economic sanctions or military threats worked against Cuba and North Korea. If they do not work against countries that are small, lack resources, and may actually be defeated militarily, why should they have worked against the USSR, a country that had all the resources in the world and was militarily untouchable? Also, if the falling (assuming it was falling, which was not the case) standard of living had played a role in the fall of the USSR, why did the much lower standard of living in Cuba and North Korea not produce the same result?

Western-centred explanations are nothing new. Many in the West still subscribe to the delusion that it was the Anglo-American supplies that turned the tide of the Soviet-German conflict during WWII. In fact, the Red Army enjoyed its greatest armament superiority in June 1941, precisely when it performed so badly against the Germans – in other words, before the supplying began. (This is covered in the "Stalin Lost Because He Prepared Too Well" chapter.)

Endnotes

1 Robert M. Gates, *From the Shadows: The Ultimate Insider's Story of Five Presidents and How They Won the Cold War*, (New York, A Touchstone Book published by Simon and Schuster, 1997).

2 George Weigel, *The Final Revolution: The Resistance Church and the Collapse of Communism*, (New York, Oxford University Press, Inc. 1992), pages 21 to 26.

3 George Weigel, *The Final Revolution: The Resistance Church and the Collapse of Communism*, (New York, Oxford University Press, Inc. 1992), page 27.

4 George Weigel, *The Final Revolution: The Resistance Church and the Collapse of Communism*, (New York) Oxford University Press, Inc. 1992), page 3.

5 A. V. Shubin, *Ot "Zastoya" k Reyformum: SSSR v 1917–1985, (From "Stagnation" to Reforms: USSR in 1917–1985),*

(Moscow, Russian Political Encyclopaedia Publisher, 2000), page 24.

6 The number is 14,453 according to Vladlen Sirotkin, Stalin: Kak Zastavit Liudeay Rabotat, (Stalin: How to Make People Work?), (Moscow, Algorithm Publishing, 2004), page 335.

7 Ronald H. Spector, "Vietnam War 1954–1975", Britannica website, published July 20, 1998, consulted on May 8, 2021, https://www.britannica.com/event/Vietnam-War.

8 A. V. Shubin, *Ot "Zastoya" k Reyformum: SSSR v 1917–1985, (From "Stagnation" to Reforms: USSR in 1917–1985),* (Moscow, Russian Political Encyclopaedia Publisher, 2000), page 32.

9 George Crile, *Charlie Wilson's War,* (Great Britain, Atlantic Books, 2007), page 487.

10 George Crile, *Charlie Wilson's War,* (Great Britain, Atlantic Books, 2007), pages 127, 2171 218, 351.

11 The USA was supplying them not only with a cornucopia of low and high-tech weapons but also with satellite intelligence, food, boots, blankets, medicine, automobiles, donkeys, communication devices, early warning devices, and other necessities. The USA even financed building of highways and bridges in Afghanistan so that ordinance can be delivered easily and delivered trees to be planted in the war zone. George Crile, *Charlie Wilson's War,* (Great Britain, Atlantic Books, 2007), pages 217, 347, 354, 355, 367, 370, 397, 398.

12 A. V. Shubin, *Ot "Zastoya" k Reyformum: SSSR v 1917–1985, (From "Stagnation" to Reforms: USSR in 1917–1985),* (Moscow, Russian Political Encyclopaedia Publisher, 2000), page 715.

13 George Crile, *Charlie Wilson's War,* (Great Britain, Atlantic Books, 2007), pages 405, 415, 419.

14 George Weigel, *The Final Revolution: The Resistance Church and the Collapse of Communism,* (New York, Oxford University Press, Inc. 1992), pages 21 to 26.

15 Mark Solonin, 22 *Yunya: Anatomya Catastrophyee, (June 22: Anatomy of the Catastrophe),* (Moscow, Yauza-Press, Eksmo, 2009).
16 A. V. Shubin, *Ot "Zastoya" k Reyformum: SSSR v 1917–1985, (From "Stagnation" to Reforms: USSR in 1917–1985),* (Moscow, Russian Political Encyclopaedia Publisher, 2000), pages 451, 453.
17 Andrei Burovsky, *Da Zdrastvooyet "Zastoy", (Long Live "Stagnation"),* (Yauza-Press, Eksmo Publishing, Moscow, 2010), page 107.
18 George Weigel, *The Final Revolution: The Resistance Church and the Collapse of Communism,* (New York, Oxford University Press, Inc. 1992), page 27.
19 George Weigel, *The Final Revolution: The Resistance Church and the Collapse of Communism,* (New York, Oxford University Press, Inc. 1992), page 29.
20 Blaine Harden, *Escape from Camp 14: One Man's Remarkable Odyssey from North Korea to Freedom in the West,* (London, Pan Books an imprint of Pan Macmillan, 2015), page 172.
21 Deirdre Shesgreen, USA Today website, published January 3, 2019, consulted on July 1, 2021, https://eu.usatoday.com/story/news/world/2019/01/02/president-trump-former-soviet-union-right-invade-afghanistan/2466897002/.
22 A. V. Shubin, *Ot "Zastoya" k Reyformum: SSSR v 1917–1985, (From "Stagnation" to Reforms: USSR in 1917–1985),* (Moscow, Russian Political Encyclopaedia Publisher, 2000), page 77.
23 George Crile, *Charlie Wilson's War,* (Great Britain, Atlantic Books, 2007), page 438; A MIG cost about 20 million dollars at the time. (George Crile, *Charlie Wilson's War,* (Great Britain, Atlantic Books, 2007), page 437.)
24 See, for example, Jacques Levesque, The Enigma of 1989: The USSR and the Liberation of Eastern Europe, California Digital Library website, page 10, https://publishing.cdlib.

org/ucpressebooks/view?docId=ft4q2nb3h6&chunk.id=d0e281&toc.depth=1&toc.id=0&brand=ucpress.

25 Barbara Demick, *Nothing to Envy: Real Lives in North Korea*, (Granta Publications, 2010), page 115.

26 Barbara Demick, *Nothing to Envy: Real Lives in North Korea*, (Granta Publications, 2010), page 67.

27 Blaine Harden, *Escape from Camp 14: One Man's Remarkable Odyssey from North Korea to Freedom in the West*, (London, Pan Books an imprint of Pan Macmillan, 2015), page 46.

28 Barbara Demick, *Nothing to Envy: Real Lives in North Korea*, (Granta Publications, 2010), page 183.

29 Barbara Demick, *Nothing to Envy: Real Lives in North Korea*, (Granta Publications, 2010), page 308 mentions North Korean diplomats being caught smuggling drugs and counterfeit money; Blaine Harden, *Escape from Camp 14: One Man's Remarkable Odyssey from North Korea to Freedom in the West*, (London, Pan Books an imprint of Pan Macmillan, 2015), page 46 talks of "criminal enterprises that funnel hard currency to Pyongyang".

30 Blaine Harden, *Escape from Camp 14: One Man's Remarkable Odyssey from North Korea to Freedom in the West*, (London, Pan Books an imprint of Pan Macmillan, 2015), page 199.

31 Barbara Demick, *Nothing to Envy: Real Lives in North Korea*, (Granta Publications, 2010), page 145.

32 Jeremy Smith, *The Fall of Soviet Communism 1985–91*, (Palgrave Macmillan, 2005), page 110.

33 Jacques Levesque, The Enigma of 1989: The USSR and the Liberation of Eastern Europe, California Digital Library website, page 9, https://publishing.cdlib.org/ucpressebooks/view?docId=ft4q2nb3h6&chunk.id=d0e281&toc.depth=1&toc.id=0&brand=ucpress.

34 A. V. Shubin, *Ot "Zastoya" k Reyformum: SSSR v 1917–1985, (From "Stagnation" to Reforms: USSR in 1917–1985)*, (Moscow, Russian Political Encyclopaedia Publisher, 2000), page 95.

35 A. V. Shubin, *Ot "Zastoya" k Reyformum: SSSR v 1917–1985, (From "Stagnation" to Reforms: USSR in 1917–1985),* (Moscow, Russian Political Encyclopaedia Publisher, 2000), page 715.

36 A. V. Shubin, *Ot "Zastoya" k Reyformum: SSSR v 1917–1985, (From "Stagnation" to Reforms: USSR in 1917–1985),* (Moscow, Russian Political Encyclopaedia Publisher, 2000) page 82.

37 George Crile, *Charlie Wilson's War,* (Great Britain, Atlantic Books, 2007), page 438.

38 The people killed in this way were predominately Ukrainians. However, some regions settled with other nationalities, including Russians, suffered as well.

39 R. J. Rummel, *Never Again: Ending War, Democide, & Famine Through Democratic Freedom,* (nonfiction supplement), (The United States of America, Llumina Press, 2005, page 100.

40 R. J. Rummel, *Never Again: Ending War, Democide, & Famine Through Democratic Freedom,* (nonfiction supplement), (The United States of America, Llumina Press, 2005, page 94.

41 Igor Bunich, *Zlatoto na Partiata (The Party's Gold),* (Sofia, Prozoretz publishing house, 1993), page 126.

42 Marina Svanidze, *Estoricheskiye Hroniki si Nikolaim Svanidze, (Historical Chronicles with Nikolai Svanidze),* Volume one, (Amphora Publishers, Saint Petersburg, 2007), page 194.

43 Peter Kenez, *A History of the Soviet Union from the Beginning to the End,* (Cambridge, Cambridge University Press, 2006), page 43.

44 Peter Kenez, *A History of the Soviet Union from the Beginning to the End,* (Cambridge, Cambridge University Press, 2006), pages 44, 45.

45 Boris Sokolov, *Pravda o Velikoi Otechestvennoi Voinye: Sbornik Statei (The Truth of the Great Patriotic War: Collection of Articles),* (St. Petersburg, Aleteiia Publishing, 1998), page 171.

46 Leonid Mlechin, *Lenin: Soblaznenie Rossii (Lenin: The Seduction of Russia)*, (Peter Publishing, Moscow, 2012), page 292.

47 Roy Medvedev, *Bleejnee Krug Stalina: Saratnikee Vajdyah. (The Inner Circle of Stalin: Associates of the Chief)*, (Eksmo, Yauza-Press, 2005), page 77.

48 Viktor Suvorov, *Tya Se Kazvashay Tatiana: Hronika Na Veleekoto Deseteeletiyeh (She Was Called Tatiana: A Chronicle of the Great Decade)*, (Fakel Express publishing, 2013), page 89.

49 Peter Kenez, *A History of the Soviet Union from the Beginning to the End*, (Cambridge, Cambridge University Press, 2006), page 167.

50 Mark Solonin, *22 Yunya: Anatomya Catastrophyee, (June 22: Anatomy of the Catastrophe)*, (Moscow, Yauza-Press, Eksmo, 2009), page 403, 405.

51 Mark Solonin, *Niet Blaga na Voyne (Nothing Good Comes from War)*, (Moscow, Yauza-Press, 2012).

52 Martin Ebon, *Svetlana: The Incredible Story of Stalin's Daughter*, (New York, Signet Books published by The New American Library, 1967), page 74.

53 Andrei Burovsky, *Da Zdrastvooyet "Zastoy", (Long Live "Stagnation")*, (Yauza-Press, Eksmo, Moscow, 2010), page 222.

54 Viktor Suvorov, *Tya Se Kazvashay Tatiana: Hronika Na Veleekoto Deseteeletiyeh (She Was Called Tatiana: A Chronicle of the Great Decade)*, (Fakel Express publishing, 2013), page 94.

55 Peter Kenez, *A History of the Soviet Union from the Beginning to the End*, (Cambridge, Cambridge University Press, 2006), page 167.

56 Kaystoot Zakoretskiy, *Tret'ia miravaya voina Stalina (Stalin's World War III)*, (Moscow, Yauza-Press, 2009), page 370.

57 Andrei Burovsky, *Da Zdrastvooyet "Zastoy", (Long Live "Stagnation")*, (Yauza-Press, Eksmo, Moscow, 2010), page 157.

58 Robert V. Daniels, *The End of the Communist Revolution, (published by Taylor & Francis e-Library, 2003)*, page 61.

59 Vladislav M. Zubok, *Neoodafshyasya Imperia: Sovietskee Sayooz v Holodnoy Voyne ot Stalina daw Gorbachova, (A Failed Empire: The Soviet Union in the Cold War from Stalin to Gorbachev)*, (Moscow, Russian Political Encyclopedia, 2011), page 393.

60 Edited by Michael Ellman and Vladimir Kontorovich, *The Destruction of the Soviet Economic System: An Insiders' History*, (M. E. Sharpe, Inc., 1998), page 57.

References

"100 Woody Allen Quotes That Highlight His Take on Life", The Famous People website, https://quotes.thefamouspeople.com/woody-allen-3439.php.

1941. Feelm Treeyeti "Aglushitilnoiyeh Malchaneyay" – Polneey Voipoosk, (1941. Third film "Deafening Silence" – full length documentary), Serialyee Ookraniee Premiere (Ukrainian Series Premiere) YouTube channel, published on April 29, 2015, https://www.youtube.com/watch?v=B9N3Zri--Cc.

"A Deputy Said 'No' to the Eternal Putin, Culture of Dignity YouTube Channel", published on June 10, 2020, https://www.youtube.com/watch?v=zCn9RNKRcJA.

"A Tsunami of Maladies Afflicting the Soul of Our Universities (THE SAAD TRUTH_676)", Gad Saad YouTube channel, published on June 19, 2018, https://www.youtube.com/watch?v=GXjzYh6p4WE&t=2601s.

"Armed and extremely dangerous Russian drivers | Road Rage in Russia", Epic Driving YouTube channel, published on March 17, 2016, https://www.youtube.com/watch?v=J2Dl2QLkKOs.

"Avgoostovskiyeh Ratinggee Adabrayneeyah" (August Approval Ratings), Levada Center website, published on August 6, 2014, https://web.archive.org/web/20140808235142/http://www.levada.ru/06-08-2014/avgustovskie-reitingi-odobreniya.

"Babies' First Names 2020", National Records of Scotland website, published on March 23, 2021, https://www.nrscotland.gov.uk/files//statistics/babies-names/20/babies-first-names-20-report.pdf.

"Balnitza v Rassee-Ujhas e Strah-Viy Takoyeh Vidilee? (Blog o Jhiznee), (A Hospital in Russia-Horror and Fear-Have You Seen Such a Thing?" (Blog About Life), Vladik Fokin-Blog o Jhiznee YouTube channel, on January 2, 2018, https://www.youtube.com/watch?v=Hx-bq-WBEsQ&list=WL&index=2.

"Bashir I Petrov Chastushki" (Bashirov and Petrov Chastushki), Yuri Hovansky's YouTube channel, published on October 4, 2018, https://www.youtube.com/watch?v=LgFxMFfoB4g.

"Boleyeh sta Rassesskiech Tankov, Katoreech 'Nyeh Bilya e Nyet'-III" (More Than a Hundred Russian Tanks, that 'were not and are not there'-3), Om TV YouTube channel, published on January 16, 2015, https://www.youtube.com/watch?v=C4nZeG_Lzbs.

"Boodnee Sverhdejavay" | Putinism kak on yest: Ad Raseeskeekh Balntiz ("A Day in the Life of a Superpower" Putinism as it is: The Hell of the Russian Hospitals), Acute Angle YouTube channel, published on 20 May 2020, https://www.youtube.com/watch?v=GNLnLID5xHc&list=WL&index=4.

"Bulgaria has Europe's largest grey economy, IMF says", IntelliNews website, published on February 8, 2018, https://www.intellinews.com/bulgaria-has-europe-s-largest-grey-economy-imf-says-136465/.

"Can't Pay We'll Take It Away" Series 02 Episode 06 HD, HDSTUFF YouTube channel, published on September 7, 2020, https://www.youtube.com/watch?v=bf05qwrHoYA.

"Chernobyl, the true scale of the accident", World Health Organization website, published on September 5, 2005, https://www.who.int/mediacentre/news/releases/2005/pr38/en/.

"Chernobyl: The end of a three-decade experiment", BBC website, published on February 14, 2019, https://www.bbc.co.uk/news/science-environment-47227767.

"Child Grooming – circular to Police Forces in 2008", published on November 12, 2018, https://www.whatdotheyknow.com/request/child_grooming_circular_to_polic.

"Child sexual exploitation by organised networks: investigation report February 2022", published on February 1, 2022, https://www.iicsa.org.uk/reports-recommendations/publications/investigation/cs-organised-networks/part-h-profiling/h4-failures-record-victim-and-perpetrator-ethnicity.

"Combination – American Boy", Gem Mediatheque YouTube Channel, published on May 7, 2016, https://www.youtube.com/watch?v=W7hAo28NCXc.

"Combination – two small sausages", Gem Mediatheque YouTube Channel, published on February 11, 2018, https://www.youtube.com/watch?v=Zbgr6Hpqcpg.

"Compressed Air Energy Storage", *Science Direct website*, https://www.sciencedirect.com/topics/engineering/compressed-air-energy-storage.

"Darya Besedina Demands Public Budget Hearings", (Darya Besedina treeyehbooyet publeechnyih slooshaneeh byujetah) Darya Besedina YouTube channel, published on October 31, 2019, https://www.youtube.com/watch?v=Qc8vjSCT1AA.

"Darya Besedina vs Mosgorduma. 'Veyaychnee Putin', 'Vashingtonskee Abcom' e Pratyestee Protiv Papravak", (Darya Besedina vs Moscow City Council. "The Eternal Putin", "Washington's Regional Committee" and the Protest Against the Amendments), RTVI Novastee YouTube channel, published on March 14, 2020, https://www.youtube.com/watch?v=Qlbp8NRNfj8.

"David Webb accused of 'white privilege' by CNN legal analyst", Fox News YouTube channel, published on January 16, 2019, https://www.youtube.com/watch?v=BAlig2jW7SA.

"Did Saltykov-Shchedrin: 'When they begin to talk about patriotism in Russia, know: somewhere they stole something'?", geospatialcollaborative website, https://geospatialcollaborative.com/did-saltykov-shchedrin-when-they-begin-to-talk/.

"Division of parents' estate between sons and daughters", February 1, 2004, https://islamqa.info/en/categories/very-important/60/answers/47057/division-of-parents-estate-between-sons-and-daughters.

"Doclatniya zapiska vayenava procurora vitiepskava garnizona o riezutatah pravierki pravavoy e abaronyee daeyaltelnasti v garnizonyeh" (Report by the Military Prosecutor of the Vietiebsk Garrison about the result of the inspection of the legal and defence activity in the garrison), from 5 July 1941, RKKA website, http://rkka.ru/docs/spv/SPV7.htm.

"Dutch Disease", Corporate Finance Institute, updated February 2, 2021, consulted on February 25, 2021, https://corporatefinance institute.com/resources/knowledge/economics/dutch-dis ease/.

"Dyela" Yusefa Stalina (2012), (The "Lifelong Achievement" of Joseph Stalin) (2012), directed by Viktor Pravdyuk, Evgeniy Chelpanov YouTube channel, published on March 25, 2020, https://www.youtube.com/watch?v=nuLT2nBe3JI.

"Environmental Movement", published on Encyclopedia website, updated on May 18, 2018, https://www.encyclopedia.com/earth-and-environment/ecology-and-environmentalism/environmental-studies/environmental-movement.

"Eta Tresh! Chto Realnoh Proeezhodit v Raseeskeekh Balnitzsach" (This Is Trash! What Really Goes on in the Russian Hospitals), published on Dnyevnik Dyeputata YouTube channel, on October 31, 2019, https://www.youtube.com/watch?v=MY9OhrMPn8U.

"Evgeniy Ponasenkov: Pro Adaptazieu Meegrantav v Evropay (S Naoochnoy Tochkee Zraynia), (Evgeniy Ponasenkov: About the Integration of Migrants in Europe (From a Scientific Point of View)", published on the Common Sense YouTube channel, published on June 6, 2016, https://www.youtube.com/watch?v=SXOMp8W5Gug.

"Expert: Kak si Paree ot ES be sizdadina Bulgarska Mafia", (Expert: How A Bulgarian Mafia was Created with EU Money), Vesti website, published on August 9, 2018, https://www.vesti.bg/bulgaria/ekspert-kak-s-pari-ot-es-be-syzdadena-bylgarska-mafiia-6085329.

"Fluctuating asymmetry and preferences for sex-typical bodily characteristics", William M. Brown, Michael E. Price,

Jinsheng Kang, Nicholas Pound, Yue Zhao and Hui Yu, National Center for Biotechnology Information website, published September 2, 2008, https://www.ncbi.nlm.nih.gov/pmc/articles/PMC2529114/.

"Fukushima Daiichi Accident", World Nuclear Organisation website, updated on April 2021, https://world-nuclear.org/information-library/safety-and-security/safety-of-plants/fukushima-daiichi-accident.aspx.

"Gibel Evropayskoy Tvleezatseeyee, Mif o Padeynee Rojdaemostee v Evropay/Evgeniy Ponasenkov" (The European Civilisation is Doomed, The Myth of Dropping Birth Rates in Europe/Evgeniy Ponasenkov), Piervay Naoochni YouTube channel, published on September 15, 2021.

"Granitza Na Zamkye" (The Border is Padlocked), 1937 film, produced by Syoozdyetfilm, directed by Vasily Jhuravlov, All soviet movies on RVISION YouTube channel, published on May 27, 2013, https://www.youtube.com/watch?v=VFnmKhkHn8A.

"Group-based Child Sexual Exploitation Characteristics of Offending", published on December 2020, Home Office website, https://assets.publishing.service.gov.uk/government/uploads/system/uploads/attachment_data/file/944206/Group-based_CSE_Paper.pdf.

"Haladealnik Pabyeajzdyet Televizar" ("The Fridge winning over the TV-set"), Krasnaya Linia YouTube channel, published on December 4, 2018, https://www.youtube.com/watch?v=MoufV4C1Igg&list=WL&index=25.

"HBOs Chernobyl: BUSTED!", Thunderf00t YouTube Channel, published on June 12, 2019, https://www.youtube.com/watch?v=SsdLDFtbdrA.

"Holodomor: Parliament recognises Soviet starvation of Ukrainians as genocide", European Parliament website, published on December 15, 2022, https://www.europarl.

europa.eu/news/en/press-room/20221209IPR64427/holodomor-parliament-recognises-soviet-starvation-of-ukrainians-as-genocide.

"How the World Went to War In 1914", Imperial War Museum website, published on February 5, 2018, https://www.iwm.org.uk/history/how-the-world-went-to-war-in-1914.

"How to Unite your Team: Advice from Napoleon", published on December 31, 2012, on The Grassy Road, https://pennyherscher.com/2012/12/31/how-to-unite-your-team-advice-fro/.

"Inaya launches brutal takedown of Insulate Britain", GB News YouTube channel, published on October 15 2021, https://www.youtube.com/watch?v=g0BM5ri-s-k.

"Inside the Kremlin: The Mind and Policies of Vladimir Putin", carthagecollege YouTube Channel, published on June 26, 2015, https://www.youtube.com/watch?v=s88pMN-3qDRQ&t=343s.

"Isobel's Story", BBC Radio 4 "File on 4" podcast, page 11, published September 27, 2022, http://downloads.bbc.co.uk/rmhttp/fileon4/PAJ_4562_PG12_Isobel.pdf.

"J. Stalin, Glalavokruzhaynieh ot Oospyehav. K Vaprosam Kalhosnavah Dveejaniah" ("Dizzy with Success. Concerning Questions of the Collective-Farm Movement"), 100(0) key documents website, Department of History, Friedrich-Alexander University, https://www.1000dokumente.de/index.html/index.html?c=dokument_ru&dokument=0007_erf&object=translation&l=ru.

"Jack Straw criticised for 'easy meat' comments on abuse", BBC News website, published on January 8, 2011, https://www.bbc.co.uk/news/uk-12142177.

"John Kerry to Russia: You Lost the Cold War, Get Over It", ABC News website, published on March 18, 2014, http://abcnews.go.com/blogs/politics/2014/03/john-kerry-to-russia-you-lost-the-cold-war-get-over-it/.

"Kirk Sorensen @ MRU on LFTR-Liquid Fluoride Thorium Reactors", on gordonmcdowell YouTube channel, published on May 24, 2011, https://www.youtube.com/watch?v=D3rL-08J7fDA.

"Kravchuk o Tom, Pacheymoo Ookrania Atkazalas ot Yadreynava Aruszhia", (Kravchuk on why Ukraine gave up their nuclear weapons), V Gasteeach oo Gardona YouTube channel (At Gordon's YouTube channel), published on October 10, 2016, https://www.youtube.com/watch?v=LGEALnD8Haw.

"Lord Pearson Question in the House of Lords on Grooming Gangs 13 March 2018", Brian London YouTube channel, published on March 17, 2018, https://www.youtube.com/watch?v=BtRcdge3hTE.

"Lyubit po-Russki", IMDb website, https://www.imdb.com/title/tt0178725/.

"Maajid Nawaz On The Muslim Grooming Gangs In Telford Scandal, a debate on the BBC", Patriotic Populist YouTube channel, published on March 24, 2018, https://www.youtube.com/watch?v=_KVtOzYn2Wg.

"Maajid Nawaz: It Is Not Racist to Talk About Muslims in Grooming Gangs", LBC website, published on December 10, 2017, https://www.lbc.co.uk/radio/presenters/maajid-nawaz/not-racist-talk-islam-grooming-gangs/.

"Matt Bunn-How Nuclear Bombs Work", Ronald Veisenberger YouTube channel, published on November 21, 2017, https://www.youtube.com/watch?v=jqLbcNpeBaw.

"Mochit Terroristav v Sarteeriyeh! Starye Soviet ot Putina" (Dipping the Terrorists in the Pit Latrine, Putin Shares Old Wisdom), '5 Canal' YouTube channel, published on May 27, 2014, https://www.youtube.com/watch?v=-2f-Q4K_J70.

"Moi e Anyeggdoti Klasna Travim – Petrov I Bashirov za Kadrom (Parodia)", (We Can Tell Jokes as Well – Petrov and Bashirov Behind the Scenes – Parody), Studia Kvartal 95

Online YouTube channel, published on November 3, 2018, https://www.youtube.com/watch?v=Vax3Y2Z9XE4.

"Mortality rate worldwide in 2012, by energy source", Statista website, published on January 29, 2021, consulted on 26 April 2022, https://www.statista.com/statistics/494425/death-rate-worldwide-by-energy-source/.

"Ne Smaysheeteh Myee Iskandiereh", ("Don't make my Iskanders laugh"), Golos Islama website, published on September 26, 2014, https://golosislama.com/news.php?id=25004.

"Neegayria v Snyegakh" Putinism kak on yest: Ad Raseeskeekh Balntiz ("A Snowy Nigeria" Putinism as it is: The Hell of the Russian Hospitals), Acute Angle YouTube channel, published on September 15, 2020, https://www.youtube.com/watch?v=L4VhuxrC3Is.

"Nuclear Power", https://www.greenpeace.org.uk/challenges/nuclear-power/.

"On your bike! Saudi women allowed to ride bicycles, buggies in public", Al Aribiya News website, April 1, 2013, http://english.alarabiya.net/en/News/middle-east/2013/04/01/On-your-bike-Saudi-women-allowed-to-ride-bikes-in-public.html#.

"ORNL Thorium Molten Salt Reactor Experiment Researchers – Dick Engel and Syd Ball – Dinner & Interview", the gordonmcdowell YouTube Channel, published on September 28, 2012, https://www.youtube.com/watch?v=ENH-jd6NhRc.

"Pakt o Nyenapadeynee Molotova na Ribbentropa. Zveyzdnyeh chas Stalina, chast 2", (The Molotov Ribbentrop Pact. Stalin's finest hour. Part 2), Mark Solonin YouTube channel, published on December 2021, https://www.youtube.com/watch?v=6hUwDIrLrms.

"Paslednyee Mief" (The Last Myth), part 2, Vladimir Sinelnikov YouTube channel, published on July 11, 2012, https://www.youtube.com/watch?v=kl4vVYgLnds&list=PL8E5DC8F66DFF2CB2&index=2.

"Paslednyee Mief", (The Last Myth), part 1, Vladimir Sinelnikov YouTube channel, published on July 11, 2012, https://www.youtube.com/watch?v=YtukSNdQ21s&list=PL8E5DC8F66DFF2CB2.

"Petroleum Technology History Part 1 – Background", http://www.greatachievements.org/?id=3677.

"Postanovleneyeah Sayezdah Narodneekh Deputatov SSSR o Paktyeh Molotova Ribbentropa ot 24.09.1989" (Decree of the People's Deputy Congress of USSR about the Molotov-Ribbentrop Pact from 24.09.1989), Documentee Dvadsatava Vyekah website (Documents from the 20th century website), http://doc20vek.ru/node/3261.

"Pragrama Sergeiya Darienka (31.10.1999). Gost: Vladimir Putin" (The programme of Sergei Darienko (31.10.1999). Guest: Vladimir Putin), RVISION YouTube channel, published on September 26, 2016, https://www.youtube.com/watch?v=wVciK18nEeA&t=493s.

"Praycrastnoyeh Dalehko" ("My Bright Future"), Lubimiyah Muzika YouTube channel, published on April 16, 2015, https://www.youtube.com/watch?v=m7A4uy6Nw0k.

"Predoopreschdeyniyeh o svastikay" (*Warning about the swastika*) from 11.11.1922, Naslediyeh A V Lunacharskava (The Heritage of A. V. Lunacharsky) website, 2021, http://lunacharsky.newgod.su/articles/preduprezhdenie/.

"Putin compares 'Western Woke' to Soviet Bolshevism (Marxism) via RT", Main Street Media YouTube channel, published on November 1, 2021, https://www.youtube.com/watch?v=O0tNi5w3mo4.

"Putin Doesn't Object to Russia Joining NATO", Kommersant Daily website, published on March 7, 2000, https://www.kommersant.ru/doc/142046.

"Putin: raseeyeski myedved nee oo kavo sprasheevat nyeh budyet. Valdie, 24.10.2014", (Putin: the Russian bear is not going to ask for permission), MIR 24 YouTube channel, published on October 24, 2014, https://www.youtube.com/watch?v=EbHMIluLYmI.

"Putin's speech after taking Crimea", RT in Russian YouTube Channel, streamed live on March 18, 2014, https://www.youtube.com/watch?v=mhrPXMQUNBA.

"Putin's Speech before the Federal Assembly recorded from the Russia 1 TV Channel", Ilya Makrin YouTube channel, published on March 1, 2018, https://www.youtube.com/watch?v=_u1IKd9vgfo.

"Reytch Stalina Na Stantsee Mayakovskaya 6 Nayabreeya 1941, polnaya vyerseeya" (Stalin's speech given in the Mayakovskaya underground Metro station on 6 November 1941, Full Version), History Lab YouTube channel, published on May 1, 2020, https://www.youtube.com/watch?v=BIc18YqgyiE. (The speech is part of the film "For the Complete Vanquishing of German Invaders", directed by L. Varlamova, produced by the Central Newsreel Studio.)

"Robert Hargraves-Thorium energy cheaper than coal at ThEC12" lecture, gordonmcdowell YouTube website, December 9, 2012, https://www.youtube.com/watch?v=ayIy-iVua8cY.

"Russia activists push state to fix potholes", Al Jazeera English YouTube channel, published on August 19, 2013, https://www.youtube.com/watch?v=eQoeBUKZQBg.

"Russia Finally Found a way to resolve all Potholes on Road", Awesome Stuff YouTube channel, published on September 4, 2018, https://www.youtube.com/watch?v=-guO722mvH0.

"Russian Bombers Did Not Carry Nuclear Weapons to British Borders – Military Source", The Moscow Times website, February 2, 2015, https://themoscowtimes.com/articles/russian-bombers-did-not-carry-nuclear-weapons-to-british-borders-military-source-43463.

"Russian nuclear accident: Medics fear 'radioactive patients'", BBC News website, published on August 23, 2019, https://www.bbc.co.uk/news/world-europe-49432681.

"Russia's T-14 Armata Tank Is Amazing (But There Is a Big Problem)", The National Interest website, published on April 6, 2019, https://nationalinterest.org/blog/buzz/russias-t-14-armata-tank-amazing-there-big-problem-51022.

"Sanksee? Ne Smaysheeteh Myee Iskandiereh", ("Sanctions? Don't make my Iskanders laugh"), RT YouTube channel, published on September 25, 2014, https://www.youtube.com/watch?v=JcMhih8E9l0.

"Sex-gang's background must be acknowledged without fear of racism" – UK MP, https://www.youtube.com/watch?v=A57hnJx8kVE, RT YouTube channel, published on August 12, 2017.

"Sexual Offences Act 2003", https://www.legislation.gov.uk/ukpga/2003/42/pdfs/ukpga_20030042_en.pdf.

"Shark Attack", article from Wikipedia website, https://en.wikipedia.org/wiki/Shark_attack#cite_note-5.

"Shrapnel from mortars, grenades and, above all, artillery projectile bombs, or shells, would account for an estimated 60 percent of the 9.7 million military fatalities of World War I." Caroline Alexander, "The Shock of War", World War I: 100 Years Later, Smithsonian Magazine website, published on September 2010, https://www.smithsonianmag.com/history/the-shock-of-war-55376701/.

"SibLAG of OGPU Report on the Economic Development of Nareem by the Special Settlers from May 1931 to June 1932, towards 7 August 1932", published on the Estoricheskiye Materialy (Historical Materials) website, http://istmat.info/node/58244.

"Slavery in the United States", Economic History Association website, https://eh.net/encyclopedia/slavery-in-the-united-states/.

"Soviet Tank BT-7 (Red Army)", yolkhere YouTube channel, published on February 3, 2012, https://www.youtube.com/watch?v=Jzpom1gZcag.

"Spanish nighttime solar energy fraud 'unlikely in UK'", The Ecologist website, published on April 16, 2010, https://theecologist.org/2010/apr/16/spanish-nighttime-solar-energy-fraud-unlikely-uk.

"Squeeze Germany Until the Pips squeak", Richard M Langworth website, published on September 14, 2014, 2020, https://richardlangworth.com/squeeze-germany.

"SSSR: Kakooyo Stranu Patayreealyee ..." (USSR: What a Country We Lost...), published on the Samoy Sock 2 YouTube channel on June 18, 2018, https://www.youtube.com/watch?v=d-S0cvQeTjFI&list=PL1E32Douoi6IINXhXWHbvyreWGCdwz-j34&index=3.

"Statistics and Data", Honour Based Violence Awareness Network website, 'http://hbv-awareness.com/statistics-data/'.

"Sukhoi Su-30MKM Dances in the Sky over Singapore with Thrust Vectoring Maneuvers – AINtv", Aviation International News YouTube channel, published on February 8, 2018, https://www.youtube.com/watch?v=gNx6DV8EcF8.

"Tanke T-64, Katoreech 'Nyeh Bilya e Nyet'-II. Russian Tanks in Ukraine! Part 2" (The T-64 tanks which 'were not and are not there'-2), Om TV YouTube channel, published on September 2015, https://www.youtube.com/watch?v=n0MzDo7HbyU.

"Tanke T-72B3, Katoreech 'Nyeh Bilya e Nyet'-I. Russian Tanks in Ukraine! Part 1" (The T-72B3 tanks which 'were not and are not there'-I), Om TV YouTube channel, published on September 5, 2015, https://www.youtube.com/watch?v=gupUasybpuw.

"The Complete Case for Nuclear", Environmental Progress website, https://environmentalprogress.org/the-complete-case-for-nuclear.

"The Great Citizen (1937)", Mair Nur-Bek YouTube, published on February 28, 2018, https://www.youtube.com/watch?v=iX-Qo1o4RrpI.

"The Molotov-Ribbentrop Pact: Secretly and Suddenly", BBC website, published on July 31, 2009, https://www.bbc.com/russian/russia/2009/08/090731_ussr_germany_pact_history.

"The Nation American journal", published on July 20, 1998, https://www.britannica.com/topic/The-Nation-American-journal.

"The pact between Stalin and Hitler: a triumph or tragedy", (Pact Stalina suh Gitlerom: trioomph eleh tragedia), Radio Liberty YouTube channel, streamed live on August 26, 2019, https://www.youtube.com/watch?v=E-7CnMRS-Xw.

"The Pension Age Raised in Russia", http://www.ng.ru/itog/2018-12-28/1_7476_itog2.html, Nezavisimaia, published on December 28, 2018.

"The Russian Civilization", Common Sense YouTube channel, published on December 9, 2013, https://www.youtube.com/watch?v=sizcDk0UZqo.

"The Soviet Story 2008 – English subtitles", The Ben Tame YouTube channel, published on August 30, 2019, https://www.youtube.com/watch?v=v7IrB_6mX4k.

"The True Cost of Wind-Ryan M. Yonk", Independent Institute YouTube channel, published on December 8, 2015, https://www.youtube.com/watch?v=WC8z9GTQOYA&list=WL&index=6.

"Things we won't say about race that are true", a 2015 Channel 4 documentary, published on March 22, 2015, Mario YouTube Channel, https://www.youtube.com/watch?v=Tb2iFikOwYU.

"This is why foreign aid is bad for less developed countries", Thomas Sowell TV YouTube Channel, published on March 13, 2021, https://www.youtube.com/watch?v=ZPxjquGHlyU.

"Thorium Containing Welding Rod" (1990s), Museum of Radiation and Radioactivity website, https://www.orau.org/health-physics-museum/collection/consumer/products-containing-thorium/welding-rod.html.

"Trump: the United States won two world wars and put communism on the knees", consulted on July 13, 2023, http://weaponews.com/news/19816-trump-the-united-states-won-two-world-wars-and-put-communism-on-the-kn.html.

"Trump: The United States won two world wars and put communism on the knees", Weapon News website, published on December 9, 2017, http://weaponews.com/news/19816-trump-the-united-states-won-two-world-wars-and-put-communism-on-the-kn.html.

"U.S. Immigration Since 1965", History tv channel website, published on June 7, 2019, https://www.history.com/topics/immigration/us-immigration-since-1965.

"Udarnaya Sila" (Striking Force) YouTube channel, https://www.youtube.com/channel/UCFxyaS_iXLK-MCLyu-fgQZg/featured.

"UK children suffered sex abuse on 'industrial scale'", BBC News website, published on March 3, 2015, https://www.bbc.co.uk/news/uk-31691061.

"UK Home Secretary Suella Braverman faces backlash over 'racist' comments about British-Pakistani men", Middle East Eye YouTube channel, published on April 4, 2023, https://www.youtube.com/shorts/Pd0EkWURmFg.

"UK's most popular baby names of 2021 so far", Independent website, published on June 15, 2021, https://www.independent.co.uk/life-style/health-and-families/baby-names-popular-uk-2021-b1866059.html.

"Ukip launch EU election campaign amid candidate controversy", Channel 4 News YouTube channel, published on April 18, 2018, https://www.youtube.com/watch?v=iRV8kwHyZJ0.

"Vegetius fl. ad 379–395 Roman military writer", Oxford Reference website, no publish date, https://www.oxfordreference.com/view/10.1093/acref/9780191866692.001.0001/q-oro-ed6-00011152.

"Voroshilovskiy Strelok", (Voroshilov Sharpshooter) (1999), Veselin Strahilov YouTube channel, published on October 9, 2018, https://www.youtube.com/watch?v=wH-FkNGo9qU.

"What's the deal with political correctness?", Reachout website, https://au.reachout.com/articles/whats-the-deal-with-political-correctness.

"Who is the biggest killer on the planet?", Hardy Diagnostics website, http://www.hardydiagnostics.com/wp-content/uploads/2016/05/The-Most-Deadly-Animals.pdf.

"Wolf whistling can now be reported as a hate crime", BBC News website, published on July 20, 2016, http://www.bbc.co.uk/newsbeat/article/36835470/wolf-whistling-can-now-be-reported-as-a-hate-crime.

"Your Children Will Be Given to the Gays if You Don't Vote: A Disgusting Agitation for Constitutional Amendment", Informational Family Policies Protal "Ivan - Chay" YouTube channel, published on June 2, 2020, https://www.youtube.com/watch?v=YqD_2G2bZTc.

"Yugoslavia–ruska pesma, prevod na sribski", Serbskijkazak (Serbian Cossack) YouTube channel, published on March 31, 2014, https://www.youtube.com/watch?v=GYQJEEOKqW-c&list=RDjGxRzx5DNLw&index=17.

"Za prozata na poetitay" (About the prose of the poets), Capital BG website, https://www.capital.bg/biznes/media_i_reklama/2000/05/12/203074_za_prozata_na_poetite/.

"Zaprayschenee Efeer Eha Maskvoiy pro Boy za Donestkee Aeraport" ("Echo of Moscow Forbidden Airtime about the battle of Donestk Airport"), Dax Ure YouTube channel, published on November 2, 2014, https://www.youtube.com/watch?v=DBNm-I56cAg.

"Zimmermann Telegram: United States-European history (1917)", Britannica website, https://www.britannica.com/event/Zimmermann-Telegram.

Abraham, John, "Biofuels can help solve climate change, especially with a carbon tax", The Guardian website, published on March 14, 2018, https://www.theguardian.com/environment/climate-consensus-97-per-cent/2018/mar/14/biofuels-can-help-solve-climate-change-especially-with-a-carbon-tax.

Abramowitz, Alan I., "Did Russian Interference Affect the 2016 Election Results", published on August 8, 2019, https://centerforpolitics.org/crystalball/articles/did-russian-interference-affect-the-2016-election-results/.

Acemoglu, Daron and Robinson, James A., "Why foreign aid fails – and how to really help Africa", The Spectator website, published on January 25, 2014, https://www.spectator.co.uk/2014/01/why-aid-fails/.

Afzal, Nazir, "Three Girls: I prosecuted the Rochdale child grooming gang – it wasn't about race", International Business Times website, published on May 17, 2017, https://www.ibtimes.co.uk/i-prosecuted-rochdale-child-grooming-gang-it-wasnt-about-race-1621370.

Allen, Henry, "Hot Disputes", published October 1, 1981, https://www.washingtonpost.com/archive/lifestyle/1981/10/01/hot-disputes-38/6621d792-a922-4093-858d-aa056663eeee/.

Apple Books Formatting Guidelines, Apple website, https://help.apple.com/itc/applebooksstoreformatting/en.lproj/static.html#itcb1219ee5c.

Atlas, Scott W., Birge, John R., Keeney, Ralph L. and Lipton, Alexander, "The COVID-19 shutdown will cost Americans millions of years of life", The Hill website, published on May 25, 2020, https://thehill.com/opinion/healthcare/499394-the-covid-19-shutdown-will-cost-americans-millions-of-years-of-life.

Avtorhanov, Abdurakhman, *Zagadkata Okolo Sm'rtah Na Stalin.* (*The Mystery of Stalin's Death*), (Interprint publishing, Sofia, 1991).

Avtorhanov, Abdurakhman, *Zagatka Smyearttee Stalina (The Mystery of Stalin's Death)*, (Moscow, Ex Libris Slovo Soviet-British co-operative venture, 1992).

Baker, Neal, "TOWN OF SIN What was the Rotherham sex abuse scandal, who were the child grooming gang and are the law changes proposed?", published on November 28, 2018, https://www.thesun.co.uk/news/4302003/rotherham-sex-abuse-scandal-child-grooming-exploitation-sarah-champion-mp/.

Batty, David and agencies, "White girls seen as 'easy meat' by Pakistani rapists", said Jack Straw, The Guardian website, published on January 8, 2011, https://www.theguardian.com/world/2011/jan/08/jack-straw-white-girls-easy-meat.

Beshanov, Vladimir, *Tankaviy Pagrom: Kuda Ischesley 28 Teysciatch Soviestskyekh Tankov (The 1941 Tank Rout: How 28 Thousand Soviet Tanks Disappeared)*, (Minsk, Harvest, 2004).

Besser, Linton, "Dead white man's clothes", Australian Broadcasting Corporation website, updated on October 21, 2021, https://www.abc.net.au/news/2021-08-12/fast-fashion-turning-parts-ghana-into-toxic-landfill/100358702.

Bindel, Julie, "Britain's honour crime shame", published January 14, 2019, https://unherd.com/2019/01/britains-honour-crime-shame.

Birstein, Vadim J., *SMERSH – Stalin's Secret Weapon*, (London, Biteback Publishing, 2011).

Birstein, Vadim J., *The Perversion of Knowledge: The True Story of Soviet Science*, (USA, Westview Press, 2001).

Blakemore, Erin, "There Are Only Two Shakers Left in the World", published January 6, 2017, https://www.smithsonianmag.com/smart-news/there-are-only-two-shakers-left-world-180961701/.

Bleiker, Carla, "Women's rights in the Islamic world", Deutsche Welle website, September 27, 2017, https://www.dw.com/en/womens-rights-in-the-islamic-world/a-40714427.

Born, Matt, "Race fears halt film on Asian sex 'grooming'", The Telegraph website on May 21, 2004, https://www.telegraph.co.uk/news/uknews/1462413/Race-fears-halt-film-on-Asian-sex-grooming.html.

Bryson, Bill, *A Short History of Nearly Everything,* (Black Swan).

Buchanan, Patrick J., *Churchill, Hitler, and "The Unnecessary War": How Britain Lost Its Empire and the West Lost the World,* (New York, Crown Publishers, 2008).

Bunich, Igor, *Zlatoto na Partiata (The Party's Gold),* (Sofia, Prozoretz publishing house, 1993).

Burke, Joe-Rojas, "Darwin's Pitbull: Richard Dawkins on evolution and unintelligent design", Oregon Live website, published on October 9, 2009, https://www.oregonlive.com/news/2009/10/darwins_pitbull_richard_dawkin.html.

Burovsky, Andrei, Da Zdrastvooyet "Zastoy", (*Long Live "Stagnation"), (*Yauza-Press, Eksmo, Moscow, 2010).

Buttar, Prit, *Between Giants: The Battle for the Baltics in World War II,* (Oxford, Osprey Publishing).

Carruthers, Bob, *Hitler's Violent Youth: How Trench Warfare and Street Fighting Moulded Hitler* (England, Pen & Sword Military, 2015, e-book edition).

Carvajal, Doreen and Castle, Stephen, "Bulgarian corruption troubling EU", New York Times website, published on October 15, 2008, https://www.nytimes.com/2008/10/15/world/europe/15iht-bulgaria.4.16989483.html.

Centenary News, First World War 1914–1918, published on May 2, 2014, https://centenarynews.com/article?id=1616.

Chadwick, Jonathan, "Producing energy from wind or solar is now CHEAPER than coal as campaigners demand power stations are shut down", Daily Mail website, published on March 24, 2020, https://www.dailymail.co.uk/sciencetech/article-8104801/Energy-renewables-cheaper-coal-says-report.html.

Charen, Mona, *Sex Matters: How Modern Feminism Lost Touch with Science, Love, and Common Sense,* (United States of America, Crown Forum, a division of Penguin Random House LLC, 2018).

Cheloukhine, Serguei, Haberfeld, M.R., *Russian Organized Corruption Networks and their International Trajectories,* (New York, London, Springer, 2011).

Chen, James, "Investopedia website", updated October 31, 2021, https://www.investopedia.com/terms/d/dutchdisease.asp.

Chenel, Thomas and Moynihan, Qayyah, "These are the 13 most corrupt countries in Europe", Business Insider website, published on February 13, 2019, https://www.businessinsider.com/these-are-the-13-most-corrupt-countries-in-europe-2019-2?r=US&IR=T.

Chenoweth, P. J., Sexual Behaviour of the Bull: A Review, Journal of Dairy Science, Volume 66, Issue 1, January 1983, page 174, https://www.sciencedirect.com/science/article/pii/S0022030283817706.

Chertkovskaya, Ekaterina, Paulsson, Alexander, Barca, Stefania, *Towards A Political Economy of Degrowth,* (London, Rowman & Littlefield International Ltd, 2019).

Chossudovsky, Michel, Prof., "Hillary Clinton: 'We Created Al Qaeda', The Protagonists of the "Global War on Terrorism" are the Terrorists", Global Research website, published on June 1, 2013, http://www.globalresearch.ca/hillary-clinton-we-created-al-qaeda/5337222.

Chuev, Sergei, *Prakliatiye Soldatiy: Praydatilee Na Staranyeh III Raykha, (The Damned Soldiers: Traitors Siding with the Third Reich),* (Moscow, Yauza-Press, Eksmo, 2004).

Conca, James, "How Deadly Is Your Kilowatt? We Rank The Killer Energy Sources", Forbes website, published on June 10, 2012, https://www.forbes.com/sites/jamesconca/2012/06/10/energys-deathprint-a-price-always-paid/#3b7cf014709b.

Conquest, Robert, *The Harvest of Sorrow: Soviet Collectivization and the Terror – Famine,* (New York, Oxford University Press Inc., 1986).

Copenhagen Consensus Centre Director Bjorn Lomborg according to "World spending $240b on green subsidies for 'virtually nil impact'", Sky News Australia website, published on August 11, 2019, https://www.skynews.com.au/details/_6071657727001.

Cowell, Alan, "Nuclear Waste Convoy Stirs Angry Protests in Germany", New York Times website, published on March 4, 1997, https://www.nytimes.com/1997/03/04/world/nuclear-waste-convoy-stirs-angry-protests-in-germany.html.

Creviston, A.S., Soverns, Tony, and Gengenbach, Gary, "DISTRIBUTED POWER, RENEWABLES, STORED ENERGY AND THE GRID BLINKLESS® SYNCHRONOUS INVERTER SYSTEM CAPABILITIES AND APPLICATIONS", page 2, Go Electric Inc website, https://goelectricinc.com/wp-content/uploads/2017/08/Distributed-Power-Renewables-Stored-Energy-and-the-Grid.pdf.

Crile, George, *Charlie Wilson's War,* (Great Britain, Atlantic Books, 2007).

Cunningham, Hugo S., "On the Transfer to the Eight-Hour Working Day, The Seven-Day Work Week, and On the Prohibition of Unauthorized Departure by Laborers, and Office Workers from Factories and Offices", published December 28, 2000, http://www.cyberussr.com/rus/uk-trud-e.html.

D'Souza, Dinesh, *The Big Lie: Exposing the Nazi Roots of the American Left,* (USA, Regnery Publishing, 2017).

Dallin, David J. and Nicolaevsky, Boris I., *Forced Labor in Soviet Russia,* (London, Hollis and Carter, 1948).

Daniels, Robert V., *The End of the Communist Revolution,* (published by Taylor & Francis e-Library, 2003).

De Klerk, F. W. giving interview to The Atlantic, published on September 9, 2017, https://www.theatlantic.com/international/archive/2017/09/north-korea-south-africa/539265/.

De Mesquita, Bruce Bueno and Smith, Alistair, *The Dictator's Handbook: Why Bad Behavior Is Almost Always Good Politics*, (New York, Public Affairs, 2012).

De Waal, Thomas, *The Caucasus: An Introduction*, (Oxford University Press, New York, 2010).

De Waal, Thomas, *The Caucasus: An introduction*, (United States of America, Oxford University Press, 2010).

Dearden, Lizzie, "Grooming gang review kept secret as Home Office claims releasing findings 'not in public interest'", Independent website, published on February 21, 2020, https://www.independent.co.uk/news/uk/home-news/grooming-gang-rotherham-review-home-office-findings-a9344896.html.

Dearden, Lizzie, "Grooming 'epidemic' as almost 19,000 children identified as sexual exploitation victims in England", published on December 28, 2019, https://www.independent.co.uk/news/uk/home-news/grooming-child-sex-abuse-exploitation-rotherham-rochdale-police-a9215261.html

Demick, Barbara, *Nothing to Envy: Real Lives in North Korea*, (Granta Publications, 2010).

Duell, Mark, "Ethnicity of child abusers MUST be recorded to tackle grooming gangs, says landmark report – after police and councils 'failed, ignored and blamed' victims as young as 12 because authorities 'didn't want to become another Rotherham'", published on February 1, 2022, https://www.dailymail.co.uk/news/article-10463833/Scathing-report-finds-extensive-failures-way-child-exploitation-tackled.html.

Dzenis, Sandra and Faria, Filipe Nobre, "Political Correctness: the Twofold Protection of Liberalism", Springer Link website, published on June 17, 2019, https://link.springer.com/article/10.1007/s11406-019-00094-4.

Ebon, Martin, *Svetlana: The Incredible Story of Stalin's Daughter*, (New York, Signet Books published by The New American Library, 1967).

Echo of Moscow radio station, vsegard1 YouTube channel, published on February 18, 2016, https://www.youtube.com/watch?v=H_rpPXBZ2ms&list=WL&index=3.

Eerkens, Jeff W., *The Nuclear Imperative: A Critical Look at the Approaching Energy Crisis (More Physics for Presidents)*, (Dordrecht Heidelberg London New York, Springer, 2010).

Ellman, Michael and Kontorovich, Vladimir, *The Destruction of the Soviet Economic System: An Insider's History*, (M. E. Sharpe, Inc., 1998).

Elsheikh, Badawy M., Journal of Radiation Research and Applied Sciences, "Safety assessment of molten salt reactors in comparison with light water reactors", Science Direct website, published on October 26, 2013, https://www.sciencedirect.com/science/article/pii/S1687850713000101.

Ermolov, Igor: *Ruskoyeh Gosudarstvoh v Nymetskom Taylieu: Estoria Lokotskovo Samo-oopravleniya 1941–1943 (A Russian State in the German Rear: History of the Lokot Autonomy 1941–1943)*, (Moscow 2009, Centrepoligraph).

European Parliament resolution on the 80th anniversary of the start of the Second World War and the importance of European remembrance for the future of Europe, European Parliament website, http://www.europarl.europa.eu/doceo/document/B-9-2019-0098_EN.html.

Fedoseyev, Anatolii, *Zapadnya: Chelovek i sotsializm (Trap: Man and Socialism)*, (Frankfurt/Main, Germany, Possev-Verlag, 1976).

Feerosov, S L, *Eestoria Rasee: Oochebnik diliya Srednyeevah Prasfessionalnava Abrazavania, (History of Russia: Textbook for Intermediate Professional Education)*, (Moscow, Yourite Publishing, 2019).

Feminism Book, The, (London, Dorling Kingsley Limited, A Penguin Random House Company, 2019).

Ferguson, Niall, *The Pity of War*, (London, The Penguin Press London, 1998).

Ferguson, Niall, *War of the World: Twentieth-Century Conflict and the Descent of the West*, (New York, The Penguin Press, 2006).

FitzGerald, David S. and Cook-Martín, David, "The Geopolitical Origins of the U.S. Immigration Act of 1965", published on February 5, 2015, https://www.migrationpolicy.org/article/geopolitical-origins-us-immigration-act-1965.

Fleegler, Robert L., *Theodore G. Bilbo and the Decline of Public Racism, 1938–1947*, The Journal of Mississippi History, Volume *68:1* (2006).

Franchi, Jaimie, "Shakers", New Georgia Encyclopaedia website, last edited on September 10, 2013, https://www.georgiaencyclopedia.org/articles/arts-culture/shakers.

Fussell, Elizabeth, "Warmth of the Welcome: Attitudes toward Immigrants and Immigration Policy", https://www.ncbi.nlm.nih.gov/pmc/articles/PMC4782982/, published on April 14, 2014.

Gage, John, "Crenshaw calls Google 'disturbing' after employee calls Ben Shapiro a 'Nazi'", June 26, 2019, https://www.washingtonexaminer.com/news/crenshaw-calls-google-disturbing-after-employee-calls-ben-shapiro-a-nazi.

Galbi, Douglas A., Ph.D., "incarcerating child-support debtors without the benefit of counsel", Purple motes website, published on March 22, 2011, https://www.purplemotes.net/2011/03/22/persons-in-jail-for-child-support-debt/.

Gaser-Bligh, Amanda, "25 Best Climate and Renewable Pages", Eon website, https://www.eon.com/en/new-energy/new-energy-world/25-best-climate-and-renewable-pages.html.

Gates, Robert M., *From the Shadows: The Ultimate Insider's Story of Five Presidents and How They Won the Cold War*, (New York, A Touchstone Book published by Simon and Schuster, 1997).

Genome Variations, Genome News Network website, *updated on January 15, 2003,* http://www.genomenewsnetwork.org/resources/whats_a_genome/Chp4_1.shtml.

Gibson, Owen, "BNP hits back over Channel 4 abuse film", The Guardian website, published on May 26, 2004, https://www.theguardian.com/media/2004/may/26/broadcasting.elections2004.

Glover, Andrew, "If You Want to Save the Planet, Drop the Campaign Against Capitalism", Quillette website, on October 29, 2018, https://quillette.com/2018/10/29/if-you-want-to-save-the-planet-drop-the-campaign-against-capitalism/.

Goodchild, Peter, *Edward Teller: The Real Dr Strangelove,* (Weidenfeld & Nicolson, 2004, Great Britain).

Graeber, David, in The Myth of Barter chapter in his book *Debt: The First Five Thousand Years* (New York, London, Melville House Publishing, 2014).

Grant, Andrew, "The scientific exodus from Nazi Germany", published on September 26, 2018, https://physicstoday.scitation.org/do/10.1063/PT.6.4.20180926a/full/.

Gray, Justin, "That's Not Funny, That's Sexist: The Controversial Legacy of Benny Hill", Vulture website, published on May 15, 2013, https://www.vulture.com/2013/05/thats-not-funny-thats-sexist-the-controversial-legacy-of-benny-hill.html.

Green, Dominic, "Why Hitler Wished He Was Muslim", Wall Street Journal website, published on January 16, 2015, https://www.wsj.com/amp/articles/book-review-ataturk-in-the-nazi-imagination-by-stefan-ihrig-and-islam-and-nazi-germanys-war-by-david-motadel-1421441724.

Hagelin, Rebecca, "Margaret Sanger Founded Planned Parenthood on Racism", Washington Times website, published on April 23, 2017, https://www.washingtontimes.com/news/2017/apr/23/margaret-sanger-founded-planned-parenthood-on-raci/.

Hamby, Alonzo L., (*For the survival of democracy: Franklin Roosevelt and the world crisis of the 1930s*), (New York, USA, Free Press, 2004).

Hamilton, Martha M. and Wiener, Aaron, "The Roots of the 'Great Replacement Theory' Believed to Fuel Buffalo Suspect", The Washington Post website, published on May 15, 2022, https://www.washingtonpost.com/history/2022/05/15/great-replacement-theory-buffalo-bilbo/.

Hanif, M., "Pakistan: where the daily slaughter of women barely makes the news", May 9, 2019, https://www.theguardian.com/commentisfree/2019/may/09/pakistan-murdered-women.

Harden, Blaine, *Escape from Camp 14: One Man's Remarkable Odyssey from North Korea to Freedom in the West*, (London, Pan Books an imprint of Pan Macmillan, 2015).

Harding, Luke and MacAskill, Ewen, "Putin revives long-range bomber patrols", The Guardian website, published on August 18, 2007, https://www.theguardian.com/world/2007/aug/18/russia.ewenmacaskill.

Hawley, Von Charles and Schmitt, Stefan, "The Chernobyl Body Count Controversy", Spiegel website, published on April 18, 2006, https://www.spiegel.de/international/greenpeace-vs-the-united-nations-the-chernobyl-body-count-controversy-a-411864.html.

Hayes, Georgina, "Ex-MP Harvey Proctor wins Met payout for false child abuse claims", The Guardian website, published on November 29, 2019, https://www.theguardian.com/uk-news/2019/nov/29/ex-mp-harvey-proctor-wins-900k-from-met-over-false-child-abuse-allegations.

Ho, Timothy, "5 Types Of Alternative Money That Have Been More Useful Than Legal Currencies We Use Today", Dollars and Sense website, published on July 2, 2015, https://dollarsandsense.sg/5-types-of-alternative-money-that-have-been-more-useful-than-legal-currencies-we-use-today/.

Hollander, Paul, *Political Will and Personal Belief: The Decline and Fall of Soviet Communism*, (Yale University Press, page 53), quote from Google books UK website, https://books.google.co.uk/books?id=vJwC34GQnhEC&pg=PA53&lpg=PA53&dq=%22like+so+much+inert+raw+material+for+their+plans%22&source=bl&ots=IjRPVHmG_B&sig=ACfU3U0Li-Y8tJa_rSsfceZjT-XFIa-GXA&hl=en&sa=X&ved=2ahUKEwidk-nE-ZL0AhXoQ_EDHRe1AWUQ6AF6BAgEEAM#v=onepage&q=inert&f=false.

Hvistendahl, Mara, "Coal Ash Is More Radioactive Than Nuclear Waste", Scientific American website, published on December 13, 2007, https://www.scientificamerican.com/article/coal-ash-is-more-radioactive-than-nuclear-waste/.

Indeed.ae website, https://www.indeed.ae/Female-jobs-in-Dubai-Free-Zone?vjk=db7ccd607cc0108e.

Inside the Kremlin: The Mind and Policies of Vladimir Putin, Carthage College YouTube channel, published on June 26, 2015, https://www.youtube.com/watch?v=s88pMN3qDRQ&t=339s.

Ivanenko, Alex, "It's Time for Elon Musk to Admit the Significance of Hydrogen Fuel Cells", Forbes website, published on November 2, 2020, https://www.forbes.com/sites/forbestechcouncil/2020/11/02/its-time-for-elon-musk-to-admit-the-significance-of-hydrogen-fuel-cells/.

Jay, Alexis OBE, "Independent Inquiry into Child Sexual Exploitation in Rotherham 1997–2013", published on August 21, 2014, https://www.rotherham.gov.uk/downloads/file/279/independent-inquiry-into-child-sexual-exploitation-in-rotherham.

Jharava, Ksenia, "Beyeleeyeh Rabeenyih: Megrantee Godamee Naseelooyoot Britanskeeh Deyevachek. Palitizia Bayeetsyah Abvneeyneeyeh V Raseesmiyeh", (White Female Slaves: Migrants Rape Young British Girls. The Police Fears Racism Accusations), Lenta.RU website, published on January 6, 2018, https://lenta.ru/articles/2018/01/06/bri/.

Journo, Elan, "Ayaan Hirsi Ali on Migration, Islam and Women as Prey", Ayn Rand Institute New Ideal website, published on August 28, 2021, https://newideal.aynrand.org/ayaan-hirsi-ali-on-migration-islam-and-women-as-prey/.

Katina, Lena, "Yugoslavia", Serbia-Russia-God-with-us YouTube channel, published on October 8, 2014, https://www.youtube.com/watch?v=NGMnojYvaVc.

Katina, Lena, "Yugoslavia", SinCity company YouTube channel, published on July 22, 2016, https://www.youtube.com/watch?v=7Jftw4VcTjI.

Kelley, Rick, "Retiring worn-out wind turbines could cost billions that nobody has", Energy Central website, published on February 21, 2017, https://energycentral.com/news/retiring-worn-out-wind-turbines-could-cost-billions-nobody-has.

Kelly, Caroline, "Ocasio-Cortez compares migrant detention facilities to concentration camps", CNN website, published on June 18, 2019, https://edition.cnn.com/2019/06/18/politics/alexandria-ocasio-cortez-concentration-camps-migrants-detention/index.html.

Kenez, Peter, *A History of the Soviet Union from the Beginning to the End*, (Cambridge, Cambridge University Press, 2006).

Kindy, David, "'Blue' Hydrogen May Not Be a Very 'Green' Energy Source After All", Smithsonian Magazine website, published on August 17, 2021, 2021, https://www.smithsonianmag.com/smart-news/blue-hydrogen-20-worse-burning-coal-study-states-180978451/.

Kraemer, Sebastian, The Origins of Fatherhood: An Ancient Family Process, Sebastian Kraemer website, http://sebastiankraemer.com/docs/Kraemer%20origins%20of%20fatherhood.pdf.

Krushelnycky, Askold, "Ukraine: Famine-Survivors Recall the Horrors of 1933 (Part 2)", Radio Free Europe, Liberty Radio website, published on May 8, 2003, https://www.rferl.org/a/1103170.html.

Latson, Jennifer, "What Margaret Sanger Really Said About Eugenics and Race", Time website, published October 14, 2016, https://time.com/4081760/margaret-sanger-history-eugenics/.

Lazarus, Ben, "'SHUT YOUR MOUTH': Corbyn ally shares message telling Rotherham sex abuse victims to be quiet 'for the good of diversity'", The Sun website, published on August 22, 2017, 17:49, Updated: August 24, 2017, 4:11, https://www.thesun.co.uk/news/4299167/corbyn-ally-shares-message-telling-rotherham-sex-abuse-victims-to-be-quiet-for-the-good-of-diversity/.

LDPR TV YouTube channel, published on March 27, 2019, https://www.youtube.com/watch?v=LL5oi1IE2Us.

Levesque, Jacques, *The Enigma of 1989: The USSR and the Liberation of Eastern Europe*, California Digital Library website, https://publishing.cdlib.org/ucpressebooks/view?docId=ft4q2nb3h6&chunk.id=d0e281&toc.depth=1&toc.id=0&brand=ucpress.

Lewis, Jeffrey, Dr., "Russia's Nuclear Powered Cruise Missile", Arms Control Wonk website, published on March 24, 2018, https://www.armscontrolwonk.com/archive/1205006/russias-nuclear-powered-cruise-missile/.

Litvin, Alter and Keep, John, *Stalinism: Russian and Western Views at the Turn of the Millennium*, (United Kingdom, USA, Canada, Routledge an imprint of Taylor & Francis, 2005).

Lunacharsky, A V "Predoopreschdeyniyeh (Warning)", Naslediyeh A V Lunacharskava (The Heritage of A. V. Lunacharsky website), http://lunacharsky.newgod.su/articles/preduprezhdenie/.

Macias, Amanda, "10 Facts Reveal the Absurdity of Pablo Escobar's Wealth", Independent website, published on December 29, 2017, https://www.independent.co.uk/news/people/pablo-escobar-worth-wealth-money-how-much-a8133141.html.

Mallapaty, Smriti, "China prepares to test thorium-fuelled nuclear reactor", Nature website, published on 9 September 2021, https://www.nature.com/articles/d41586-021-02459-w.

Markov, Georgi, *Zadochnee Reportagee za Bulgaria, (In Absentia Reports About Bulgaria)*, (Sofia, Profizdat Publishing, 1990).

Marris, Sharon, "Fukushima worker dies of cancer caused by radiation seven years after disaster", Sky News website, published on September 6, 2018, https://news.sky.com/story/fukushima-worker-dies-of-cancer-caused-by-radiation-seven-years-after-disaster-11491282.

Marshall Plan European-United States history, Britannica website, published on January 14, 1999, https://www.britannica.com/event/Marshall-Plan.

Marten, Kimberly, "The Puzzle of Russian Behavior in Deir al-Zour", War on The Rocks website, published on July 5, 2018, https://warontherocks.com/2018/07/the-puzzle-of-russian-behavior-in-deir-al-zour/.

Marx, Karl and Engels, Frederick, "Manifesto of the Communist Party", Marxists Internet Archive website, https://www.marxists.org/archive/marx/works/download/pdf/Manifesto.pdf.

Marx, Karl and Engels, Frederick, "Preface to the 1882 Russian Edition" of the Communist Manifesto, Marxists Internet Archive website, 2010, https://www.marxists.org/archive/marx/works/download/pdf/Manifesto.pdf.

Materials-Based Hydrogen Storage, Office of Energy Efficiency and Renewable Energy, Energy Gov website, https://www.energy.gov/eere/fuelcells/materials-based-hydrogen-storage.

Mavrokefalidis, Dimitris, "US startup unveils battery made from nuclear waste that could last up to 28,000 years", Energy Live News website, published on September 2, 2020, https://www.energylivenews.com/2020/09/02/us-startup-unveils-battery-made-from-nuclear-waste-that-could-last-up-to-28000-years/.

McDonald, Ronan, "The Scarlet Letter", https://www.britannica.com/topic/The-Scarlet-Letter-novel-by-Hawthorne

McDuff, Phil, "Ending climate change requires the end of capitalism. Have we got the stomach for it?", The Guardian website, published on March 18, 2019, https://www.theguardian.com/commentisfree/2019/mar/18/ending-climate-change-end-capitalism.

McGrath Matt, "Climate change: Electrical industry's 'dirty secret' boosts warming", September 13, 2019, BBC News website, https://www.bbc.co.uk/news/science-environment-49567197.

McKelvie, Geraldine, "Huddersfield grooming scandal is just the start – sick child rape gangs are littered across our country", published on October 20, 2018, https://www.mirror.co.uk/news/uk-news/huddersfield-grooming-scandal-just-start-13450338.

McLoughlin, Siobhan, "Freedom of the Good: A Study of Plato's Ethical Conception of Freedom", UNM Digital Repository website, published in 2012, https://digitalrepository.unm.edu/cgi/viewcontent.cgi?article=1014&context=phil_etds.

McNabb, David E., *Vladimir Putin and Russia's Imperial Revival,* e-book, (London, New York, CRC Press, Taylor and Francis Group, 2016).

Mechanical and Organic Solidarity, Britannica website, https://www.britannica.com/topic/mechanical-and-organic-solidarity.

Medvedev, Roy, *Bleejnee Krug Stalina: Saratnikee Vajdyah. (The Inner Circle of Stalin: Associates of the Chief),* (Eksmo, Yauza-Press, 2005).

Medvedev, Roy, *Let History Judge: The Origins and Consequences of Stalinism,* revised and expanded edition, (Columbia University Press, 1989).

Miller, James E., "Why not split harmful carbon dioxide into harmless carbon and oxygen?", Scientific American website, published on July 9, 2009, https://www.scientificamerican.com/article/splitting-carbon-dioxide/.

Mittiga, Ross, "Political Legitimacy, Authoritarianism, and Climate Change", Cambridge website, published December 6, 2021, https://www.cambridge.org/core/journals/american-political-science-review/article/abs/political-legitimacy-authoritarianism-and-climate-change/E7391723A7E02FA6D536AC168377D2DE.

Mlechin, Leonid, *Lenin: Soblaznenie Rossii* (*Lenin: The Seduction of Russia),* (Peter Publishing, Moscow, 2012).

MNC Jobs Gulf website, https://www.mncjobsgulf.com/jobs/female-accountant-on-husbands-or-fathers-sponsorship-abu-dhabi-1292663.

Montefiore, Simon Sebag, *Titans of History: The Giants Who Made Our World,* (London, Weidenfeld & Nicolson, 2017).

Mooney, Chris, "Turns out wind and solar have a secret friend: Natural gas", The Washington Post website, published on August 11, 2016, https://www.washingtonpost.com/news/energy-environment/wp/2016/08/11/turns-out-wind-and-solar-have-a-secret-friend-natural-gas/.

Moyer, Laurence, *Victory Must Be Ours: Germany in the Great War 1914–1918,* (London, Leo Cooper, 1995).

Moyo, Dambisa, *Dead Aid: Why Aid Is not Working and How There Is a Better Way for Africa,* (New York, Farrar, Straus and Giroux, 2009).

Muller, Gerald, "The atmospheric steam engine as energy converter for low and medium temperature thermal energy", Faculty of Engineering and the Environment, University of Southampton website, https://eprints.soton.ac.uk/348565/1/Muller%2520RENE%25202013.pdf.

Munro, Andre, "State monopoly on violence", Britannica website, https://www.britannica.com/topic/state-monopoly-on-violence.

Murray, Brian, "The Paradox of Declining Renewable Costs and Rising Electricity Prices", Forbes website, published on June 17, 2019, https://www.forbes.com/sites/brianmurray1/2019/06/17/

the-paradox-of-declining-renewable-costs-and-rising-electricity-prices/#668aae7661d5.

Murray, Douglas, *The Strange Death of Europe,* ((London, Bloomsbury Continuum, 2017).

Nayak, A.K., Bal Raj Sehgal, *Thorium-Energy for the Future,* (Singapore, Springer Nature Singapore Pte Ltd, 2019).

Nikoulin N. N., *Vospomenania O Vineyneh (Memoirs About the War),* (St. Petersburg, The State Hermitage, 2008).

Norfolk, A., "Revealed: Conspiracy of Silence over UK Sex Gangs", The Times Digital Archive, published on 5 January 2011, https://go.gale.com/ps/i.do?p=TTDA&u=wikipedia&v=2.1&it=r&id=GALE%7CIF0504169030&asid=1610341200000~904a260a.

Oberhaus, Daniel, "Germany Rejected Nuclear Power – and Deadly Emissions Spiked", Wired website, published on January 23, 2020, 2021, https://www.wired.com/story/germany-rejected-nuclear-power-and-deadly-emissions-spiked/.

Ohanian, Lee, "Seattle Schools Propose to Teach That Math Education Is Racist – Will California Be Far Behind?", Stanford University website, published on October 29, 2019, https://www.hoover.org/research/seattle-schools-propose-teach-math-education-racist-will-california-be-far-behindseattle.

Oliveira, Thiago Dumont and Suprinyak, Carlos Eduardo, "The nature and significance of Lionel Robbins' methodological individualism", Science Direct website, published on October 19, 2017, https://www.sciencedirect.com/science/article/pii/S1517758016301436#!.

Oliver, Maggie, *Survivors: One Brave Detective's Battle to Expose the Rochdale Child Abuse Scandal,* (London, John Blake Publishing, 2019).

Patterson, James T., *Grand Expectations: The United States, 1945–1974,* (Oxford University Press, New York, Oxford, 1996).

Phillips, Kristine, "'He is honest – but smart as hell': When Truman met Stalin", Washington Post website, published on 17 July 2018, https://www.washingtonpost.com/news/retropolis/wp/2018/07/17/he-is-honest-but-smart-as-hell-when-truman-met-stalin/.

Pornhub website, https://www.pornhub.com/view_video.php?viewkey=1910676746.

Porubcansky, Marc, "795 million people don't have enough to eat – why that's actually good news", Minnpost website, published on June 8, 2015, https://www.minnpost.com/foreign-concept/2015/06/795-million-people-don-t-have-enough-eat-why-s-actually-good-news/.

Potter, Alex and Dulai, Shaminder, "Me Against My Brother", published on September 29, 2014, , https://www.newsweek.com/photos-me-against-my-brother-274000.

PriceWaterhouseCoopers Belgium, PriceWaterhouseCoopers Netherlands, Directorate General For Internal Policies Policy Department D: Budgetary Affairs, "How does organised crime misuse EU funds?", https://www.europarl.europa.eu/document/activities/cont/201106/20110616ATT21560/20110616ATT21560EN.pdf, Brussels, © European Parliament, 2011.

Proctor, Kate and Stewart, Heather, "No 10 denies claims Boris Johnson groped Sunday Times journalist", The Guardian website, published on September 30, 2019, https://www.theguardian.com/politics/2019/sep/29/no-10-denies-claims-boris-johnson-squeezed-thigh-journalist-charlotte-edwardes.

Radnedge, Aidan, "Police Probe Vile Ukipper Rape Threat", Metro newspaper, published on May 8 2019.

Radzinsky, Edvard, *Stalin*, (Great Britain, Hodder & Stoughton, 1997).

Raseeskiyeh Balnitzee-Papali v ad Pree Jhisnee (The Russian Hospitals-We Found Ourselves in Hell While Alive), hoffMAN

YouTube channel, published on February 19, 2018, https://www.youtube.com/watch?v=j6E4uRnFeGU&list=WL&index=3.

Reisman, George, *Why Nazism Was Socialism and Why Socialism Is Totalitarian*, (The Jefferson School of Philosophy, Economics and Psychology, CA, USA, 2014).

Reuters staff, "U.S. imposes duties on structural steel from China, Mexico", Reuters website, published September 4, 2019, https://www.reuters.com/article/us-usa-trade-steel/us-imposes-duties-on-structural-steel-from-china-mexico-idUSKCN1VP2R7.

Revere, Evans J.R., "Endgame: A Reflection on U.S. Strategic Choices and the North Korean Threat", page 15, https://www.brookings.edu/wp-content/uploads/2018/02/fp_20180202_endgame_strategic_choices_north_korean_threat.pdf.

Rhodes, Richard, *The Making of the Atomic Bomb*, (New York, Simon and Schuster, 1988).

RIA Novosti, "Putin Pashuteel O Saddamye Husseinye E Yadrehynom Arujhee" (Putin Joked About Saddam Hussein and Nuclear Weapons), published on October 3, 2019, https://ria.ru/20191003/1559415828.html.

RIA Novosti, "Putin Raskriteekaval Ziyavleneeya O Razvyazeevanee Stalineem Voinee" (Putin Criticised The Statement About Stalin Instigating The War) published on October 3, 2019, https://ria.ru/20191003/1559415462.html?in=t.

Robinson, Paul, "How Russia Might Have Stopped World War I", The American Conservative website, published on February 4, 2014, https://www.theamericanconservative.com/articles/how-russia-might-have-stopped-world-war-i/.

Romei, Valentina, "Half of women in England and Wales do not have children by age 30", published on January 27, 2022, https://www.ft.com/content/2928092e-1d57-4dff-9062-f66d8f64fb48.

Rosenbaum, Ron, "Stalin's Cannibals: What the new book Bloodlands tells us about the nature of evil", published on

February 7, 2011, https://slate.com/human-interest/2011/02/stalin-cannibalism-and-the-true-nature-of-evil.html.

Roser, Max, "Fertility Rate", *OurWorldInData website, published on December 2, 2017,* https://ourworldindata.org/fertility-rate.

Ross, Alex, "How American Racism Influenced Hitler", published on April 30, 2018 issue, https://www.newyorker.com/magazine/2018/04/30/how-american-racism-influenced-hitler.

Rotter, Charles, "Wind farm turbines wear sooner than expected, says study", Watts Up With That website, published on December 29, 2018, https://wattsupwiththat.com/2018/12/29/wind-farm-turbines-wear-sooner-than-expected-says-study/.

Rummel. R. J., *Death by Government,* (New Brunswick, New Jersey, Transaction Publishers, 1995).

Rummel. R. J., *Death by Government,* (New Brunswick, USA, London, UK, Transaction Publishers, 2009).

Rummel. R. J., *Never Again: Ending War, Democide, & Famine Through Democratic Freedom,* (nonfiction supplement), (The United States of America, Llumina Press, 2005).

Russkiya Balntiza, Katoroyou Prievrateelee v Ad! Plesen, Greebok, Gnieleyeh Matrasi! Oojhas e Shok! (A Russian hospital turned into hell! Fungus, Mould and Rotten Mattresses! Horror and Shock!), Cultura Dostoynstva YouTube channel, published on May 25, 2020, https://www.youtube.com/watch?v=59S_DvHBLQc&list=WL&index=1.

Saad, Gad, Professor, "A Tsunami of Maladies Afflicting the Soul of Our Universities (THE SAAD TRUTH_676)", Gad Saad YouTube channel, published on June 19 2018, https://www.youtube.com/watch?v=GXjzYh6p4WE&t=2601s.

Saharov, Andrei, *Sabraniyeh Sacheenaynyee, Vaspamenania* (Complete Works, Memoirs) Volume 1, (Moscow, Vremya, 2006).

Sample, Ian, "Clean, abundant and free", The Guardian website, published on April 30, 2008, https://www.theguardian.com/technology/2008/apr/30/greentech.scienceofclimatechange.

Savin, Vladislav, *Razgadka 1941: Preecheeney Catastrophee. (Solving the Mystery of 1941: The Reasons for the Catastrophe),* (Moscow, Yauza-Press, 2010).

Schmidt, Katharina Isabel, "Henry Maine's 'Modern Law': From Status to Contract and Back Again?", published on June 13, 2017, https://academic.oup.com/ajcl/article-abstract/65/1/145/3867144?redirectedFrom=fulltext.

Senior, Jayne, *Broken and Betrayed: The True Story of the Rotherham Abuse Scandal by the Woman Who Fought to Expose it,* (London, Pan Books an imprint of Pan Macmillan, 2016).

Service, Robert, *A History of Modern Russia: From Nicholas II to Putin,* (The Penguin Group, 2003).

Shalamov, Varlam, *Kalimskiyeh Raskazee (Kolyma Stories),* Completed Works in Four Volumes, (Moscow, Vagrius, 1998).

Shalamov, Varlam, *Kolyma Stories,* (New York, New York Review Books, 2018).

Shapiro, Fred, "Quotes Uncovered: Big Government and Peculiarities", Freakonomics website, published on October 1, 2009. https://freakonomics.com//2009/10/01/quotes-uncovered-big-government-and-peculiarities/?utm_source=feedburner&utm_medium=feed&utm_campaign=Feed%3A+-FreakonomicsBlog+%28Freakonomics+Blog%29.

Shellenberger, Michael, "The Real Reason They Hate Nuclear Is Because It Means We Don't Need Renewables", Forbes website, published on February 14, 2019, https://www.forbes.com/sites/michaelshellenberger/2019/02/14/the-real-reason-they-hate-nuclear-is-because-it-means-we-dont-need-renewables/?sh=67ca4f1c128f.

Sherden, William A. *Best Laid Plans: The Tyranny of Unintended Consequences and How to Avoid Them,* (California, Colorado,

England, Praeger, 2011), Chapter 6, section "The Balance of Power".

Shesgreen, Deirdre, USA Today website, published January 3, 2019, https://eu.usatoday.com/story/news/world/2019/01/02/president-trump-former-soviet-union-right-invade-afghanistan/2466897002/.

Shevchenko, Vitaly, "Little green men" or "Russian invaders"?, BBC News website, published on March 11, 2014, https://www.bbc.co.uk/news/world-europe-26532154.

Shirer, William L., *The Rise and Fall of the Third Reich: A History of Nazi Germany*, (New York, London, Toronto, Sydney, Simon and Schuster Paperbacks, 1990).

Shubin, A. V., *Ot "Zastoya" k Reyformum: SSSR v 1917–1985, (From "Stagnation" to Reforms: USSR in 1917–1985)*, (Moscow, Russian Political Encyclopaedia Publisher, 2000).

Simpson, Craig, "Wikipedia may delete entry on 'mass killings' under Communism due to claims of bias", published on November 27, 2021, https://uk.news.yahoo.com/wikipedia-may-delete-entry-mass-203714321.html.

Sirotkin, Vladlen, *Stalin: Kak Zastavit Liudeay Rabotat, (Stalin: How to Make People Work?)*, (Moscow, Algorithm Publishing, 2004).

Slepakov, Semion Spili, published on the Serg Lus YouTube channel on October 10, 2018, https://www.youtube.com/watch?v=fMyFMyrvhh8.

Smith, Erika D., "Column: Larry Elder is the Black face of white supremacy. You've been warned", published on August 20, 2021, https://www.latimes.com/california/story/2021-08-20/recall-candidate-larry-elder-is-a-threat-to-black-californians.

Smith, Helen, *Men On Strike: Why Men Are Boycotting Marriage, Fatherhood, and the American Dream – and Why It Matters*, (New York, London, Encounter Books, 2013).

Smith, Jeremy, *The Fall of Soviet Communism* 1985–91, (Palgrave Macmillan, 2005).

Smotriaev, Michail, "Rassheeraynier NATO: Abmanool Lee Zapad Gorbachova?", (NATO's Enlargement: Did The West Deceive Gorbachov?), Russian Service of BBC website, published on December 26, 2017, https://www.bbc.com/russian/features-42483896.

Sokolov, Boris, *Accupatzia: Pravda e Mifoye (The Occupation: Truth and Myths)*, "Squabble for Lebensraum" chapter, Military Literature website, http://militera.lib.ru/research/sokolov3/01.html.

Sokolov, Boris, *Pravda o Velikoi Otechestvennoi Voinye: Sbornik Statei (The Truth of the Great Patriotic War: Collection of Articles)*, (St. Petersburg, Aleteiia Publishing, 1998).

Solonin, Mark, "Ceance Ahotneechay Magee" ("A Hunting Magic Seance"), published on March 7, 2018, personal website of Mark Solonin, https://www.solonin.org/article_seans-ohotnichey-magii.

Solonin, Mark, *22 Yunya, ili Kogda nachalas' Velikaya Otechestvennaya Voyna? (June 22, or when the Great Patriotic War began?)*, (Moscow, Yauza-Press, 2005) (in Russian).

Solonin, Mark, *22 Yunya: Anatomya Catastrophee, (June 22: Anatomy of the Catastrophe)*, (Moscow, Yauza-Press, Eksmo, 2009).

Solonin, Mark, *Kak Sovietskee Sayooz Pabedil v Voyne, (How The Soviet Union Won the War)*, (Moscow, Yauza-Press, 2019).

Solonin, Mark, *Niet Blaga na Voyne (Nothing Good Comes from War)*, (Moscow, Yauza-Press, 2012).

Solzhenitsyn, Aleksandr, *The Gulag Archipelago, 1918–1956: An Experiment in Literary Investigation*, (The Harvill Press, London, 1986).

Sombart, Werner, *Torgashi e Geroyy: Razdoomeyah Patriota, (Merchants and Heroes: Thoughts of a Patriot)*, (Complete Works, Volume 2), (Saint Petersburg, Vladimir Dal Publishing, 2005).

Sowell, Thomas, "Racism Isn't Dead – But It Is on Life Support", https://www.nationalreview.com/2015/11/racism-america-history/, November 18, 2015.

Sowell, Thomas, "Thomas Sowell: Even with slavery, power is limited", Washington Examiner website, published on April 21, 2010, https://www.washingtonexaminer.com/thomas-sowell-even-with-slavery-power-is-limited.

Sowell, Thomas, *Applied Economics: Thinking Beyond Stage One*, (The United States of America, Basic Books – a member of the Perseus Books Group, 2009).

Sowell, Thomas, *Basic Economics: A Citizen's Guide to the Economy*, Chapter 10 Controlled Labour Markets, Minimum Wage Laws, (United States of America, Basic Books, 2004).

Sowell, Thomas, *Basic Economics: A Common Sense Guide to the Economy*, (New York, Basic Books, 2011).

Sowell, Thomas, *Intellectuals and Society*, (Basic Books – a member of the Perseus Books Group, New York, 2011).

Spector, Ronald H., "Vietnam War 1954–1975", Britannica website, published July 20, 1998, https://www.britannica.com/event/Vietnam-War.

Standage, Tom, *Seriously Curious: The Economist Explains the facts and figures that turn your world upside down,* (London, Profile Books Ltd, 2018).

State Archive of Russian Federation, Fund 9414, Inventory 1, Case 1805, Sheet 66, quoted after www.memo.ru/history/NKVD/GULAG/artcles/Chapter3prim.htm.

Stewart, Andrew, *Empire Lost: Britain, the Dominions and the Second World War*, (London, New York, Continuum, 2008).

Steyn, Mark, *America Alone: the end of the world as we know it*, (United States of America, Regnery Publishing, Inc. 2006), Chapter 1.

Stierlitz Forever, the All-Russia Centre for Study of the Public Opinion website, published on October 21,2019, https://wciom.ru/index.php?id=236&uid=9953.

Sudoplatov, Pavel, *Spiyetzaparatsii: Lubyanka e Kremil 1930–1950s (Special Operations: Lubyanka and Kremlin 1930s-1950s),* (Moscow, Olma-Press, 1998).

Sumner, William Graham, *Protectionism: the-ism Which Teaches that Waste Makes Wealth,* (New York, Henry Holt and Company, 1888).

Suvorov, Viktor, *Dien M: Kakda nachalas vtayara meeroviya voyna? (M-Day: When Did World War II Begin?),* (Moscow, AST Publishing, 2000).

Suvorov, Viktor, *Icebreaker,* (London, Hamish Hamilton Ltd, 1990), Internet Archive website, https://archive.org/stream/IcebreakerWhoStartedTheSecondWorldWar/SuvorovViktor-Icebreaker.WhoStartedTheSecondWorldWar_djvu.txt

Suvorov, Viktor, *Icebreaker,* (London, Hamish Hamilton Ltd, 1990).

Suvorov, Viktor, *Ochishcheniye: Zachem Stalin Obyisglaville Svyoo Armyoo? (Cleansing: Why Stalin Decapitated His Army?),* (Moscow, AST Moscow Publishing, 2007).

Suvorov, Viktor, *Ochishcheniye: Zachem Stalin Obyisglaville Svyoo Armyoo? (Cleansing: Why Stalin Decapitated His Army?),* (Moscow, AST Moscow Publishing, 1998).

Suvorov, Viktor, *Poslednata Republika: Zashto Savetskiyat Sayooz Zagoobi Vtorata Svetovna Voina? (The Last Republic: Why the Soviet Union Lost World War II?),* (Fakel Express publishing, Sofia, 1996).

Suvorov, Viktor, *Razgrom (Defeat),* (Moscow, AST publishing, 2010).

Suvorov, Viktor, Samohubeastvoh: Zechem Gitlyer Napal na Savietski Syooz? (Suicide: Why Hitler Invaded the Soviet Union?), (Moscow, AST publishing, 2003).

Suvorov, Viktor, Solonin, Mark, Burovsky, Andrei, *Why They Fear Viktor Suvorov,* (Moscow, Yauza-Press, 2012).

Suvorov, Viktor, *The Chief Culprit: Stalin's Grand Design to Start World War II,* (Annapolis, Maryland, Naval Institute Press, 2013.

Suvorov, Viktor, *Tya Se Kazvashay Tatiana: Hronika Na Veleekoto Deseteeletiyeh (She Was Called Tatiana: A Chronicle of the Great Decade)*, (Fakel Express publishing, 2013).

Suvorov, Viktor, *V Syankata Na Pobedata (Shadow of Victory)*, (Sofia, Fakel Express publishing, 2003).

Suvorov, Viktor, *Vzemum Si Dumitay Nazad, (I Take it Back)*, (Sofia, Fakel Express publishing, 2004).

Svanidze, Marina and Svanidze, Nikolai, *Estoricheskiye Hroniki (Historical Chronicles): 1981–1983*, (Amphora Publishers, Saint Petersburg, 2014).

Svanidze, Marina, *Estoricheskiye Hroniki si Nikolaim Svanidze, (Historical Chronicles with Nikolai Svanidze*), Volume two, (Amphora Publishers, Saint Petersburg, 2007).

Svanidze, Marina, *Estoricheskiye Hroniki si Nikolaim Svanidze, (Historical Chronicles with Nikolai Svanidze*), Volume one, (Amphora Publishers, Saint Petersburg, 2007).

Szondy, David, "Feature: Small modular nuclear reactors – the future of energy?", New Atlas website, published February 16, 2012, https://newatlas.com/small-modular-nuclear-reactors/20860/.

Tankersley, Jim, "Trump's Metals Tariffs Added Some Jobs and Raised Consumer Prices", New York Times website, published on May 30, 2019, https://www.nytimes.com/2019/05/30/us/politics/norway-trump-aluminum-tariffs.html.

Tatu, "Yugoslavia", QuattroSol YouTube channel, published on December 10, 2011, https://www.youtube.com/watch?v=gjb93LrE8h4.

Tatu, "Yugoslavia", Viacheslav Sukhanov's YouTube channel, published on April 2, 2014, https://www.youtube.com/watch?v=BCTvMcSccNE.

Thaller, Shannon, "Canadian school CANCELS event with ISIS survivor Nadia Murad because her harrowing description of torture and rape 'would be offensive to Muslims and foster Islamophobia'", published on November 26, 2021, https://www.dailymail.co.uk/news/article-10247301/School-CANCELS-event-ISIS-survivor-Nadia-Murad-saying-visit-offensive-Muslims.html.

The Operation Linden Report, IOPC website, published in June, 2022, https://policeconduct.gov.uk/operation-linden-report.

Tsyganok, Anatolii, 'K kakoi voyne gotovilas' Krasnaya armiya? Chast' pervaya,' Polit.ru, June 18, 2006 (in Russian), http://www.polit.ru/analytics/2006/06/16/whichwar.html, retrieved September 4, 2011.

University of Sussex, "Chemists Have Found a Productive Use for Stockpiles of Nuclear Waste", SciTechDaily website, published on January 10, 2020, https://scitechdaily.com/chemists-have-found-a-productive-use-for-stockpiles-of-nuclear-waste/.

Vance, Kevin, "Sec. Clinton Stands By Her Praise of Eugenicist Margaret Sanger", Washington Examiner website, published on April 15, 2009, https://www.washingtonexaminer.com/weekly-standard/sec-clinton-stands-by-her-praise-of-eugenicist-margaret-sanger.

Vehicle Tuning YouTube channel, published on April 30, 2015, https://www.youtube.com/watch?v=9G3qmjO1Mu8.

Vine, David, "Where in the World Is the U.S. Military?'", Politico Magazine website, published on July/August 2015, https://www.politico.com/magazine/story/2015/06/us-military-bases-around-the-world-119321/.

Voelcker, John, "Steam Under The Hood", May 13, 2008, https://www.popsci.com/scitech/article/2008-05/steam-under-hood/.

Wahl, Madeline, "How Rape Jokes Contribute to Rape Culture", HuffPost website, published on April 30, 2014, https://www.huffpost.com/entry/how-rape-jokes-contribute_b_5240592?guccounter=1&guce_referrer=aHR0cHM6Ly93d3cuZ29vZ2xlLmNvbS8&guce_referrer_sig=AQAAAGnSHjIMcc7FvnUjD2ZUnECIsNp0VmyIFY1cjKRwzqGfma953Bt1zxncjckdrQZr

gRMMhHMnzRiQobscBVFh5vy_aid8botH5D1sJP-q-C8WKm44dRbCpwQKdmnhPM-jhAb60I8QdVwXqlGU2emeMW_o0ngHkpEfydsdIjqSc4Th.

Wardle, Lynn D., "Relationships between family and government", Core website, published in the Fall 2000, page 16, https://core.ac.uk/download/pdf/232621187.pdf.

Watson, Ellen L., Roy F. Weston, Inc., "TRANSPORTATION OF RADIOACTIVE WASTE – PLANNING FOR CONFLICT", http://www.wmsym.org/archives/1998/html/sess24/24-05/24-05.htm.

Weaver, Kevan, Ph. D, "A Solution to the Nuclear Waste Problem", TerraPower website, published October 29, 2015, https://terrapower.com/updates/a-solution-to-the-nuclear-waste-problem/.

Weigel, George, *The Final Revolution: The Resistance Church and the Collapse of Communism*, (New York, Oxford University Press, Inc. 1992).

Whitman, James Q., "Hitler's American Model: The United States and the Making of Nazi Race Law", https://press.princeton.edu/books/hardcover/9780691172422/hitlers-american-model.

Wolfgang, Ben, "Bill Clinton expresses 'terrible' regret for pushing Ukraine to give up its nuclear weapons", Washington Times website, published on April 5, 2023, https://www.washingtontimes.com/news/2023/apr/5/bill-clinton-expresses-terrible-regret-for-pushing/.

Woods, Thomas E. Jnr, PhD, lecture "The History of Foreign Aid Programs (Lecture 13 of 15) Thomas E Woods, Jnr." LibertyInOurTime YouTube channel, published on June 10, 2012, https://www.youtube.com/watch?v=fft3l-sao6c&list=PLpmOMu_Jxhdnq2A2Ug-3ETXsOs-eqWzrn&index=13.

World Steel Prices, MEPS website, https://mepsinternational.com/gb/en.

Yefim Gordon, *Tupolev Tu-95/–142*, (New York, Polygon Press, IP Media Inc, 2003).

Zakoretskiy, Kaystoot, *Tret'ia Miravaya Voina Stalina (Stalin's World War III)*, (Moscow, Yauza-Press, 2009).

Zamboni, Jon, "The Advantages of a Large Sample Size", Sciencing website, published on May 15, 2018, https://sciencing.com/advantages-large-sample-size-7210190.html.

Zeffman, Henry, "End your hostility to West, Theresa May tells President Putin of Russia", on June 29, 2019, https://www.thetimes.co.uk/article/irresponsible-russia-must-halt-hostilities-warns-may-frrrk7v2h.

Zhelev, Zhelyu, *Fascismut (The Fascism)*, (BZNS Publishing, Sofia, 1990), page 244.

Zubok, Vladislav M., *Neoodafshyasya Imperia: Sovietskee Sayooz v Holodnoy Voyne ot Stalina daw Gorbachova, (A Failed Empire: The Soviet Union in the Cold War from Stalin to Gorbachev)*, (Moscow, Russian Political Encyclopedia, 2011).

Zurcher, Anthony, Echo Chambers, BBC News website, published on March 20, 2014, https://www.bbc.co.uk/news/blogs-echochambers-26676051.